# LEADING BY EXAMPLE:
## *RENOVATING THE AMERICAN DREAM*

BY

# JOHN KENT KIDWELL

ISBN: 1477688781
ISBN-13: 9781477688786
Library of Congress Control Number: 2012911225
CreateSpace Independent Publishing Platform
North Charleston, South Carolina

Dedicated to my father, H. Kent Kidwell. Thank you for teaching me the American Dream.

I pledge allegiance to the flag of the United States of America, and to the republic for which it stands, one Nation under God, indivisible, with liberty and justice for all.

# Contents

INTRODUCTION:

# THE AMERICAN DREAM

*"The American Dream is that dream of a land in which life should be better and richer and fuller for everyone, with opportunity for each according to ability or achievement...it is not a dream of motor cars and high wages merely, but a dream of social order in which each man and each woman shall be able to attain to the fullest stature of which they are innately capable, and be recognized by others for what they are, regardless of the fortuitous circumstances of birth or position."*

**- James Truslow Adams in *The Epic of America*, 1931.**

The American Dream is more than a patriotic, national ethos. At its roots, the American Dream is a core belief in the unique opportunity being a citizen of the United States affords each American; that our unyielding democratic ideals are a promise of prosperity for our people.

The notion of the American Dream itself is derived from the circumstances giving rise to the very birth or our great nation, in the way our American colonies declared themselves dissolved of the political shackles which had long bound them to the tyrannical hands of Britain. This unprecedented leap of faith was the first step toward the realization of a free, yet governed people, and it made the American Dream possible.

The second sentence of the Declaration of Independence so boldly and brilliantly states that, "We hold these truths to be self-evident, that all men are created equal, that they are endowed by their Creator with certain unalienable Rights, that among these are Life, Liberty and the pursuit of Happiness."

This core belief in the unalienable rights of the individual, that governments derive their just powers from the consent of the people, is not only one of the guiding principles so luminously propounded by the founding fathers into the framework of America's ordered liberty, it is also the pillar upon which this great nation has built the most influential, powerful, free, and wealthy society this planet has ever hosted.

It is the idea that if one works hard enough, if he or she is willing to roll up their sleeves, society should leave the individual free to reach his or her full potential. This philosophy, this potent and powerful mindset, undeniably, is the backbone of America's success, for it is the blood, sweat, and tears of the individual that has engineered our nation's prosperity.

The American tradition of protecting and promoting this capitalistic mindset, coalesced with ordered liberty, has proven to be our recipe for success. It's changed our infrastructure, innovated how we cultivate resources, heat our homes, and power our businesses—and it has spread throughout the globe. Individual innovation has given birth to a seemingly endless potential for individual wealth, and as a designed consequence, our nation has reaped a collective reward.

The power of the individual being set free to put his mind to something and be unhampered in the pursuit of that goal, gave us the light bulb, the telephone, the automobile, the airplane, and the Internet. It's the collective mind frame that if we want to, we can put a man on the moon. Our potential, from the individual, systemically to the apex of government, is limitless.

The concept of the American Dream, though, has fundamentally evolved over our history. Contemporarily, the American Dream is widely considered merely to be the ability to bring prosperity to oneself by dint of living within our borders. In common parlance, in fact, the American Dream is widely used as a description of personal achievement so as to convey the pride of home ownership; our society's ostensible symbol of individual success.

I myself live in this "American Dream." Nestled in a quiet cul-de-sac in a middle-class, suburban neighborhood just off of Route 66, Northern Virginia's major artery leading into the heart of the nation's capital, sits my single family, center-hall Colonial with a two-car garage. I'm only missing the white picket fence. Parked in the garage are two Ford vehicles, one of which I'm proud to say is a hybrid. And when I sit on my backyard patio, enjoying my personal oasis, proud that all of this is paid for by my salary as an attorney at law, I'm grateful for my little piece of heaven, my tangible piece of the American Dream.

But there's so much more to my American Dream—and everyone else's for that matter. The majesty of the American Dream transcends the basic achievement of material plenty. The simple fact that I am lucky enough to have a respected job and beautiful home tells nothing of my core beliefs, my upbringing, and my complete respect and appreciation for all that I am so privileged and free to have.

Personally, it is my parent's story that resonates as symbolic of the very underpinnings of the American Dream. You see, for me, and I believe it to be the case for so many Americans, family is where the American Dream is born and from where it emanates. Because, if I had to boil a definition of the American Dream down to a single word, that word would be *hope*. A hope to be free of the shackles of tyranny or religious persecution; hope for a better life for oneself and most of all, hope for a better life for our children. This hope, this American Dream, drove our ancestors to brave the icy clutches of the Atlantic in pursuit of a New World, and the vision lives on today as more people continue to immigrate to our shores in pursuit of a better and freer life than to any other nation on the planet.

In the 1960s, my mother, Gerd Dahling Kidwell, boarded a ship from Norway, not much unlike the seafaring explorer Leaf

Ericson had centuries before. Leaving behind her home country, she came to America as an au pair for a British family.

One particularly hot summer evening, my mother went out with a group of her Norweigan girlfriends to have a drink at the Bavarian Inn in Washington, DC. It was there that she caught the eye of a tall, handsome, United States Army specialist: my father, H. Kent Kidwell. Stationed in Fort Mede, and off for the evening, he and his Army friends were out on the town.

I'll never forget the story, and of course, the story is different depending upon whether my mother or father tells it. But, as I chose to remember it—my father, confident as he was, strutted over to my mother and offered to buy her a drink. Already Americanized, and thusly opportunistic, my mother accepted the young gentleman's offer. It wasn't long after my mother's drink had arrived that my father asked her out. She pretended like she couldn't understand him at first. Now that she had her drink of course, she politely thanked him for the cocktail and ignored him.

But if my father was one thing, he was persistent. He asked her again. She said no. He went away and then came back later in the evening to ask her out again. Same answer. And so this playful back and forth went on for the entire evening until finally she said yes. The rest of the story, as they say, is history.

My father's stubborn persistence, I believe, came as a direct result of his childhood. My father grew up in many households, but he first lived with his mother in the tiny, Appalachian mountain town of Great Cacapon, West Virginia. Great Cacapon is an unincorporated town nestled in the Blue Ridge valley on the shores of the Cacapon River, a stone's throw north of where the river meanders into the mighty Potomac. The town straddles a quiet, two-lane road, Route 9, and if you blink, you'll miss it.

As an adult, my father built a small log cabin about ten miles north of Great Cacapon. In fact, I wrote the first words of this thesis sitting on the cabin's screened porch, overlooking a five-acre field, a now-vacant cow pasture, valleyed in the shadow of a tree-hugged mountain towering over the Cacapon River.

My father purchased the land upon which the cabin is now built in 1987, and since then our family and friends have made the two-hour drive from Northern Virginia to visit as often as possible. Anybody and everybody who has ever been to this remote sanctuary will attest that as soon as you turn off Route 9 onto the gravel road, roll the car windows down to hear the crackle of the rocks under the tires, and that first breath of fresh mountain air blows in your face, you are immediately at peace. In that very moment, the hustle and bustle mindset of any beltway-insider will melt away.

From there you travel about a mile and a half down a meandering, dirt-and-gravel trail, greeted by herds of deer sometimes exceeding forty-strong, until you come to the Kidwell property.

Before the cabin was built, we'd pitch tents in the field just off the river's embankment. I'll always remember the first night we pitched tents on the property. We stopped at a butcher's shop on the way up to get the obligatory steaks, which we grilled on a miniscule portable Weber. It was just the four of us: my mom, dad, sister, and me, and least I forget, the family dog, Barrister.

My mother boiled water which she'd scooped straight from the river. "This water is so pure kids," my father was sure to boast, "that the number one source of pollution is cow manure." To this day, I'm not sure how that was supposed to make us feel like the water was clean, but I digress. That night we all woke up in about two inches of water that'd leaked into our poorly erected tents from a torrential downpour. The perfect family memory. I was seven.

Being that the cabin is only ten miles from Great Cacapon, we'd often drive into town. "The first house on the left, the yellow one," my father would tell us, our great-grandfather built with his bare hands. He used to ring the town's church bell and apparently moonlighted as a boxer at fights staged on the very property where our cabin is now built.

We always stopped in at Magio's, a small general store, even if we didn't really need anything. At the clerk's counter, the storeowner, Mrs. Magio, set a jar filled with water and a shot glass at rest on its bottom. If you could drop a quarter in the water and make it into the shot glass, you'd get a free piece of candy. I always loved playing because, even if I lost, my mother would let me pick out a Superman comic book.

Magio's has been closed for some time now. Like many of the buildings in the small town of Great Cacapon, the windows are boarded up and the edifice is falling into a state of disrepair. The town's rate of decline seems to have accelerated in recent years.

My father did not grow up wealthy in the 1940s version of this little town in West Virginia. It was just him, his younger brother, Tom, and his mother—his parents had divorced. He never talked about it much, but my father opined that he never really knew his father, barely remembered him.

When he was sixteen years old, his mother burned their house down after falling asleep with a lit cigarette in hand. Soon thereafter she passed on, and with his father dead of cancer, he was, for all intents and purposes, orphaned with a younger brother to look after.

My father bounced around from house to house, living with this aunt and that, until he was taken in by his mother's second husband, John Manuel, after whom I'm named.

John Manuel was a businessman. In fact, one of my father's first jobs was as a trash collector at the "Big M," a drive-in movie theatre owned by my grandfather and, until recently, operating in Churchville, Maryland. He taught my father respect, the value of hard work, discipline, and above all, to always look up the definition of a word he didn't know—a habit my father passed on to me.

My father's checkered childhood left him with a chip on his shoulder. I imagine it would any young man. He was smart and determined, and he had something to prove. It's as a result of my grandfather's role as a surrogate father figure—the fact that he taught my father the importance of dignity and discipline—that my father's determination was channeled positively.

In 1962, after his second year of undergraduate study at Washington College in Chestertown, Maryland, my father joined the United States Army in its fight against the Viet-Cong in Vietnam. He served three years as an Army specialist, during which time he studied Russian at the Defense Language Institute in Monterey, California, prior to being stationed in Turkey with the task of intercepting messages from the Soviet Union which was supplying the National Liberation Front in their guerilla war against American troops.

It was while on military leave that my father met my mother at the Bavarian Inn in Washington, DC. She worked as a dental assistant while my father continued to serve. And when he returned, he married her in front of a general district court judge in Arlington, Virginia, no witnesses, no friends, just he and his bride.

The Department of Veterans Affairs paid for my father to finish out his undergraduate studies at George Washington University, and in 1968 he graduated with a degree in political science.

At first he was going to get a master's in political science and become a professor—he'd even been accepted into the program. But at the last minute, he decided, on second thought, he'd rather become a lawyer.

While my father attended the George Washington University School of Law, he and my mother built a life out of nothing. Collectively, they literally had nothing, not even a sofa to sit on. But she worked and he studied, and they built a life.

In 1971, my father joined Harrell and Muchler, a small general-practice law firm located in Bailey's Cross-Roads, Virginia. In 1977, he became partner and in 1985, he bought the firm and was its leader until I took over.

My father and mother, an orphan from West Virginia and a first-generation, Norwegian immigrant, started with nothing, and in this land of opportunity, through perseverance and devotion, they built a family.

I grew up in what would likely be considered middle-class America. By no means ever rich, some years more frugal than others, but we were never poor. We were always comfortable, living in a larger-than-average house, in a quiet, safe, suburban neighborhood. The first thing my father taught me, aside from basketball, of course, was the importance of family.

My family is very traditional, the kind that, unfortunately, is waning in modern America. We sat down at seven o'clock every night to have a family dinner. My mother would set a candle-lit table and cook a four-course meal. We gathered, said grace, and then ate. Then it would begin…

My father would commence by asking questions. The first to answer twenty correctly would win—what, I still don't know. Respect, I guess. My sister and I would lean forward in eager anticipation and he'd ask away. He'd quiz us on the Bill of Rights and spout off the preamble to the Constitution. Sometimes there'd be no questions, instead he'd pontificate on the concept of state rights versus federal powers, Lockean philosophy, and the notion of ordered liberty, or regale us with a story gleaned from one of his court cases.

Over the years we kept the same basic traditions. Dinner every night, with some meals in front of the TV for sure, some missed here and there because, well, that's just life, but for the most part, at the kitchen table with a candle lit. Family Time!

My friends loved to come over, not just for my mom's culinary prowess, but also for the twenty questions and story times, even if it meant no hats at the dinner table and always being required to ask to be excused from the table.

It's at that table that I learned the importance of family, the significance of respect, rules, and hard work. My parents instilled in me the considerate ways of life that, today, are regrettably ignored by so many of us. In that warm, loving environment, I not only learned, but I also lived the American Dream.

As a young adult, I had the occasion to travel to various destinations in the third world. What struck me as truly inspirational was that no matter how destitute and seemingly hopeless an existence some of these people appeared to live, they were always smiling and somehow, despite it all, genuinely happy. That tells me something about the human spirit.

Still, witnessing with my own eyes the extreme poverty some of these people were enduring was profoundly saddening. They had so little—no electricity, no running water, and little food. There was insufficient shelter and the shelter that existed would have twenty years ago been condemned uninhabitable in even our worst ghettos. An inexplicable guilt grew deep into the pit of my stomach. Why me? Why do I deserve any better?

As a political science major in my undergraduate studies at the University of Mary Washington, I studied the acute poverty of the less fortunate, but it was truly witnessing the outwardly blighted existence of so many across this world that widened my eyes to fully appreciate and actually understand the true majesty of the American Dream. Talking to the forgotten souls of Murmansk, Russia, and eating with the Andean mountain guides of Peru, listening to how they revere America and what we as a nation stand for, has helped me to realize the influence our dream of liberty has as it reaches across our borders and spreads hope.

I've learned that the American Dream is also the unique ability of each generation to reaffirm our enduring spirit; to carry forward that noble idea, that precious, God-given truth that all are equal, all are free, and all deserve a chance to pursue their dreams by dint of being a citizen of this great nation. I am a product of this liberty—all members of my generation and the generations before me residing in these United States and protected as to our unalienable rights are a creation of this truth.

Collectively, each individual American is the American Dream, having been raised up on the shoulders of the generation preceding them. As it endures today, the American Dream, simply put, is the culmination of generations before who benefited from the luxuries afforded in freedom and who carried forward liberty's torch. Why me? Why do I deserve better? To the latter—I don't! To the former—because I am fortunate enough to be an American!

The hard work my parents put into building a life from nothing and raising my sister and me in a compassionate, ordered household gave me the chance to go to school in one of the top-ranked public school systems in the nation. It also afforded me the opportunity to attend college, and it instilled in me the drive to practice law. It fostered in me the ability and the determination to build a better life for myself, my family, and—what I truly believe to be an essential element of the American Dream—the philanthropic aspiration to build a better life for everyone around me.

Yet, the American Dream, however defined, is in numerous ways under siege. Our nation is facing crisis in every direction, from the War on Terror and economic depression, to climate change and educational, institutional, and infrastructural decay.

In many ways the shining light on the hill is flickering in the dark, teetering on the brink of a blackening abyss borne of domestic decay and international pressures. To many, and certainly for me, it's become palpable. Something is wrong—worse than normal.

The sun that once graced the amber waves of grain is graying behind a looming storm of mounting predicament. There is a measurable sapping of confidence across our land, both in the confidence that our future will be bright and in the confidence that our people have in our government as a just institution. Sleepless nights are replete with the nagging nightmare that America's decline is inevitable, that the next generation must lower its sights, expect to die younger and endure into a diseased planet. In the wake of the Great Recession, homes have been lost, jobs evaporated, businesses shuttered, and families turned upside-down in economic depression.

The reports of massacres the likes of Virginia Tech, Fort Hood, the Tragedy in Tuscon, and Sandy Hook Elementary seem to be increasing in regularity, and the media continuously bombards us with reports of global warming and looming economic catastrophe. We find ourselves in the midst of a neverending war against terror. Globally, we are witness to famine, water shortages, genocides, and the spread of tyranny and extremism—none of which seem to have been curtailed by the efforts of those fighting the good fight.

It's nearly become overwhelming, and when the citizens of this nation turn to their political leaders, too often they find them deaf to their cries. Our elected officials are so deeply entrenched in party line, more concerned with demonizing the other side, rather than uniting us to the common goal of tackling these critical issues.

But, America is too important, and we as a people are too resilient to simply fade into the dark. What we as a nation stand for—life, liberty, and the pursuit of happiness, and as the shining light of the last best hope for the remainder of humanity—must be preserved.

Our system of government is flawed, but more perfect than any other on this globe. Therefore, it is up to this generation to again pick up liberty's torch and collectively face the enemies of freedom that lurk in the dark. Let us give the Greatest Generation a run for its money, for the current status quo, a norm of division, hatred, and faction, must be shunned so that we may continue the pursuit of a brighter future for us all. We must climb back atop that hill and shine the light, embracing our flaws, facing the escalating issues and daunting tasks before us as one nation, under God, with the common goal of tackling them for a more perfect union for our people and for all peoples across this world.

For it is also a constituent of the American Dream that all who have the privilege of freedom also have the honor and duty to fight for it.

CHAPTER ONE:

# LEADING BY EXAMPLE

*It is impossible to read the history of the petty republics of Greece and Italy without feeling sensations of horror and disgust at the distractions with which they were continually agitated, and at the rapid succession of revolutions by which they were kept in a state of perpetual vibration between the extremes of tyranny and anarchy.*

*If now and then intervals of felicity open to view, we behold them with a mixture of regret, arising from the reflection that the pleasing scenes before us are soon to be overwhelmed by the **tempestuous waves of sedition and party rage.***

**- Alexander Hamilton, in *Federalist Paper No. 9*, 1786.**

Throughout the whole of human history, man has been confronted with myriad obstructions to the realization of true and complete liberty. From tyranny on one end to anarchy on the other, a spectrum of societal constraints have to date impeded our advance to the full realization of a free and ordered society for all.

Today is no different. But, as the fruits of the American Dream we now enjoy are built upon the shoulders of our learned predecessors, we are also privy to the lessons of history's past. And it is through an understanding of our history that we can forge a more perfect union for our future.

The collective conscience of our founding fathers, memorialized in our Declaration of Independence, espoused in the *Federalist Papers*, and ratified in the Constitution, was not simply conjured in

1

a vacuum and birthed in a single, brilliant, and random epiphany. Rather, these learned men were inspired by scholarly predecessors such as Montesquieu, John Locke, and the Barons who penned the Magna Carta. Our founding fathers gleaned from the anthology of erudite minds that began paving the intellectual road to liberty long before the Philadelphia Convention in 1787.

Alexander Hamilton wrote to his fellow New Yorkers in *Federalist Paper No. 9* that, "the science of politics, however, like most other sciences, has received great improvement. The efficacy of various principles is now well understood, which were either not known at all, or imperfectly known to the ancients."

It was the wisdom of earlier prophetic political minds that informed our founding fathers to the necessity of distributing power into distinct departments, the implementation of legislative checks and balances, and the representation of the people in the legislature by congressmen of their own appointment.

In their collective genius, our founding fathers engineered a Constitution meticulously calculated to act as a guided means through which the benefits of republican government could be retained and its imperfections lessened in adherence to a blueprint for a free society.

Ironically, the most ardent impediment to the continued evolution of liberty in the United States is our government, and the obstruction arises out of the very danger warned of in *The Federalist Papers* nine and ten as necessitating the need for our federal form of government in the first place. This enemy to liberty is factionalism, and it is wreaking a cancerous havoc on our federal government!

Before I delve deeper into this issue, it is necessary to define what a faction is. James Madison defined factions in *Federalist Paper No. 10* as "...a number of citizens, whether amounting to a majority or minority of the whole, who are united and actuated by some common impulse of passion, or of interest, adverse to the rights of other citizens, or to the permanent and aggregate interest of the community."

To me, though this definition is accurate, it does not elucidate the whole truth. To understand factions, one must first appreciate their qualities. Since factions are a collection of individuals forged in common goal regardless of the common good, it follows that the pedigree of all factions stems from the very nature of man. Factions, comprised of individuals, are governed by the same animalistic instincts driving their apparatus—survival of the fittest, plunder if necessary!

I do not impetuously make this indictment for again, it is the chronicles of history that bear witness to the roots of this universal truth. The incessant wars and genocides that rage even today, the duplicity in commerce that created the need and want for slavery, and the sweatshop "workers" of modern society, are all testaments to this unfortunate attribute of man. A fatal tendency is born into our very DNA it seems, a primeval instinct that impels us to satisfy our desires and prosper at the expense of others if necessary.

"Now since man is naturally inclined to avoid pain—and since labor is pain in itself—it follows that men will resort to plunder whenever plunder is easier than work," wrote the French economist Frederic Bastait in his masterpiece titled, *The Law: A Classic Blueprint for a Free Society*. He went on to further state that, "The proper purpose of law is to use the power of its collective force to stop this fatal tendency to plunder instead of to work. All the measures of the law should protect property and punish plunder."

Our founding fathers were innately aware of the dangers of factions, arguing for a strong central government capable of thwarting this stalwart antagonist to the sovereignty of liberty. But what happens when the federal government implemented as a means to prevent faction becomes rotten and unproductive because of the influence of factions? Make no mistake—this is exactly what has happened!

The reason why Americans are currently so disgusted with their government is because of the very instability, injustice, and utter confusion that factions have introduced into today's public arena. There is a multitude of factions influencing the three branches of the federal government, all taking different form (some more pol-ished than others), after two-plus centuries of politics. There are the religious camps, the gun and tobacco lobbies, to name a few, but there are two factions that have cloaked the American Dream in shadow more than any other.

These two factions are the accumulation of nearly every camp desirous of influencing policy in America. They are the accretion of the lobbies, deriving their power from nearly every American who exercises their right to vote. Nothing gets done without their say—Nothing! Because without them, the lobby would simultane-ously have no sounding board and no gavel. These dueling fac-tions of which I speak are none other than the Republican and Democratic national parties.

As I write this thesis, we, the American people, find ourselves more alienated from the federal government than perhaps at any other point in American history. And, unfortunately, the distrust is only deepening. Why, then, is the electorate so disgusted with the government? Because the Democrats and Republicans, while both have gained, lost, and regained control of government, respec-tively have done little or nothing to address the critical issues fac-ing our nation. And what they have managed to do, they have done inefficiently and without proper moral compass.

Just as our colonial predecessors found themselves governed by the tyrannical hand of a distant monarchy, we too are increasingly presided over by the growing reach of a federal government which for a majority of the electorate is geographically and ideologically detached. And while the federal government increasingly infringes upon our personal liberties and impedes our ability to prosper on our own hard work in the name of great social equalization, it simul-taneously ignores public unrest and has for far too long refused to address mounting tribulations facing the constituency as a whole.

We are witness to sky-rocketing debt and deficits on the fed-eral and state levels with nothing done to address the crisis except for the establishment of an investigative commission (which costs more money), and which has no legal authority to stop the bleeding. Financial reform, even though it is undeniably necessary and critical to the continued prosperity of our economy, was filibustered by congressmen betrothed to and indebted to financial institutions with interests contrary to the common good. Now those same congressmen vow to dismantle the regulations that were put in place. The invasion of illegal aliens continues with nothing done, forcing states like Arizona to take matters into its own hands. Finally, after months and months of partisan bickering and unfounded fear mongering over phantom death panels, healthcare reform was passed, but with no public option and with only the support of one-third of the electorate. Nothing has been done to address climate change, campaign finance reform, free trade reform to bring jobs back to America, and the list goes on and on. Overseas, nothing has been done about Iran's nuclear program; nothing done to effectively deal with North Korea; nothing done to further peace in the Middle East; nothing done to address the genocides sweeping Africa, and again, the list goes on and on.

The question that presents itself, then, is why is nothing being done? The answer lies in the entrenched interests of party line—the endless campaign for votes in the next election. The very reason why factions have been able to get such a strong hold on our government.

Here is a current example. The president, as executive in chief, has the Constitutional authority to police America's borders to protect the interests of the American people. Notwithstanding this power, George W. Bush, a Republican, did nothing to effectively control the mass invasion of illegal immigrants swarming across the border. Now, Barack Obama, a Democrat, is also doing nothing. Nothing is being done by both parties for the same exact reason: the fastest growing demographic in America is the Hispanic vote, and if either party cracks down on illegal immigration, it risks losing that vote for generations. Unacceptable!

It is entirely unacceptable when government, an institution designed and tasked to serve the people, acts contrary to the public's interests for the sole purpose of maintaining its own existence.

You see, it has all come down to political posturing. As a Senator, if I block a bill proposed by the other party from passing, I get to boast about that to my constituents, maybe even run a campaign ad regarding how ineffective the candidate for the other party is. If I don't vote for the bill and it passes but turns out to be a failure, again, I win. It's almost like a sick, twisted prisoner's dilemma American politics finds itself in. And while the Democrats worry about the prospects of the Democrats retaining or losing control of Congress and the Republicans worry about the same, who worries about the well-being of the American citizens?

In addressing the dangers of factions, James Madison wrote in *Federalist Paper No. 10,* "The instability, injustice, and confusion introduced into the public councils (by factions), have, in truth, been the mortal diseases under which popular governments have everywhere perished; as they continue to be the favorite and fruitful topics from which the adversaries to liberty derive their most specious declamations." This same danger wields a sharpened sword at Liberty's neck today. We must therefore act expeditiously to control the effects of these factions, or face the disintegration of the United States just as history witnessed the fall of the Roman Empire.

The political posturing of both parties stands in the way of America's continued progression, stifling the very innovation that laid the foundations of our now distressed American Dream. The holding of the party line for the vote in the next primary, not to mention the next general election, over the good of the constituency as a whole has endured for far too long as a systemic cancer in our democracy, becoming the seed from which outsized distrust in our government has grown.

To solve this growing problem, or lessen its effects, many would argue the answer lies in the insertion of a third, fourth, or a seemingly endless parade of political parties into the foray of American politics. The swift rise of the popular Tea Party is a testament to this line of thinking. Yet, while at first blush enticing, this would not necessarily solve the problem, and could in fact exacerbate it.

More parties would mean only more factions, in varying degrees of strength, yes, but added internal strife nonetheless. Eventually, these now numerous factions, for the sake of maintaining or gaining control of Congress, would forge ungodly alliances at the expense or, in the very least, without proper regard for the needs of the people. These alliances would be less capable of tackling critical issues, as they'd be even further removed from the reality of the issues facing their constituents. Instead of focusing on environmental legislation, they'd be focused on maintaining the alliance, forced into backroom deals and compromises of every kind before they even got around to how they would campaign on a single platform to win the next election.

History, again, has taught us this lesson, for we need look no further than the aligning of the Nazi and Conservative Nationalist parties in Germany that paved the way to the passage of the Enabling Act of 1933, empowering Hitler to his dictatorship.

In building upon the sage advice of James Madison, "The inference to which we are brought is, that the *causes* of faction cannot be removed, and that relief is only to be sought in the means of controlling its *effects*." Adding more parties would be like adding fuel to the fire because it would do nothing to regulate against the effects of faction.

Over two centuries after the ratification of our Constitution, and with only twenty-seven amendments, it is understandable that certain effects of faction were not anticipated within its framework.

We have to remember that in 1787, the population of the United States was less than four million. Now, with more than double that living in New York City alone, there are companies that employ more workers than lived in some of the states at the time of the ratification of the Constitution. The complexities of an international commerce and communication system that is evolving in stride with the explosion of technology, combined with the stress of nearly four hundred million residing within our borders could hardly have been contemplated by the founding fathers any more than the Athenians could have predicted the cause of the first World War.

The complexities of today highlight the sections of the Constitution that were vague and requires of us critical thought as to the areas not mentioned within its four corners. But, let me be clear, these societal intricacies in no way require us to abandon the sagacious construct therein formulated.

Among the purposes of the government, as organized under the Constitution, is the charge to protect against the dangers of faction. Therefore, learning from history, and building upon the scholarly shoulders of our founding fathers, we must thicken our government's shield to guard against the effects of faction. And, in order to do so, we must amend our system of government.

I speak of a revolution. Not a revolution borne of sword or gun, but one of intellect and renewed dedication to the soul of our ordered liberty. Just like the decaying inner cities of our nation require a face-lift, a second look, so too does our government if we are to continue to form a more perfect union.

Perhaps, though, the better analogy would be to say that we must revitalize our government by giving it well aimed doses of medicine because it is not that our system of administration is erroneous or ill advised, instead, it is sick with ever-spreading cancers.

To be clear—I do not advocate revolution by way of dismantling the Constitution. To do so would be contrary to every morsel of my being and to everything I know in my heart to be good and just about the government of these United States.

Instead, I propose a dramatic revolution within the political party that I believe has traditionally adhered more closely to the principals propounded in the Constitution itself, but today is unfortunately contributing to the ailments that plague our society. And, learning again from history, ironically I propose, among other things, that the Republican Party return to its conservative roots in order to fundamentally revise American politics and change the direction our nation is headed. I believe that the Republican Party's failure to do so will mean more than the simple devolution of the party into irrelevance, but will spell the far more horrifying consequence of America's systemic demise.

In this thesis, my goal is to lay out a new platform for the Republican Party. A platform that is truer to Republican values than what is being practiced today, but also one that draws lines in the sand where needed and erases the negative mindset that purveys American politics on both sides of the aisle. Starting at the grassroots level, the platform must be used by the Republican Party to revitalize the electorate while tackling the mounting critical issues facing us as a nation. This platform will usher in a new era of liberty and prosperity for Americans and do so by more closely adhering to the legislative intent behind the Constitution, as well as buttress core principles, such as checks and balances, that constitute the backbone of our system of governance.

The Republican Party has lost its way, and failure to react accordingly will only result in the continued degradation of the American Dream. As Republicans, it is no longer sufficient to say no to everything the Democrats proffer, or to demonize them because they did it to us when we were in office. Americans deserve so much more and better than what we've been providing as their entrusted leaders. They know it, and we know it!

Very clearly, if we are to tackle the issues facing our nation, Republicans and Democrats alike, our government, our institutions, all of us, must transcend the infighting that has kept our great nation from progressing as it should. We must pull ourselves from the mud and work toward perfecting our union, rather than sitting idle and resting on our laurels. We have a choice, here and now. Do we continue to wallow in our mediocrity and allow our once-great nation to disintegrate as mighty Rome did centuries before, or do we reaffirm our ideals and fight harder than we have ever fought to restore the American Dream in all its wonder for ourselves and renovate it for future generations?

Part of me would like to quote a founding father here, but if another shoe fits, wear it. As Spiderman's uncle once said, "With great power comes great responsibility." Nothing could be more true. The United States of America, as the strongest and most affluent nation on this planet, has a unique responsibility as a beacon of hope for all mankind. But we as a nation cannot be the light shining on the hill for all other nations to bear witness if individually, as Americans, we are lost in the dark, and worse yet, our government is leading us into a deepening abyss. And so, it is up to us, Republican, Democrat, Independent—all Americans to pick up Liberty's torch and forge a path out of the shadows. We must become the path once more. We must LEAD BY EXAMPLE!

# CHAPTER TWO

# THE ROLE OF GOVERNMENT

*The powers not delegated to the United States by the Constitution, nor prohibited by it to the States, are reserved to the States respectively, or to the people.*

**- 10th Amendment to the Constitution (1791)**

Tour the vastness of America, from sea to shining sea, and you will find that Republicans on the West Coast will almost universally answer the same as Republicans on the East Coast when asked what it is they believe the core principle of the Republican platform to be. "Small government," they will answer.

This central belief is echoed in every Young Republican or County Republican Committee meeting across this great land. On our campaign brochures and bumper stickers, you will usually find key phrases such as "cut government spending," or "Washington is spiraling out of control." In one form or another, the concept finds its way into nearly every Republican campaign.

But what do we mean when we say government needs to be smaller? At first blush, you may think this to be a rhetorical question. But it is not!

I ask the question because, unfortunately, as Republicans, and certainly as a nation, we've forgotten the answer and seem to remember only the slogan. So many of us no longer fully understand the power of this political "sound bite," and it is evidenced by the way we have been leading our constituents.

During the Bush presidency, government spending at the federal level increased at a historic pace, and concomitantly, the deficit spiraled out of control. Did the federal government shrink? Now there's a rhetorical question!

Now, when I bring this up at the county meetings, my fellow Republicans are quick to point out that President Obama is much worse, and Nancy Pelosi is tantamount to a socialist antichrist. The disdain expressed for the Democrats is visceral. And, to be frank, I find it distasteful.

I find it repugnant because the former affability and deference in politics is not just missing, but will soon prove extinct when the hatred of the "other side" is systemic, right down to the grassroots, as a preached and learned incantation. What's worse is that the ones who lose out are the people. "We must retake America," my fellow Republicans will shout, and I agree, but they go further to rant that the Democrats are liars, socialists, communists, evil. This is plain ridiculous. The fact that one is misguided does not make one evil.

It is necessary that we, as Republicans, break free from this need to vilify the Democrats. This is necessary for many reasons, but of paramount importance is the fact that the problem in government does not stem only from the Democrats' misguided ways. Unfortunately, the problem lies on both sides of the aisle. Both are spending too much and doing so while presiding over the expansion of our federal government into arenas entirely outside its appropriate reach. Both parties are running afoul of the true purpose of government and, as such, it is unacceptable to point out the inequities of the Democratic Party with a blind eye to the problems permeating our own.

So, back to my "rhetorical" question: What do we mean when we say "small government"? And to be more succinct, I suppose I should ask—what should we mean?

One answer to the question is rooted in the Bill of Rights. The 10th Amendment to the Constitution is clear: "The powers not delegated to the United States (Federal Government) by the

Constitution, nor prohibited by it to the States, are reserved to the States respectively, or to the people." Seems pretty explicit, right?

Thomas Jefferson described the 10th Amendment as "the foundation of the Constitution" and added, "To take a single step beyond the boundaries thus specially drawn...is to take possession of a boundless field of power, no longer susceptible of any definition."

Jefferson's formulation is where we glean the doctrine of "strict construction," an adherence to the actual or intended meaning of the language found within the four corners of the Constitution.

But, just as the definition of the American Dream has proven to be complicated, so too has the doctrine of strict constructionism. In fact, the meaning of "strict construction" may be different depending on who uses it and in what context. A justice of the Supreme Court asking counsel at oral argument whether a statute should be construed strictly is likely using the term differently than a candidate on the campaign trail using the term as a surrogate for a broader set of conservative values.

The problem with the Republican campaign trail today is that so many of us have not only lost the true understanding of what we mean when we say "small government," but we have also misconstrued the purpose of Jefferson's words.

From Nixon to Regan and through the Bush administrations, our Republican presidents have promised to appoint strict constructionist judges to the Supreme Court. Yet, even Ronald Regan's 1986 appointee to the Supreme Court, Antonin Scalia—the justice often touted as the intellectual anchor of the conservative wing, and the justice most identified with the term—has himself said that he is "not a strict constructionist and no one ought to be," calling the philosophy "a degraded form of textualism that brings the whole philosophy into disrepute."

One can understand, and even appreciate, Justice Scalia's words, as they seem to be a reaction to the political misuse of the term as a coded label to earn votes while simultaneously misrepresenting the true spirit of the philosophy as a theory of Constitutional interpretation.

Again, canvass the whole of the electorate spanning the nation, and innocently, our fellow Republicans will almost universally say that strict constructionism requires that only the exact language found in the Constitution may be followed. This is wrong! And the problem with this message being mistaken is that its true definition and meaning absolutely must form the foundation upon which the true and correct Republican platform ought to be reconstructed.

Instead, strict constructionism is a philosophy that emphasizes judicial restraint and fidelity to the original *intended* meaning of the Constitution.

Allow me to give an anecdote for clarification:

As an attorney at law, when a client asks me a question to which I do not know the answer (which, by the way, let me point out the rarity of this occasion, wink)...what do I do? The first thing I do is go into my firm's library and pull the Virginia Code to look for a statute on point. I pull the actual book instead of using a search engine at first for a very particular purpose: to learn the legislative intent behind the subject statute!

When I look up a particular code section, I not only get the black letter/strict language of the legislation, but I am also able to read a description of the history behind the enactment of the statute as well as case law on point. In reading through and understanding the legislative intent behind the strict, stone-etched statute, I am able to extract the full meaning of the codified law. As a lawyer, this is invaluable.

The same modus operandi absolutely must be followed in the application of the Constitution to how we, as Republicans, lead this great nation, and promote the varying actions of state and local government in relation to that of the federal government.

When we say, "small government," in addition to an understanding of the proper purpose of government, whether on a local, state, or national level, we must also be conveying the necessity of adherence to the intended meaning of the 10th Amendment as a means to hamper the federal government's ability to hinder our individual ability to carry forward liberty's torch.

Why is this so important? Because we, as a nation, are losing control. Individual liberties are being trampled by a federal government expanding at unprecedented speed. State sovereignty is being usurped through over-utilization of the interstate commerce clause. Deficit spending is out of control, states have become reliant upon federal funding, and the balance of power has shifted, wherein the federal government ostensibly has all the power and the states only those explicitly granted to them. In different form, and in a different millennium, we are finding a tea party necessary to show our disdain for a tyrannical hand taxing us without properly representing us.

Turning once more to the annals of history, we are thereby able to extract the legislative intent behind the adoption of the 10th Amendment. And it is vital that we do so, because an understanding of the intended meaning behind these final words in the Bill of Rights educates us as to the true and proper purpose of government under our Constitution. This precise knowledge is what we as Republicans have lost, and we must regain it in order to empower us to lead by proper example again.

To begin, one needs to look no further than the Declaration of Independence itself. Our decision to absolve ourselves of any allegiance to Great Britain was made in reaction to "a long train of abuses and usurpations" by the British Crown, evincing "a design to reduce them (us) under absolute depotism." Jefferson next penned a list of grievances to which petitions for redress had long been unanswered and which established factual evidence of the establishment of an absolute tyranny over the colonies by the British Crown.

The tyranny of a far-off government that ruled over the lives of the colonists without regard to justice and the common good, which stripped us of all representation, voice, and security, necessitated the waging of the Revolutionary War. And when our independence was won, we were justly reticent to create a central government to preside over the union of the states, much less grant it powers over their sovereignty.

This fear of a strong central government was further evidenced by the delay in the endorsement of the Articles of Confederation. Although the Articles of Confederation were adopted by Congress on November 15, 1777, it was not until March 1, 1781 that Maryland became the final state to sign, thusly forming the union of the states as a single nation for the first time. The delay was caused by the ongoing war, but also as a consequence of strong public sentiment in opposition to vesting powers in a national government presiding over the sovereign states.

As a result, Article II of the Articles of Confederation declared that "each state retains its sovereignty, freedom, and independence, and every power, jurisdiction, and right, which is not by this Confederation expressly delegated to the United States, in Congress assembled."

This intent that the central government has few and well defined powers was so universal, in fact, that the government proved too weak to function. Because the central government had no power to collect taxes, for example, the Articles of Confederation were dissolved and replaced by the Constitution.

And finally, the history of the ratification of the Constitution itself lends to the legislative intent behind the enactment of the 10th Amendment. An ideological battle raged between the Federalists and Anti-Federalists, who disagreed as to whether a Bill of Rights was even necessary to the ratification of a Constitution that vested powers in a federal government.

In *Federalist Paper 84*, Alexander Hamilton asserted that ratification of the Constitution did not mean the American people were surrendering their rights, and, therefore, protections were unnecessary: "Here, in strictness, the people surrender nothing, and as they retain everything, they have no need of particular reservations."

Anti-Federalists such as Patrick Henry, on the other hand, publicly argued against the Federalist-proposed Constitution as a clear threat to individual rights, expressing fear that the president would become a king much the same as the tyrannical King George from whom they had just won their independence.

The desirability of a Bill of Rights was powerful and widespread, a sentiment the Anti-Federalists capitalized on in the 1788 ratification convention in Massachusetts. The Federalists were forced to agree to the Massachusetts Compromise, permitting delegates with doubts as to the Constitution to recommend amendments to be considered by Congress subsequent to ratification. Notwithstanding this compromise, North Carolina refused to ratify the Constitution until clear progress was shown toward the codification of a Bill of Rights.

And so, in 1789, the First United States Congress met in New York City's Federal Hall, first, and foremost, with the task of considering proposed amendments to the Constitution, the majority of which pertained to the protection of individual rights. As a result, the Bill of Rights, penned by James Madison, and based in large part on George Mason's *Virginia Declaration of Rights*, were adopted.

The legislative intent behind the enactment of the Bill of Rights, which includes the 10th Amendment, then, is quite clear. Learning from then recent history, Americans were aware of the dangers a disassociated, central government with vast, undefined and unquestionable powers, posed to the liberty for which they had just fought and won. They understood the necessity of explicitly outlawing the encroachment by the government onto those liberties, and in doing so, intended to delineate the limits of the federal government's powers.

Through a long line of Supreme Court rulings, ranging from *Wickard v. Filburn*, wherein the court ruled that the Congress, via the commerce clause, could regulate the production of wheat on a family farm; to *Garcia v. San Antonio Metropolitan Transit Authority*, where the court forever changed the standard of review of the constitutionality of a federal law to whether that law is "destructive of state sovereignty or violative of any constitutional provision," the intended meaning and application of the 10th Amendment to the provision of federal governance has changed drastically.

However, while many of my contemporaries quibble in the fascinating intricacies of each of these cases and the effects they have on the way in which the federal government goes about its business, I posit that the true meaning of the 10th Amendment, the legislative intent behind its enactment, comes from a historical understanding of the very purpose of government itself. As such, any "construction" of the 10th Amendment, or the Constitution, and the powers therein granted to the federal government and reserved to the states, must be based upon the proper purpose of government, and be rooted in a proper understanding of that purpose.

In other words, I believe the best way to understand the 10th Amendment is to gain an understanding of what law is meant to accomplish and what government's true and limited purposes ought to be. This knowledge of the true purpose of government was the antecedent to the Declaration of Independence, the Constitution and the Bill of Rights, for without it the founding fathers could never have penned any of the documents as they did, nor would they have structured our system of ordered liberty as they did.

The legislative intent behind the 10th Amendment, then, is found in an understanding of the role of government. Moreover, an understanding of the proper purpose of government allows us to regulate how we, as Republicans, promote certain actions as government leaders.

What, then, is the role of government? What ought to be its purpose and its limits? As Republicans, we must re-learn the answer to these questions, for it is out of a misguided and ill-informed understanding of the role of government that the Democrats are operating to project what we call "socialism" onto our society.

Government, by very definition, is political direction and control exercised over the actions of the members, citizens, or inhabitants of communities, societies, and states. This political direction and control is both created and exercised in the application of law. To understand government, and its proper purpose, then, we must delve even deeper to define law.

Building from history, I again find that it is unnecessary for me to re-invent the wheel when defining law. In his thesis, *The Law*, French economist and statesman, Frederic Bastait, defined law as "the organization of the natural right to lawful defense. It is the substitution of a common force for individual forces." He went on to say that "this common force is to do only what the individual forces have a natural and lawful right to do; to protect persons, liberties, and prosperities; to maintain the right of each, and to cause justice to reign over us all."

Government, being the administrator of the law, therefore, can only have, as its purpose, the protection of persons and their liberties and prosperities, and do so by the administration of justice. It is when the government attempts to do more than this that it not only tramples the rights of some of the constituents it is sworn to protect, but also becomes a legal framework for injustice.

To be more clear, a legal framework for injustice arises when the government sworn to protect liberty destroys that liberty through the enactment and execution of laws designed to give government more power than it ought to have. It is on this slippery slope that the government is able to transfer property in whatever form— land, money, etc.—from the person who owns it, without his consent or compensation, to someone else, and do so legally. And it is well down this slippery slope that our federal government now finds itself.

This "legal plunder," as Bestait called it, is born of two roots: the first is human greed. Law itself is necessitated by this first root. And it was the legislative intent of our founding fathers to guard against this greed by creating a system of checks and balances through the division of power amongst the executive, legislative, and judicial branches of government. The second cause of legal plunder grows from the seed of false philanthropy. Today, though, it has become the mentality of too many, Republicans and

Democrats alike, that the government should not only be just, it should also be philanthropic. The government, for the better part of a century now, has been utilized as a tool to extend welfare to all.

This is certainly not to say that welfare for all is a bad thing—no, I'm instead pointing out the problem with how this philanthropic ideal is currently being implemented. Unfortunately, a paradox occurs when the federal government tries to create welfare for all. Ironically, by taking more and more from the haves and giving to the have nots (legal plunder), the government makes things worse for everyone.

Going back to why I find it distasteful when Republicans vilify Democrats: Given the state of affairs in America, how much has been left undone and needs to be tended to; it is no wonder that the Democrats find it necessary to utilize the government toward social agendas designed to establish a greater welfare for their constituents. Their "socialist" agendas I don't think are born from any hatred for America and the continued prosperity of our people. To the contrary, they are trying to fight, as they know how, for the continued prosperity of our people. Their intentions are admirable, not evil, and we, as Republicans, must understand and certainly respect this if we are ever to work in concert with them to effectively address the critical issues facing our nation. Simply put, it is not a question of whether these critical issues need to be addressed, rather, it is a question of how!

My applause for the Democrats, therefore, stops there. The Democrats may not be immoral and plot through malevolent conspiracies, but they are certainly misguided. And, unfortunately, their well-intentioned imprudence has grave consequences, many of which we now face.

The Democrats' use of the federal government to not only promote, but require social change through federal programs that reach across state borders into communities and households, is born of false philanthropy. Many of the ills in our society that these federal programs are intended to address desperately need to be addressed, no question, but it is not the role of the federal government to address them through ever expanding agencies designed to mediate the welfare of us all.

The problem with socialism and the redistribution of wealth, as policy, is that it not only erases the incentives to innovate, but causes great displacements in capital, labor, and even populations as both intended and often as an unintended consequence.

A historical example of this is the Smoot-Hawley Tariff Act of 1929, which is commonly considered as one of the contributing causes of the Great Depression. The law was passed by Congress to institute the highest tariff in US history. It taxed thousands of imported items at increased rates with the intent to increase our nation's revenue on imported commodities. The idea was to make American goods less expensive than foreign goods, putting money in the pocket of American industry rather than foreign. Seems like a pretty good "philanthropic" intention, right?

Unfortunately, foreign nations passed retaliatory tariffs and refused to import many of our leading American exports, such as cars and radios. Retaliatory tariffs were passed by countless countries, and the European continent even went so far as to repudiate its war debt from World War I. The result: American exports plunged over 50% from 1929 to 1932. The unintended consequences, though, were far more extensive.

The tariff hike crippled leading American industries. The Act, for instance, spiked the tariff on countless items used in the manufacture of Ford and General Motor's vehicles. US automakers not only sold fewer cars to Europe as a result of retaliatory tariffs, they also had to pay higher prices for crucial components in their end product. This cost, of course, was passed on to the American consumer who now had fewer and ironically more expensive options, as well as less money.

A second historic example arises out of President Roosevelt's New Deal intended to combat the Great Depression. In 1933, he succeeded in passing the Agricultural Adjustment Act (AAA). In essence, AAA worked as follows: some farmers were paid to not plow and produce from part of their land; produce prices were set to pre-depression levels; processors were taxed to pay for the massive cost of the program; and the secretary of agriculture was vested with vast power to set the processing taxes, peg the price of countless commodities, and determine how much land farmers should not harvest.

AAA was passed in a philanthropic effort to combat the farm problems exacerbated by the Great Depression. The problem, boiled down to its roots, was that there were too many farmers producing too much. Too much? Here's how. Farmers could not sell their farms and move to the cities as they had in the years leading up to the Great Depression as a result of the housing crash. As a result, each farmer produced as much as he could in an effort to sell as much as he could with hopes of earning enough to put food on the table. Problem was, every farmer was doing that, and the market was saturated, driving prices further and further down. Unfortunately, the economic law of supply and demand was working against the farmer.

Moreover, the Smoot-Hawley Tariff Act, which caused the unintended consequence of retaliatory tariffs, meant that foreign nations were no longer buying farmer's overproduction.

AAA, then, was designed to rein in overproduction by paying farmers not to produce and lift farm prices by setting them to a more affluent period, pre-depression. But, again, an unintended consequence reared its ugly head.

Giving the secretary of agriculture the power to make contracts with millions of processors, farmers, and distributors to set prices, levy taxes, and legislate parity, resulted in an unprecedented expansion in the Department of Agriculture. The Washington bureaucrats, in an effort to regulate supply and demand on a national level, and despite their compilation of voluminous data ranging from average-acre-yield to production aggregates, turned the US from a top food export to a major food-importing nation.

Everything from cotton, corn, and wheat, to pork and beef production in America declined rapidly. Why? 1) The bureaucrats proved inept at accurately predicting what prices were reasonable, taking into consideration weather variation and world production levels; 2) farmers switched from producing crops set at a low price to higher-pegged commodities, and they farmed their best acres, leaving fallow their already unproductive acres; and 3) competition between farmers was rendered futile because prices were fixed and kept in parity with the prices of other industrial and consumer products. While the farmers earned more for their reap, AAA sewed the reality of higher costs and greater scarcity in food and other commodities. With America still enduring the Great Depression, AAA resulted in many impoverished Americans going hungry. Also, with fewer commodities being produced and sold, unemployment rose as textile companies were forced to lay off their workers.

Contemporarily, continued Federal tinkering farming controls and education spawn a litany of unintended consequences that plague each sector respectively. Further, there can be no doubt that the government bailouts in reaction to the financial crisis of 2008 are already producing unintended consequences. For instance, despite the prolonged "solvency" of many of our lending institutions, very little has trickled down to the consumer and lending has continued to dry.

Given all of the above, I have come to a conclusion—an epiphany in the form of a short and simple phrase. It boils the purpose of government down to one short truism defended by the very history of America's birth and the legislative intent behind the framing of our Constitution. The phrase is straightforward and easy to digest—it is therefore my hope that Republicans can better understand and thusly enact this "sound bite" as an elucidation of the phrase, "Small government." Without further ado:

**<u>The true purpose of government is to protect, not to do!</u>** This is especially true of the federal government, which is meant to act on only certain explicitly defined powers.

Now, of course, it is near impossible to pare the parameters of appropriate government action into a sound bite, and as such, it is necessary to explain further what it is that I mean if only to avoid being misunderstood. As previously discussed, the government should act only by the execution of the law. This is because law, in its purest form, is designed to provide equal justice for all.

Now, in applying the law, the government has two tools at its disposal, both of which, if wielded unwisely, are extremely dangerous. The first is force, utilizing the police and military, and everything between. The second is regulation.

Regulation can be a tricky beast, however. Over regulation of an industry is undeniably crippling to its ability to produce and compete both in domestic and global markets. In fact, the process of studying, organizing, preparing, and then regulating and fumbling through waves of litigation has impeded American progress at an escalating and alarming rate since the 1940s. An intricate and growing web of bureaucracy has eroded our great tradition of ingenuity and "roll up our sleeves and get it done" attitude, and it is why Japan is nearing 8,000 miles of high-speed train line while we have only 563 miles of high-speed rail planned, yet, to date, largely unbuilt. Senseless over regulation is why our vast natural gas reservoirs remain veritably untapped and why NASA estimates it will take us twenty-plus years to put a man on the moon again, compared to just nine in the 1960s, before the microchip was even invented. Regulation, therefore, in many respects, is a problem that must be dealt with if America is to move forward competitively in the global marketplace.

Yet, regulation is necessary! It has its legitimate purpose, and that purpose is to protect. To protect against the overzealous, yes, but truly, regulation is properly utilized only when it tells one person or group that it cannot infringe upon the liberties of another. Regulation properly guards the liberties of all against the desires of any particular group (faction) to directly harm another, or even to act in a way that is reasonably calculated to lead to a great harm to the constituency.

The formulation of regulation to protect against direct harm is theoretically easier—more "black and white." Thou shalt not kill, by way of example. But, regulation limiting one group from acting in a way that is reasonably calculated to lead to a great harm to the constituency is more difficult. An example of this latter version of regulation would be a regulation that, because of the moral hazard inherent therein, forbids loan originators from lending to individuals with horrible credit only to turn around and sell that imprudent risk to another institution.

How do we know when we've gone too far in regulating against foreseeable harm in order to protect the many? At what point is it simply too much regulation, where innovation, indeed progress, is halted and an erosion of our American tradition of independent, productive, and competitive grit evinces a palpable threat to our future prosperity? The answer, actually, is quite clear.

Regulation, properly formulated, warns people that the force of the law will be used against them if they do something untoward. Regulation, improperly formulated, forces people to do something.

Sometimes, the formulation of regulations proves quite difficult, because of the gray area. We almost ask our elected officials, if you really think about it, to be prophetic, to foresee impending, even if lurking doom. But, this is the job of our legislators, is it not? Every elected official is tasked to be truly judicious and consider, with extreme scrutiny, the merits of any proposed legislation. Unfortunately, in these days of more than 2,000-page bills prepared by staff members at the guidance of lobbyists, we aren't receiving that level of service from our congressmen and women.

Turning back to the 10th Amendment and the legislative intent behind its enactment: When a federal system of government is established wherein the national government is given only defined powers and explicitly forbidden to exercise any other powers, it follows that the federal government should not be permitted to expand through the creation of agencies and programs designed to do that which it was not explicitly granted the power to do.

Unfortunately, though, the expansion of the federal government is currently escalating at an even greater pace than subsequent to the Great Depression. The result, as we all are aware, is a government that is hemorrhaging money, building unconscio-

25

nable debt, and doing so in the provision of wasteful, ineffective, and or outright broken systems.

The crisis with regard to our federal government is twofold: not only are critical issues not being addressed, we see that those tasks the federal government does take on are handled inefficiently. The government's response to the devastation caused by Hurricane Katrina and the BP oil spill in the Gulf of Mexico, for example, exemplifies a federal government stretched too thin, unprepared, and incompetent at doing what is actually in its proper role to perform.

Now, many would respond to the above by simply advocating for the review of government inefficiencies and the development of standard operating procedures designed to cut waste and red tape. There is no doubt that this is desperately needed, for the government is so wasteful it is mind numbing. For example, why is it so difficult to fire a government employee?

The answer is two-pronged—one, it's easier to just move them to another agency; and two, there is just too much paperwork, making it time prohibitive. Well, have you ever heard of a work-at-will system where the employer can lay a worker off for a reason as well as for no reason—of course with certain restrictions, such as discrimination? I don't know about you, but I would feel a lot safer and more confident in my government if lazy, unproductive, and disingenuous federal employees could actually be fired. Maybe this would elevate the level of customer service we receive when we call the Internal Revenue Service or visit our local Social Security Office (with all due respect to the many hard working individuals in those agencies).

However, the problem is unfortunately more systemic than can be solved by efficiency evaluation and implementation. And the problem has nothing to do with Democrats v. Republicans, incompetence, or even corruption, though these factors certainly aggravate the situation.

The problem lies in competing interests and detached government. The reason why our founding fathers found it prudent to vest the overwhelming majority of government power in the individual states, rather than a central government, was because they had just lived through the reality of a government betrothed to the citizens of Britain over the interests of the citizens of the colonies, and so detached from the colonial realities, it proved tyrannical.

Why is it so important to vest more powers in the state, rather than the federal government? Didn't Alexander Hamilton, John Jay, and James Madison, in *The Federalist Papers,* advocate for the creation of a central government to unify the states into one nation better able to guard against the dangers from foreign force and influence, mediate dissention and hostilities between the states, and safeguard against domestic insurrection and faction? Well, yes, but these were arguments to forge a union in lieu of America disintegrating into a number of confederacies with competing interests, less capable of defending against foreign interests and other pressures as a result of infighting much the same as was the reality of the warring city-states in ancient Greece. Further, they were arguments in support of explicit powers to be granted to a central government. They certainly were not arguments in support of granting all or even vast power to the federal government.

It is prudent to vest the majority of powers in the state governments respectively because a federal government must take into consideration the competing interests of all the states in order to make a determination as to how it will regulate any given matter. To be fair, the federal government must consider the reasonable interests of the citizens of not just California, New York, or Virginia, but it also must consider the voice of every person in every state. In doing so, the government is rightfully endeavoring to be just and representative of its constituents.

Unfortunately, this venerable undertaking is the exact cause of government inefficiency. This is where red tape comes from, because, to gather the voices of 300 million, there must be forms. There must be government employees to categorize these forms, and of course, there must be a committee to develop protocols for the procedures to submit, decipher, and consider those forms. And so on.

After millions and millions are spent, a system is finally implemented. And what do we get? We get a system that addresses little if any of the particular concerns brought to Congress' attention by the interested localities, but instead mandates in a way that theoretically won't upset any particular group. The result is a wasteful program that does not address that which it was created to address, or is severely hampered in its philanthropic intent to so do. The program burdens the entire nation, and therefore is answerable to the entire nation, depriving it of any ability to succinctly address the problems facing the region that originally requested help.

Why? Again, human nature! If I am required to pay for a program, I will require a say in how that program is run. Multiply that by 300 million, and suddenly thousands of Maine lobster fisherman, through their representatives in Congress, are telling farmers in California how to irrigate their crops. What we get is a far-off, isolated, but all-too-interested government engaged in false philanthropy, creating a result contrary to their altruistic purpose. What we get is a catch-22!

The problems, though, do not stop there. Unfortunately, and as a direct result of government programs designed to provide for the welfare of all, human nature rears yet another ugly head—entitlement.

Entitlement programs, as they are sometimes called, are programs that are initially designed to address a particular problem plaguing a region or group of individuals. The program is created, and, so as to not discriminate, other groups and individuals are granted access to the program upon demand. The program grows, and grows. It becomes more and more inefficient, wasteful and ironically, less capable of addressing the concerns of those it is "helping." Congress, in its right mind, then, may attempt to cut spending on that program.

But woe to the Congressman who votes to cut spending for such a program. He or she will be maligned for cutting funding to schools, welfare, veterans aid, or whatever program is to be cut. There will be riots in the streets. We are witness to this in Greece, France, England—all over Europe, and it has already begun here in the United States.

If a Republican votes to cut a program, the Democrat opponent will campaign on a platform crucifying him for cutting off the funds, and vice versa. Why? First, because insofar as political posturing is concerned, it is successful. It is Propaganda 101. But, to truly answer the question, I find it prudent to further analyze why these programs become entitlement programs.

An entitlement program is a federal program that guarantees a certain level of benefits to persons or entities who meet requirements set by law, such as Social Security, farm price supports, or unemployment benefits. If an individual or group meets the legal requisites for receipt of government aid, it leaves no discretion with Congress on how much money to appropriate. Moreover, some entitlements carry permanent appropriations.

The reason why government programs are nearly impossible to dismantle, whether or not they fit into the narrow definition of an entitlement program, is because they breed dependency into the minds and hearts of those they "help."

Once you become dependent upon something or someone else doing a particular thing for you, it is human nature to rely upon that external force to always do it for you. Why should I save money for retirement if the government is doing it for me? Why should I work if the government will ostensibly pay me not to work? Going back to the concept of plunder, and why government is necessary to guard against man's animalistic instinct to take from others instead of producing for themselves—we plunder and we sit idly while things, gadgets, robots, and governments do for us because, just like water, it is in our nature to follow the path of least resistance.

Now, fast-forward five, ten, twenty, or thirty years into the future to when people have become entirely dependent upon any particular program, and try to dismantle that program. Good luck! Those dependent upon the program will riot in the streets and fight tooth and nail for that which they feel they are entitled to.

Analogy time! One of my favorite channels to watch is the Discovery Channel. Recently, they aired a series titled *Life*, in which Oprah Winfrey narrates to some of the most visually stunning high-definition footage of the world that surrounds us. In one particular episode which analyzed the intricacies of mammals and how we've evolved to become the dominant species on the planet, we find ourselves following the lives of myriad animals ranging from dolphins and whales to meerkats and cheetahs. The thesis of the episode is that the key to mammal's success as a class is not just in the size of our brains, but actually results from our exhibiting the most complex social behaviors out of any in the animal kingdom. In other words, we are successful because we live and die by the strength and weakness of our families and our capacity to use and share wisdom across generations allows us to flourish.

At one point, we find ourselves learning of the close-knit family dynamic which shapes the African Elephant's ability to rule the landscape. We follow a herd of six or seven elephants lead by a matriarch, the oldest and wisest female, and her daughter which has just birthed a one-day-old baby elephant. Soon, the baby elephant gets stuck in waist-deep mud at the edge of his first watering hole. The mother quickly comes to the rescue, extending a trunk to push the baby elephant out of the mud. Unfortunately, she is only pushing her baby deeper and deeper into the mud. Finally, the matriarch pushes the mother out of the way and simply lets the baby figure out how to escape the mud on his own.

This tale of a baby elephant's struggle is a perfect analogy for our federal government. You see, despite the mother's good intentions, it was best for her to let her baby figure it out on his own. Let's assume she helped him out. What would happen the next time he got stuck in the mud, or the time after that? If the baby elephant could always rely on his mother to get him out of the mud, he would understandably become dependent upon it and never have the incentive or chance to figure it out for himself. Then, one day, he gets stuck in the mud and his mom isn't around, resulting in him baking to death, unable to escape the Sun's rays to shade or water.

Likewise, what happens when the federal government is unable to bankroll inefficient entitlement programs through the expansion of our deficit? All those people so dependent upon the program will be left out to dry.

Moreover, just as the mother elephant made things worse for the baby elephant, the federal government, through action, often makes it harder for individuals and localities to efficiently govern and produce for themselves as they need and see fit.

Understanding the dangers of a strong, vast, and expanding federal government in the context of today's modern politics, and the roadblock it places in the path toward more perfect liberty and justice for all is essential to the rebirth of the Republican platform. The federal government must be reduced in size and efficiencies implemented post-haste.

But what of the critical issues facing our nation? Let me be clear—the challenges facing our nation are many, and they absolutely be met! It is not sufficient to argue that government should be smaller, that deficit spending must be choked off, and in that same breath ignore the critical issues of our time. It is the failure to meet these critical issues, decade after decade, that has lead us to this pivotal moment in our nation's history.

Now is not the time to cut government funding, many will argue. How, they will ask, can we tackle the mounting problems facing America while simultaneously reducing the size of the federal government? The Democrats will argue that the issues cannot be met without the further extension of the federal government's long arm into growing jurisdictions or an emergency increase in the debt ceiling. But they are dead wrong!

The answer is found in our very own backyards, our local town, city, and county governments and most of all, in our state governments. As was the intention of our founding fathers, the true power in government to effect change is laid in the state. For it is each locality and each state that best knows how to govern the intricacies of the varying geographies within their borders.

Unfortunately, the current paradigm of American governance has shifted to where the federal government increasingly administers programs that should be left to the states, either by holding the operation of those programs ransom with the carrot that is federal aid, or through the outright commandeering of those functions. We are increasingly delving into a system of governance where the reality is that of the American management of states. Instead, as was the legislative intent behind the Tenth Amendment, it not only should, but absolutely must be the Virginia management of Virginia, New York of New York, California of California, and so on!

Yet, states as well as the individuals comprising each state are looking to the federal government to do more and more. Congressmen and Senators are increasingly taking the burdens of America on their shoulders, directing the awesome force of federal government at the states in reaction to the simple fact that states are failing in the tasks provided them, such as the administration of proper education. And so, the Democrats have taken up liberty's torch, having seen that so much is being left undone at state and local levels, erroneously using the interstate commerce clause of the United States Constitution to mandate what should be done.

And it is not just the Democrats who increasingly are seeing it fit for the federal government to engage in the false philanthropy of providing for the welfare of all through government mandate. The Republicans, though their appropriations are aimed at different pockets, are equally as guilty of using the treasury coffers to fund inefficient programs outside the proper scope of federal government.

The Republicans have lost their way. Deep down, in our stomachs, we have always known the flawed thinking of "socialism."

We've read Orwell's masterpiece, *1984*, we've been taught about the dangers of communism, but we've lost the tongue for being able to express what we even mean by "small government" in an age when government is rapidly expanding, often at our direction.

In order for the Republican party to regain its strength as more than just a viable party, but one that actually leads this great nation once again to prosperity, our platform must begin with revolutionizing local and state politics. The core of American politics must be infused with a revitalized and re-focused Republican platform that understands that the role of government is to regulate in order to protect, not to do everything for its constituents. This mentality will enable the implementation of fiscal responsibility in state and local budgets as well as empower those governments to more succinctly tackle the critical issues facing their respective regions.

Why is this so important? In fiscal year 2010, state governments collectively ran a budget deficit approaching $55 billion—the result of both Democrats and Republicans allowing government to expand into improper arenas. In doing so, we are thereby strapping state governments in their ability to perform properly the functions they ought to be performing.

In particular, the near bankruptcy of the majority of our states is analogous to the mother elephant and her newborn stuck in the mud. The states, addicted to federal funds, almost unanimously turned to Troubled Asset Relief Funds and other sources of bailout moneys to delay their bankruptcies. But, now, the federal government is increasingly unable, or at least unwilling to borrow money from China to underwrite the states and pull them from the mud. What now?

There is no question that the federal government has the authority, as well as the duty, to govern in certain arenas. But, it is with the states that the majority of power must remain if we, as Americans, are to continue to honor the intentions of our sage founders.

Empowering each region to budget for that which is of greater importance to their constituents will allow each region the flexibility to tackle their laundry list of problems in the order they see fit. The result—pockets of happy constituents popping up across counties, cities, towns, and states. Further, as each of these local and state governments are directly accountable by their respective taxpayers as to money spent and a proximal demand for results directly effecting the region, it stands to reason that these governments will have more incentive to efficiently and expeditiously address the relevant issues than the federal government could plausibly ever have.

This will further result in each locality creating new and innovative ways to tackle the issues plaguing their region. It will be up to each state to determine the level of invasiveness of their regulations and what programs to implement, reform, or scrap altogether. One county or one state may develop craftier solutions than the other, and as capitalism goes, the next state over will be free to build upon the advances of the next. This is the true American way. The alternative, nationwide, top-down standard operating platforms—the trend of today, not only stifles innovation, but also sets in stone today's system(s) as the best we can hope for.

As Republicans, we must rise from the ashes, begin at the grassroots, and institute fundamental change in every locality in this nation. We must change politics from the inside out, from its core, starting with town, city, and county government, right to the doorsteps of our state capitols. We must fight to free local and state government from the strings of entitlement programs and a host of inefficient systems, thereby bringing state budgets into fiscal responsibility.

As the states become more fiscally responsible and resolutely focused on tackling the critical issues facing the residents within their borders, there will be less for the federal government to do, freeing up the treasury to invest in what it properly should and providing the necessary opportunity to reduce the federal deficit. Then, and only then, will there be less of a need for states to reach out to the federal government for aid. Best of all, perhaps, utilizing state and local governments as they were originally intended will work to remove the Democrats' desire to spend on false philanthropy from Capitol Hill.

# CHAPTER THREE

# LOBBYING, CAMPAIGN FINANCE REFORM OR TERM LIMITS: HOW TO STOP CORRUPTION

*For of those to whom much is given, much is required. And when at some future date the high court of history sits in judgment on each one of us—recording whether in our brief span of service we fulfilled our responsibilities to the state—our success or failure, in whatever office we may hold, will be measured by the answers to four questions:*

*First, were we truly men of courage—with the courage to stand up to one's enemies—and the courage to stand up, when necessary, to one's associates—the courage to resist public pressure, as well as private greed?*

*Secondly, were we truly men of judgment—with perceptive judgment of the future as well as the past—of our own mistakes as well as the mistakes of others—with enough wisdom to know that we did not know, and enough candor to admit it?*

*Third, were we truly men of integrity—men who never ran out on either the principles in which they believed or the people who believed in them—men who believed in us—men whom neither financial gain nor political ambition could ever divert from the fulfillment of our sacred trust?*

*Finally, were we truly men of dedication—with an honor mortgaged to no single individual or group, and compromised by no private obligation or aim, but devoted solely to serving the public good and the national interest?*

**- John F. Kennedy in a speech delivered to a Joint Convention of the General Court of the Commonwealth of Massachusetts on January 9, 1961.**

After graduating from the University of George Mason School of Law, I sat for the Virginia State Bar in the winter of 2006 and was sworn in at the Supreme Court of Virginia as a licensed attorney. Listening to the commencement speech of the Honorable Chief Justice Leroy Rountree Hassell, Sr., the first African American appointed to the court, a tremendous sense of honor came over me. I distinctly remember looking around at my fellow juris doctors readying to be sworn in to the sacred practice of law in the Commonwealth, thinking, "Here we are, the next agents of justice."

However, I had already been steeped in the practice of law since January of 2005, having petitioned the Supreme Court for permission to practice in my third year of law school under the guidance of an attorney already admitted to the bar. Petitioning the court was unfortunately necessitated by the unexpected near death of my father that winter.

In a matter of weeks, my father had gained somewhere near fifteen pounds of water weight. We later learned that this was a result of extreme heart failure brought on by the idiopathic triggering of a superfluous electrical pathway in his heart. As a result, his resting heart rate would spike upward of two hundred, instead of the normal sixtyish beats per minute. His heart literally turned to mush, losing its elasticity and ability to pump oxygen and blood to his vital organs. His ejection fraction, the measure of how much blood the heart pumps out with each pump versus the amount it withholds, plummeted, his organs shut down, and on Christmas Eve, 2004, he literally died.

My father was revived and immediately airlifted to Fairfax Hospital, renowned as having one of the best cardiology departments in the world. He underwent emergency heart surgery for the insertion of a balloon pump. The next morning, Christmas day, the on-call pulmonary specialist told me, point blank, that my father would not last an hour.

Well, he did. And after nearly a month of induced coma, he came home on February 7th, my birthday, and we opened our Christmas presents with family on Easter. To this day, his doctors are in awe at his recovery…he became, quite literally, a walking miracle. So let me pause to say, to all, no matter how dire a situation seems, remember, there is always hope! I digress, except to say that the exact same is true of the present and future of our great nation.

My father was the senior partner, manager, and owner of my law firm, Kidwell, Kent & Curran. It's a small, general practice firm, consisting then of only three attorneys, myself, my father, and J. Charles Curran, a dear friend and mentor. As such, upon the event of my father's sudden sickness, it fell upon me to take up the mantle by tackling his caseload and managing the firm.

When I took over, approximately 85% of the firm's income was derived from real estate-oriented revenue. In 2004, the height of the real estate boom, we were conducting an average of four residential or commercial real estate settlements a day. But, as luck would have it, in 2006, the exact summer I was sworn into the practice of law, the real estate market collapsed in the wake of what is now commonly referred to as the sub-prime lending scandal.

Almost overnight, my firm went from conducting four settlements a day to conducting as little as four in a month. The bubble had burst and what ensued was the precipitous decline of our economy into the "Great Recession." And now the feared "Double-Dip Recession."

The economic fallout across our nation has been unprecedented—somewhere between seven to ten million homes now sit vacant in a rising tsunami of foreclosures as unemployment lines rap around city blocks in haunting similarity to the soup lines of the Great Depression.

Suddenly, there I was, a young, ideological attorney fresh out of law school, beyond green behind the ears and faced with the task of reviving a law firm staring down the throat of looming bankruptcy. The livelihood of my entire family hinged on the income generated by Kidwell, Kent & Curran—my sister was our senior real estate processor, my father the owner, and now my economic fortunes were equally as entwined with the success or failure of our small family business. Failure was simply not an option.

What was I to do? I decided immediately that the best thing to do was diversify. Just like any savings plan, stock portfolio, or otherwise, the answer, I thought, lied in delving headfirst into new areas of law not previously or long since practiced at our firm.

I found myself practicing domestic relations, handling divorces, child custody, and spousal abuse cases. I defended alleged drug dealers, some innocent, some not, prosecuted squatting tenants, and even "chased ambulances," to use the term loosely, to land personal injury cases. But all of it left somewhat of a sour taste in my mouth. So, I moved on to different pastures where I hoped that my legal expertise could better serve justice.

Through friends in worship, I was invited to local churches and assisted living facilities to conduct seminars on estate planning and charitable giving, and I traveled to regional real estate brokerages to coach agents on the legal minefields of the increasingly litigious market.

Being that the firm's primary focus has been on real estate law for decades, I suppose it was natural for me to find expertise in one of the fastest expanding phenomena of the emerging real estate market: the short sale.

A short sale, simply put, is when a lender that has a mortgage, or deed of trust, secured as a lien against a particular parcel of real estate, allows the owner of that property to sell the property *short* of what they owe on their mortgage. The owner's real estate agent will list the property as contingent upon third party approval, that is, the lender's approval, of any ratified contract of purchase and sale. Once a contract is in hand, a package containing the owner's W-2s, tax returns, pay-stubs, account statements, and a letter explaining why they are in economic hardship is sent to the lender for consideration.

The short sale has become one of the largest market shares of all homes sold in the wake of the sub-prime lending scandal and is utilized as an alternative to foreclosure. The lender, in essence, reviews the hardship package and if it determines that it will yield more income on its investment by allowing the short sale than by instituting foreclosure, the lender approves the sale, often with stipulations requiring the borrower to execute a new note promising to pay back the deficiency over time.

In one form or another, the thought had long been swelling in my head, but I will never forget the day I was driving back to the office after having conducted a seminar on the short sale process at a local Long and Foster Realty brokerage. My head was racing with recent memories of the clients crying in my conference room, pleading for me to save them from being ousted from their American Dream. The mounting pressures of scraping to cover payroll, pouring what little savings I'd accumulated into the firm to keep it afloat—it all just hit me. I pulled off the road, ironically into the parking lot of a Bank of America, and looked into the rearview mirror.

"How did this happen," I asked myself aloud, staring at the too-tired reflection of a man in his twenties. <u>And there it is: How did this happen</u>? How did America, what I'd grown up to know is indisputably the greatest nation on this planet, the sole remaining superpower, and the epicenter of economic opulence, come to this? How were so many people out of work? And personally, how the hell was I going to survive the worst economy since the Great Depression? How was I going to do so in a firm dependent on real estate, the very market that had been enduring through the Great Recession two years longer than every other industry and in many respects, caused the recession?

How did this happen? The answer, of course, is multi-pronged and complex. That being said, there is one major cause of the

Great Recession that speaks volumes of the rampant corruption and backdoor dealing that has permeated the body politic of the United States Congress.

The corruption of which I speak is not necessarily born of malevolent intent or even self-dealing, though this certainly exists and is an issue. Unfortunately, it is a corruption that is systemic, proliferated as an inbuilt feature of our political system, and it is debilitating to the proper purpose and function of our government.

Sadly, the political underpinnings of the Great Recession, just the same as those of the Great Depression, are cases in point of this ingrained corruption of which I speak, and that is precisely why it is so absolutely imperative that we come to recognize the severity of the issue and address it with first priority!

It is against this corruption that the protestors comprising the ubiquitous and spreading Walk on Wall Street movement, should be protesting—and I hope that they read my message to assist in their finding a more enlightened voice to their cause. I understand their anger because I myself am the prototype Small Business, literally off Main Street, being stomped out in this economy. However, I do not agree with many of their destructive rioting, as it is misplaced and dangerous. Most comprising the movement, and therefore the movement itself, need to better understand what they are truly fighting for—and more importantly, why it is so imperative that all of us fight for it.

The world, the economy, government, and politics—they are all intertwined in a highly volatile, complex system, where one directly affects all others. Therefore, to understand the critical status of our debt-ridden economy, the Walk on Wall Street members, Republicans, Democrats—every American—first needs to understand, on a deeper level, exactly how we got into this mess. While some blames and complaints are definitely well placed, it is premature to scapegoat corporations as the sole culprit. To a large extent, in fact, the Walk on Wall Street should be a Walk on Congress.

In the years leading up to the Great Recession, extensive deregulation of the financial industry opened the door for the short-term, profit-motivated masterminds of Wall Street to conjure and implement exotic schemes that literally mortgaged the very security of the United States, and by extension thereof, the world economy. It was a gamble that fueled the boom of the real estate market as well as an explosion of personal credit debt, and it was every tax-paying American that eventually paid the pot when the wager was lost.

How was this allowed to occur? As the Leaders of the Group of Twenty cited in their "Declaration of the Summit on Financial Markets and the World Economy," in November, 2008:

> During a period of strong global growth, growing capital flows, and prolonged stability earlier this decade, market participants sought higher yields without an adequate appreciation of the risks and failed to exercise proper due diligence. At the same time, weak underwriting standards, unsound risk management practices, increasingly complex and opaque financial products, and consequent excessive leverage combined to create vulnerabilities in the system. Policy-makers, regulators and supervisors, in some advanced countries, did not adequately appreciate and address the risks building up in financial markets, keep pace with financial innovation, or take into account the systemic ramifications of domestic regulatory actions.

Quite literally, the watchdogs on Capitol Hill were asleep at the wheel and in many cases, they found it in their best interests to simply look the other way. Senators were relentlessly and effectively lobbied to pull the teeth from statutes aimed at quelling the foaming mouth of the profit-at-all-cost machine that is Wall Street. The Securities and Exchange Acts of 1933 and 1934 (enacted in response to the 1929 Stock Market Crash), as well as subsequent financial reforms, were simply not enforced, and a host of new legislation opened the door for moral hazard and unregulated risk. Why?

As a result of a $70 trillion "stash" of worldwide fixed income investments seeking higher yields than those offered by US Treasury bonds, Wall Street rose to the occasion, bringing forth financial innovation in a move to link this glut of money to the real estate market. This represented a seemingly endless tide of gold to line the pockets of everyone in the mortgage supply chain from the mortgage broker selling the loans, the banks funding the brokers, to the goliath investment banks backing them, and as a result, the behavior of lenders changed swiftly and dramatically. Lenders offered unprecedented loans, both in type and volume, even to undocumented immigrants, and the government did absolutely nothing to stop it!

As a result, the sub-prime lending scandal ensued. The unbridled deregulation and outright failure to enforce the laws already on the books allowed lenders to loan money to individuals or companies looking to invest in residential or commercial properties with "teaser" interest rates below prime (the prime interest rate as reported by the *Wall Street Journal* bank survey). Commercials blitzed our televisions and soon millions of Americans were looking to take out a second or third line of credit on their home or to purchase as many properties as they could with hopes of flipping them for a profit. We were enticed with interest only loans or adjustable rate mortgages, (ARMs), with beginning teaser rates so amazing, how could we not jump into the pot?

Even more, when we clicked on the site of the newest Internet brokerage ready to lend us money, we found we weren't even required to prove our financial solvency. Traditionally, borrowers taking out conventional loans would be required to put somewhere around 20% of the value of the property down, but, by 2005 the median down payment for first-time homebuyers was around 2%, with nearly 50% of loans made with no down payment at all. We were almost being provoked to mortgage our futures.

But, the enticement didn't stop there! We flocked to the brokers when they first offered stated income, verified assets (SIVA) loans, requiring only that we state our income without providing any proof other than having some money in the bank.

Then, the no income, verified assets (NIVA) loans came out. Unbelievably, lenders no longer even required proof of employment. Borrowers just needed to show proof of money in their bank accounts. Finally came NINA, or No Income No Assets loans. These NINA loans, often referred to as "Ninja" loans, allowed us to borrow money without having to prove or even state any owned assets. All that was required for a mortgage was a credit score, and not even a good one!

Another industry was primed to capitalize on the seemingly endless flow of financing to the common consumer, the residential homebuilder. Demand exploded into full out frenzy and builders began throwing up houses at record pace. Better yet, with demand soaring, housing prices were skyrocketing for the already invested, and homeownership reached an all-time high. All seemed beautiful in the boom world of supply and demand.

But, as we all now know… it was all horribly wrong!

I distinctly recall one particular mortgage offered from a fly-by-night brokerage to first-time clients of my law firm. It took me literally an hour to decipher the convoluted terms of the Note being offered to my clients and what I read was beyond alarming. So, when my clients came to the settlement table, I asked them what they thought the terms of their loan were. As you might have guessed, what they thought they were signing up for was completely different from what they were actually being asked to sign.

My clients explained that they were purchasing their first home, recently married and willing to extend themselves a little as she was expecting and they needed the extra room. They were under the impression they were getting a thirty-year loan with a fixed interest rate at 2.75% per annum with interest-only payments required for the first three years. Not even close!

In reality, the circuitous note they were presented with was interest-only for the first thirty days, fixed at 2.75% interest for the first year, and adjustable every six months thereafter, at prime plus 5% and with a cap at 18% interest per annum.

This note was alarming on multiple levels. To start, the margin, being the lender's scope of profit on the loan, at the time, was usually set at prime plus 2.5% to 2.75%, this was prime plus 5%. Second, and more alarming, the loan was amortized over thirty years at the greater of the margin plus 5% or 9.25%, and was due, in full, in fifteen years. This meant that while the interest rate was kept artificially low, as a teaser, for thirty days of only interest and then principal and interest at 2.75% for a year, the principal balance would actually increase at a startling rate. After paying on their loan for two years, they would have owed tens of thousands more than the amount of their original loan and greater than the value of their house.

Why not just refinance immediately? They could, but, by the very terms of the note's prepayment penalty clause, they would have been required to pay a hefty fine if they did so within two years and especially if they did so with another lender.

And third, as the stack of forms for them to sign ambiguously indicated, the loan had already been sold, twice, to two different loan servicing providers, prior to their signing. This note was a product of predatory lending to say the least.

The worst part about this scenario was the fact that my clients had absolutely no idea what they were about to sign and would not have had any idea unless I had taken the time, in my capacity as an attorney at law, to explain the terms of the note at settlement. These were well-educated individuals, both with master's degrees, and settled in well-respected professions. I advised them not to sign the documents and, to date, they remain as clients.

But, imagine if these two individuals were a young, entrepreneurial minority couple tantalized at the prospect of finally being able to attain the very icon of the American Dream—their first home. Imagine further that they were told that their mortgage payment for a $600,000 residence, a home large enough for themselves, their children, and their parents, would only run them $1,200 a month. Even better, if they went with the settlement company that the builder of their brand new American Dream recommended, the builder would contribute $5,000 to their closing costs. A sweet deal, right? No!

First, the settlement company recommended by the builder would most certainly be a subsidiary or otherwise be affiliated with the parent builder company, and the settlement company would "kick back" a majority of the title insurance earned at closing. To make a personal gripe, this is allowed only through a loophole in the Real Estate Settlement Procedures Act that the Housing of Urban Development (HUD) continually fails and refuses to properly police!

Because of the affiliation between the builder and settlement company, the settlement company had no care for the interests of the borrower/purchaser. Not representing the borrower, the settlement agent, even if asked about the terms of a note or deed of trust at settlement, would not be bound by any fiduciary duty to accurately explain the documents to the borrower. In fact, they are barred in doing so because doing so constitutes the unauthorized practice of law. And, as for the $5,000 in settlement costs, well, the builders simply upped the price of their new homes to cover this amount, charging a little more here and there for extras or even deliberately excluding a necessity from the initial offer to entice the buyer to upgrade from the base model. Brilliant capitalism in grand excess!

The result: borrowers signed documents they simply did not understand, and in three months, a year, maybe two, or even three, suddenly they were not required to pay the promised $1,200 a month for their mortgage, but rather, $4,200 a month. When the clock tolled and their mortgages shot up, millions of borrowers across the country were suddenly unable to pay, and this dawned the crash of the real estate market.

Between 1997 and 2006, the average value of real estate in the United States increased by an astonishing near 125%. The mentality, then, was that houses would increase in value not primarily on par with inflation as they had historically, but rather, as super-investments promising the highest rates of return around. You could refinance your house, take out a second or third line of credit, with no proof of income, buy a car with the change in your pocket, put your kid through college, and in six months, your house would be worth another sixty thousand. For a period of years, in fact, this was the reality, but it was nothing more than a thin and beautiful veil masking the inexorable and ugly truth.

While the price of real estate skyrocketed, the average income of an individual in that same timeframe did not. In fact, it stayed absolutely flat! From 1980–2000 the national median home price range averaged approximately three times median household income. This ratio accelerated to over four and a half times median household income by 2006.

It was not long before the builders that were throwing up homes at record pace on the naïve speculation that demand for homes would continue to climb without an attendant rise in income, simply outpaced demand. Suddenly, there were too many homes and too few people willing or able to make the investment. Supply and demand had finally broken through the frenzy to unveil the dreadful truth.

The coalescence of these factors resulted in a sudden downward pressure on the value of real estate across the United States. The nail in the coffin, so to speak, would come when the first wave of adjustable rate mortgages (ARMs) reset. Countless homeowners found themselves suddenly unable to pay their mortgage and when they turned to their lenders to refinance to a lower, more manageable rate, they were now being told that the principal balance on their outstanding loans were in excess of the plummeting value of their home. Since the lender could not sufficiently secure the loan necessary to refinance the outstanding adjustable rate mortgage, they would not extend the necessary financing. The housing bubble had officially burst!

A positive feedback loop began whereby those unable to refinance defaulted on their loans, and foreclosures spread like wildfires, further driving down the value of forest after forest of homes. Second, third, fourth, and continuing waves of adjustable rate mortgages reset, and those homeowners were also unable to refinance. They defaulted and the foreclosure of their homes fed right back into the downward spiraling market, further pulling the value of real estate into the tank.

By fourth-quarter 2007, over 15% of sub-prime ARMs were in foreclosure or over ninety days delinquent. By second-quarter 2008, a staggering 25% were delinquent. In 2007, lenders instituted foreclosure proceedings on over 1.2 million properties, a dramatic 79% increase over the year prior. In 2008, lenders instituted 2.3 million foreclosures and 2.8 million in 2009.

The saga, as we all know, does not end there. We've unfortunately become all too familiar with the terminology that has been thrown around in the wake of the sub-prime lending scandal. Toxic loans, mortgage-backed securities, and credit default swaps, to name a few. This is because an additional and major catalyst of the sub-prime crisis, beyond the abovementioned predatory and deregulated lending practices, was the advent of banks entering into the mortgage bond market.

The traditional mortgage model involved a bank originating a loan to the borrower and retaining the entirety of the default risk. The significant risk of losing their investment in the secured real estate understandably forced banks to lend cautiously. But, this traditional model crumbled under a new "originate to distribute" model as a result of banks entering the mortgage bond market.

Banks were now able to sell the mortgages and distribute credit risk to investors through what we all now know as the mortgage-backed security (MBS). Suddenly the lenders issuing mortgages no longer retained any risk and by selling the mortgages to investors, they could immediately replenish their funds, enabling them to issue more loans and generate mountains of transaction fees. This unfortunately created a moral hazard in the industry as loan

47

originators were now only concerned with generating money for their pockets via origination charges without parallel regard for the quality of the underlying credit.

But, even with the advent of the MBS, the regulated banking industry had only so much money to go around. As such, the security market from 1992 to 2004 expanded at a steady but marginal rate. But now, in order to satiate the demand of foreign and domestic investors Wall Street was going to have to come up with something genius. Millions of lobbying dollars spent and in comes the 2004 United States Securities and Exchange Commission (SEC) decision on the Net Capital Rule allowing United States investment banks to issue substantially more debt. It was this exact debt that was utilized by the investment banking industry to purchase volumes of mortgage-backed securities.

The share of sub-prime mortgages passed to third-party investors via mortgage-backed securities increased to approximately 75% in 2006. American homeowners, consumers, and corporations owed nearly $25 trillion in debt with traditional depository banks retaining only $8 trillion of that total and an astonishing $10 trillion came from the securities markets.

Now, my aim is not to delve into the pros and cons of allowing investment banks to issue debt and purchase mortgage-backed securities. In fact, aside from the debt element, I am not so sure that I do have any theoretical problem with it if properly regulated. But, what is extremely important to understand is why the securities bazaar comprising the lion's share of the market was and remains such a crisis from a policy standpoint, especially insofar as it contributed to the Great Recession.

Politically speaking, the problem is a complete and utter lack of regulation of what is commonly referred to as the shadow banking system. The shadow banking system is a network of lenders, brokers and opaque financing vehicles such as hedge funds and investment banks which by definition do not accept deposits like the common depository bank and are therefore not subject to the same regulations.

In allowing investment banks to underwrite massive amounts of debt, they were, in reality, given cart blanche permission to procure mortgage-backed securities and essentially intertwine themselves into the same pool as depository banks without the requirement of adhering to nearly as stringent of regulations. And they capitalized on this opening!

In the years leading up to the crisis, the top four US depository banks moved over $5 trillion in assets and liabilities "off-balance sheet" into the shadow banking system, enabling them to bypass scores of regulations. Why would they do this? Money!

The ability to issue large amounts of debt opened the door, but the investment banks were investing in mortgage-backed securities based upon a false assumption that housing prices would continue to rise in the foreseeable future, and that borrowers would also continue to make their mortgage payments. In doing so, the investment banks were engaging in financial leverage: borrowing at a lower interest rate and investing the proceeds at a higher interest rate. This strategy proved profitable during the housing boom. In fact, the New York State Comptroller's Office reported that Wall Street executives took home bonuses totaling $23.9 billion in 2006 alone.

Now, hindsight is 20/20, sure, but given the stagnation of individual income as compared to the staggering escalation in housing affordability, it should have been clear to the investment banks that their bet was, in the very least, a short-lived risk. In reality, though, lenders certainly didn't care because they were raking in processing fees. And the investment banks, they were concerned only with short-term profit and the executives, it seems, concerned more with their year-end bonus rather than the long-term financial viability of their firms, let alone the consequences of a predictable real estate meltdown.

The entire financial system, from mortgage brokers to investment bank executives and Wall Street risk managers, was undeniably tilted toward short-term risks for the sake of the almighty buck while ignoring long-term obligations and underlying risks to main street America. They were playing with trillions of dollars, all held as debt over each American's head, and our government failed completely to regulate their actions—actions which evidently were governed by greed and reeked of moral hazard. This is what the Walk on Wall Street movement is protesting—even if they don't realize it.

Then, it hit the fan! The investment banks' brilliant financial leverage strategy, as we now know, resulted in almost incalculable losses when real estate values plummeted and mortgages began to default. Unregulated, these shadow banking entities were unconscionably vulnerable because they borrowed short-term in liquid markets to purchase long-term, illiquid, and risky mortgage-backed securities. The downturn in housing and rising foreclosure rates resulted in investment banks being subject to rapid deleveraging, requiring them to sell their long-term assets at depressed prices.

The extent of the vulnerability the investment banks were allowed to risk is astonishing. The top five investment banks in the United States reported over $4.1 trillion in debt for fiscal year 2007 alone, nearly a third of total US gross domestic product! And as a result, the top three US investment banks, institutions "too big to fail," faced financial meltdown in the wake of the sub-prime lending scandal. Lehman Brothers went bankrupt, sending the stock market into a downward spiral and Bear Sterns and Merrill Lynch were sold at fire sale prices.

What was the result for the average American? In the first three quarters of 2008 alone, owners of stocks in US corporations suffered nearly $8 trillion in losses.

Unfortunately, the rabbit hole spirals deeper. As I said before, Wall Street was literally betting on our economy, and doing so with our money. More concisely, while underwriting trillions in bad debt to purchase mortgage-backed securities, they were hedging their bets by simultaneously wagering with the other hand that the very mortgages leveraged as a carrot to the masses as a means to buy into the American Dream would fall into default and a "credit event" would occur. These loans, doomed for default, were understood by this other hand to be "toxic" and they were betting that we'd fail to make our mortgage payments!

Quite literally, this other "hand" of Wall Street wanted us to fail to meet our mortgage obligations and fall into default. They didn't care if this meant foreclosure for countless hardworking families; that wasn't their problem, because the pushers of the Credit Default Swaps (CDS) made their money at sale of the product and investors raked in the doe the instant default became reality.

Now, when I said that deregulation of the financial industry resulted in exotic products, perhaps the starkest example would be the credit default swap. The credit default swap is an extremely complicated product, one that requires a mathematical formula spanning the length of numerous blackboards to set out. But, boiled down to its roots, a credit default swap is a bilateral contract between the buyer of the contract and the seller of the contract, for protection. The protection buyer purchases the contract from the seller of the CDS and is required to pay a quarterly spread or fee to the seller. The CDS contract then references a third party, or "reference obligor," such as a borrower on any mortgage loan. If that third party, which, by the way, is in no way shape or form a party to the CDS contract, defaults on their mortgage payment, the seller of the CDS pays the buyer par value for return of the subject CDS bond, an amount that usually reaches into the many millions. In short, we fail to pay our mortgage, and some investor gets filthy rich!

According to a 2010 International Swaps and Derivative Association (ISDA) market survey, over $62 trillion of outstanding credit default swaps have flooded the financial industry, but this approximation is likely low, as not all of them are documented using the ISDA standard promulgated forms—not to mention the additional proliferation of basket default swaps, credit-linked notes, and loan-only credit default swaps. All of these exotic products are not traded on the open exchange and are therefore not reported to any government agency tasked to regulate them.

So, while wildly unregulated in the sale of the CDS, the same Wall Street companies were simultaneously selling the mortgage-backed securities to other investors—perhaps one of the most sickening displays of moral turpitude imaginable! Not even the best of magicians could pull off this sleight of hand! With one hand, Wall Street was convincing investors that the underlying credit comprising trillions of dollars' worth of mortgage-backed securities were sound, and with the other hand, they were convincing their other clients to invest in a CDS, a product with its value fundamentally linked to mortgage default.

Was everyone asleep at the wheel, or were heads just turning in the other direction? Why would any congressman or woman allow this to happen? Unfortunately, the answer, plainly and simply, is <u>systemic</u> corruption!

Allow me to indulge once again in an analogy with the predicate of an axiom that we all know, "History repeats itself."

The 1929 stock market crash, which signaled the beginning of the Great Depression, was in large part caused by problematic stock trading practices permitted under a laissez faire regulatory scheme. Perhaps the most notorious of these practices was the unchecked convention of buying stocks on the margin.

Buying on the margin consists of purchasing stocks or other securities with capital borrowed from a broker and utilizing other securities as collateral. The aim, of course, is to amplify profit on the positive equity potentially earned on any particular holding. To begin, the net value, or the difference between the value of the security and the broker's loan, is equivalent to the amount of one's own cash used. This disparity is required to stay above a minimum margin requirement designed to protect the broker against a fall in the value of the security.

Here is an example:

James purchases stock in a corporation for $1,000, using $200 of his own savings, and $800 borrowed from his broker. Here, the net value (share minus loan) is $200. As a requirement of the loan, the broker demands a minimum margin requirement, or leverage rate, of $100.

Suppose the stock, for whatever reason, drops to $850. The net value is suddenly only $50 (net value [$200]—stock value loss of [$150]). James is forced by the terms of the broker's loan to either sell the stock or pay out of his pocket to bring the investment back to the minimum margin requirement.

As a byproduct of laissez faire regulation, margin requirements were extremely loose in the 1920s. Brokers required investors to put down only 5–10% of their own money, whereas today, in response to the Great Depression, the Federal Reserve's margin requirement limits debt to 50%. So, when the stock market began to contract at the tail of the roaring twenties, many investors received margin calls. If these investors could not deliver their own money to their brokers within a certain timeframe their shares would be sold. Unfortunately, the market was quickly saturated with market call after market call and as many individuals did not have the equity to cover their margin positions, their shares were sold at rapidly declining prices. A positive feedback loop ensued, causing further market declines and additional margin calls.

Sound familiar? The fall of the real estate market which pulled us into the Great Recession is analogous to the crash of the stock market which lead to the Great Depression in that the sub-prime lending scandal ostensibly was all about buying stock, investment in real estate, on the margin, with money that was not truly in existence but speculated to eventually, if not soon, arrive. Both the boom of the roaring twenties and the boom of the early 2000s were built upon speculative equity.

Sure, the details are quite different, and unquestionably contemporary financial markets are vastly more complex, but the root cause for the meltdowns, in both the Great Depression and Great Recession, remain strikingly similar.

The Securities and Exchange Acts of 1933 and 1934 were promulgated in order to guard against exactly the economic fallout that has occurred in the Great Recession. Yet, despite being privy to the lessons of history's past, statute after statute was pushed through Congress to give entire swathes of the financial industry exemptions from regulation, and almost unfettered freedom to conjure and implement exotic products as well as expand into supplementary markets without regard for the intrinsic conflicts of interest therein created or the long-term risks to the stability of the financial market as a whole.

It is critical to the analysis of the current economic crisis, however, to note that the government's release of their necessary regulatory grip on the financial industry did not happen merely overnight. Instead, the deregulation and adoption of ill-advised legislation has been a steady process lead by a gloriously mounted lobbying effort of major Wall Street firms and a concomitant and growing lack of political will to enforce or enact legislation to guard against market excess and conflicts of interest.

For example, Jimmy Carter's Depository Institutions Deregulation and Monetary Control Act of 1980 (DIDMCA) phased out a number of banking restrictions, expanded their lending powers, and raised the deposit insurance limit from $40,000 to $100,000, thereby reducing the lender's risk per loan. In 1982, Congress passed the Alternative Mortgage Transactions Parity Act (AMTPA), which allowed non-federally chartered housing creditors to write adjustable-rate mortgages. The Act was the subject of major criticisms surrounding banking industry deregulation argued to have contributed to the savings and loans crisis, yet it remains in full force and effect. By 2006, approximately 80% of all sub-prime mortgages were adjustable-rate mortgages.

The 106th Congress, under Bill Clinton, passed the Gramm-Leach-Bliley Act in 1999, effectively repealing major portions of the Glass-Steagall Act of 1933. The Glass-Steagall Act was enacted after the Great Depression with the purpose of separating commercial banks and investment banks in order to avoid latent conflicts of interest amid the lending activities of the former and rating activities of the latter. Economist Joseph Stiglitz criticized the repeal of the Act, blasting its repeal as the "culmination of a $300 million lobbying effort by the banking and financial services industries..." (Stiglitz, *Vanity Fair*, "Capitalist Fools"). The

Act's repeal has been central to the proliferation of complex and opaque financial instruments such as the credit default swap.

Deregulation (which I will hereinafter use when referring both to the failure of our government to enforce existing laws and the enactment of ill-advised legislation) of the financial industry has been steady and deliberate at the lobby of major market players. Finance, insurance, and real estate sectors spent over $2.5 billion lobbying congress between 1998 and 2006, leading all other sectors, including the health sector. Is it any wonder why Wall Street got its way, despite the glaring signs of impending doom?

It depends only upon the lobby, the National Rifle Association, or any one union for example, and in whose "pocket" they lie, whether the Democrats or Republicans will vote in favor of any particular lobby and their special interests. So, while it is convenient to point across the aisle at the other side, the reality is that the problem permeates both political parties. At the push of lobbies, our elected officials, more and more, are persuaded to deregulate in the name of free market capitalism, and further seem to believe that deregulation is necessary.

As a registered Republican, though, and it pains me to say— many of Congress' misguided behests are personifications of an absolutely precarious philosophy that exists as a staple within the contemporary Republican platform. It exists on both platforms, as I just mentioned, but I speak here of the mentality within the party of which I am a devout member.

I've volunteered in a number of Republican campaigns in the Northern Virginia region; from local board of county supervisor, school board, delegate, and state Senate races to campaigns for election to the United States Congress. At every committee meeting, fundraiser, or local rally, I hear one version or another of the same pronouncement; an absolute decree that government, as a whole, both at the state and federal level, should not in any way, shape, or form regulate the free market. This, obviously, is a subset of the cry for smaller government, both of which I happen to agree with...to a degree.

A very real problem within the Republican Party exists in the fact that many seem to blindly believe that ANY regulation is tantamount to socialism. There is absolutely no question that the ever expansion of government is entirely corrosive of the economy. However, there is a fine line between over-regulation and under-regulation. To espouse the removal of all regulatory "schemes" as a platform is ill informed, shortsighted, and simply dangerous. To do so is to espouse anarchy.

As a lawyer, I am perhaps uniquely aware of the need for "regulation." Regulation is simply another word for law, which I have already said is created to protect persons, liberties, and properties; to maintain the right of each, and to cause justice to reign over us all. With the exception of the Almighty in the afterlife, there can be no justice if not by way of man enforcing the laws of man.

Practicing in criminal law highlights it most perhaps, but a truism of man's nature is equally as apparent in varying degrees when I sit as a mediator between a husband and wife beyond reconciliation and well down the unfortunate road to divorce: Homo Homini Lupus—Man is wolf to man! It is unfortunate that this platitude necessitates regulation, but it is naïve to promote resultant anarchy through the espousal of the absolute removal of government regulation of the free market. Unfortunately, so many of us are doing this in order to win a vote.

Reducing the size of government is a big-ticket item today, and it ought to be. I believe in it so ardently that I tackled the issue first and foremost in this thesis. But, reduction in government does not necessarily mean or require the eradication of regulation. To argue as such is simply illogical and presents a false choice. Nevertheless, let me clarify.

There are basically two types of regulation: 1) regulation to protect and 2) regulation requiring action or inaction. The former is within the true and proper purpose of government. The latter is beyond the scope of government function and in all cases ought to be abolished*. Taxes, I suppose, would fit into the second category, and so I asterisk my statement to note that there are certain limited, and I do mean absolutely limited, exceptions to that rule that must be strictly defined and instituted to perform a clearly identifiable and narrow purpose.

The Great Recession was caused by a deregulation of the first type of abovementioned regulation—regulation to protect. What ensued?

By November 2008, individual Americans lost more than 25% of their net worth, the S&P 500 was down 45% from its 2007 high, and housing prices had dropped 20% from their peak two years earlier, shedding nearly $5 trillion in speculated value. Total retirement assets dropped by 22%, from approximately $10 trillion in 2006 to $8 trillion in 2008. In short, just as in the wake of the 1929 stock market crash, we were left out to dry.

In response, the federal government announced a $600 billion program in November 2008 to purchase the mortgage-backed securities financed by Fannie Mae and Freddie Mac in the hopes of lowering mortgage rates. By March 2009, the Federal Reserve's balance sheet was expanded to further purchase agency (GSE) mortgage-backed securities, bringing its total purchase of toxic securities up to $1.25 trillion and counting. On February 17, 2009, the American Recovery and Reinvestment Act was signed into law by President Obama, with $787 billion earmarked for spending. All of this is at the enormous expense of the individual American taxpayer. We have been caught paying the wager lost by corporate America!

Now, let me pause. Reading to this point, you may think that I am 100% against free market capitalism and that you may as well stop reading this and turn to Karl Marx's *Communist Manifesto*. Quite to the contrary! I believe that in order for liberty to prevail, all men and women must be free to attain to the fullest stature of which they are innately capable and that in order to do so, free market capitalism must reign supreme. The most essential pillar to build upon liberty's foundation is that of free market capitalism!

As I said before, America is built upon the idea that if one works hard enough, if he or she is willing to roll up their sleeves, society should leave the individual free to reach his or her full potential. This philosophy, this potent and powerful mindset, undeniably, is the backbone of America's success, for it is the blood, sweat, and tears of the individual that has engineered our nation's prosperity. I am absolutely, 100% against the abolition of free market capitalism, in any way, shape, or form!

Can you tell I'm a lawyer? Now that I'm through with my disclaimer…

Above, I've used terms to describe Wall Street as the profit-at-all-cost machine and thrown executives under the bus by highlighting their exorbitant bonuses and terming their lemming's as the short-term, profit-motivated masterminds of Wall Street who conjured and implemented the exotic schemes that literally mortgaged the very security of the United States, and by extension thereof, the world economy. Do I question their motives? Do I question their moral compass? Do I question their risk assessments? Yes! But, to be frank, as a businessman myself, I not only understand their position, I also appreciate it.

You see, Wall Street, when you boil it down to its most fundamental roots, is not so different from Main Street, despite what CNN would like us to believe. Just like my small, family-run, general practice law firm, Wall Street goliaths are motivated by one overriding concern—money! Quality of product and customer loyalty aside (which is of utmost importance at Kidwell, Kent & Curran = shameless plug), Wall Street is, by the very nature of free market capitalism, married to the profit margin. Who will buy stocks if their futures are forecast to deteriorate? Nobody! (Except for the ridiculous practice of shorting stocks, which, as a side note, is in itself a moral dilemma.)

Corporations trading on the open market, and the board members sworn to uphold the salient interests of their firm, then, are beholden to the stockholder. Stop, then, and put yourself in the shoes of a stockholder. Many of us, in fact, should find this easy, as we do, in one form or another, own stocks. They might be in mutual funds, held in a brokerage account, or casually traded on our iPhone apps. What do we all wish for, and ultimately demand? We demand that the stock turn us a profit or we dump it, period, no ifs, ands, or buts!

Multiply our individual want of short-term profit on any particular stock by $70 trillion worldwide. This is what Wall Street was looking at. And some of the smartest people in our nation, graduated from the likes of Yale and Harvard, conjured schemes to make you and I money as we demanded. Fortuitously, of course, they also made themselves heaps of cash.

Simply put, Wall Street did what free market capitalism demanded—they met demand by providing supply of money! On this factor alone, I cannot and will not fault them. In fact, to an extent, I applaud them.

You see, those of us who are stockholders, in any form, can be broken down into two selves: 1) the stockholder, and 2) the individual. I point this out because our stockholder self, demanding short-term, if not long-term profit, but profit nonetheless, has interests inherently contrary to that of our individual self. Allow me to explain.

Our stockholder self wants whatever corporation we have invested in to do all it can to make a profit. We'd like to think, in theory, that this means pure innovation to outdo the competitor. But, in reality, our stockholder self knows this may include investing in risky endeavors that yield a short-term profit, skirting environmental regulations, or increasing profit margins by cutting employee wages or procuring cheaper materials.

Meanwhile, our individual self wants higher wages even though our company is cutting costs to cow-tow to their investors, and we complain when they outsource to India or look to China for cheaper materials.

We go to Walmart to buy clothes on the cheap, but complain when they come into our town and destroy the small businesses comprising our downtowns. Why? Because, on each end, whether as the consumer or as the supplier, money seems to be our governor.

Look at the price of a hybrid vehicle. On average it is three to five thousand dollars more than the same car without a hybrid engine. If it were the same cost, aside from adrenaline junkies, we'd all probably buy the hybrid. But even most "tree huggers" can't choke down the extra green involved in purchasing the same car, with less horsepower, for thousands more. Why? Because money talks!

So, given an opening in the law, which allows you to make money, perhaps even a lot of money, and do so 100% legally, will you take it? What if it is perhaps morally questionable and the risks are exceptional? What if nobody questions it? Will you go for it and become rich? I know you'd like to say no.

So, imagine you are a board member, one of, say, twelve, elected to your position with the solitary direction of finding ways for your company to make money for those invested. Now this opening presents itself; an opening that means millions and millions to your stockholders, and, oh yes, yourself. The unbridled risks that eventually backfired and thrust us into the Great Recession are proof that those on Wall Street, in any case, went for it.

It is a function of man that we try to better our position always, and, unfortunately, will do so at the cost of our fellow man if necessary. Homo Homini Lupus—Man is Wolf to Man! This animalistic instinct necessitates government, law, regulation! The history of the Great Depression taught us many lessons and, if headed, many warnings could have prevented the Great Recession. Why did Congress not listen? Why did they allow such extensive deregulation despite the lessons of history? Again, the answer is faction!

As James Madison argued in *Federalist Paper No. 10*, the problem of faction is, "most likely, not least, severe in a small republic, for it is in a small republic that a self-interested private group would be most likely able to seize political power in order to distribute wealth or opportunities in its favor!" He was arguing that the policies of a federal government, comprised of the states, would not easily be hijacked by the interests of any one state, whereas, the states, individually, would be at risk of falling prey to noxious factions within.

The problem is this: Wall Street, and the individual corporate conglomerates that comprise it, being so "in bed" with the federal government is tantamount to a small republic. In making the federal government a "good ol' boys" network indebted to their money, lobbies are able to pull the strings of our congressmen and women and bring them into their very fold. The result is a faction, a small republic if you will, (many of them with a workforce the size of any one of the 13 colonies), that is divorced from the reality of its constituents and more concerned with distributing the common wealth to itself. Money for power, power for money! And such is the nature of politics. But it does not have to be so.

*"The Journey from Congress to K Street,"* was published in 2005 by Public Citizen, a non-profit government watchdog group. Their report analyzed hundreds of lobbyist registration documents filed in compliance with the Lobbying Disclosure Act and the Foreign Agents Registration Act, finding that since 1998, 43% of the 198 members of Congress who left government to join "private life" have registered to lobby. Not only is there a job awaiting our elected officials after their term is through, but there is a seemingly endless parade of money thrown their way to convince them to vote in favor of the lobby while in office. Between 1998 and 2006, the top thirteen lobbying sectors spent a combined $15 billion-plus on persuading Congress this way and that, not even including campaign contributions.

The lamentable, clear fact is that corporate interests are taken into consideration by dint of their unmatched spending power at the apparent disregard of concern for the common constituent. Money does buy access in Washington, access that amplifies corporate influence which often results in swaying congress to promote the interests of the few at the immediate or eventual expense of the many. The question that presents itself, then, is how can this be dealt with?

There are three distinct avenues, and all of which, by their very nature are intrinsically entwined, I believe the corrupting weight of corporate money on the federal legislative process can be pacified:

1. Lobbying Reform;
2. Campaign Finance Reform; and
3. Term Limits.

I will tackle each proposed course in order, analyzing the need for each, the debates surrounding them, and then make specific proposals respectively.

**Lobbying Reform:**

While I have so far been critical of the effect lobbying has had on the decisions made by our elected officials, let me be clear in stating that I believe lobbying, per se, is not the underlying problem in Washington. Rather, the **EFFECT** lobbying is allowed to have on our elected officials as a result of our political system is to blame.

To clarify, the root of the problem is not born of the fact that any particular lobby has the ability over their competitor to shovel millions of dollars into the pockets of our politicians, for this is a natural and positive byproduct of capitalism and true to democratic ideals, rather the problem is that our politicians need that money to survive. Our elected officials' need for money to survive in the political forum renders them voiceless without the say of their "financiers," resulting in the average constituent, you and I, being disenfranchised.

I believe that lobbying is essential to our republic, as the informed discussion of public issues and debate are integral to the operation of our democracy. Lobbyists are often experts in a given subject capable of examining various economic, commercial, and other functional interests and often advise Congress on how to formulate legislation. To that end, lobbying in America serves a very useful purpose. However, when lobbying, as it has become in not all but many respects, turns merely into above-board bribery, it undermines the legislative process and is ultimately destructive of our democracy.

Lobbying, which by definition is the act of soliciting or trying to influence the votes of members of a legislative body, is a powerful form of speech and petition, and therefore the act, in and of itself, is protected by the First Amendment.

*Congress shall make no law respecting an establishment of religion, or prohibiting the free exercise thereof; or abridging the freedom of speech, or of the press; or the right of the people peaceably to assemble, and to petition the Government for a redress of grievances.*

### – First Amendment to US Constitution

Because the discussion of public issues and debate are so integral to the operation of the system of government established by our Constitution, any prohibition of speech, including the petition of government itself (aka lobbying), must serve a legitimate, narrowly tailored purpose. Though I would have it no other way, this serves as a very large hurdle for lobbying reform to overcome.

In order to analyze the impediment to lobbying reform presented by the First Amendment, we must start with case law. An expanding line of Supreme Court cases has ruled the following as it pertains to the curtailing of speech:

To begin, there is the doctrine of no prior restraint. Essentially, government cannot punish someone before they have spoken or try to prevent them from speaking as to do so would constitute censorship and would result in society always being deaf to a particular message. However, the government can, in varying degrees, promulgate laws regulating the content of speech and content-neutral speech.

Content-based regulation centers around the limitation or punishment of speech because of the content of the message or the stance of the speaker. In order for any such curtailment to be constitutional, the regulation must pass the test of strict scrutiny. Strictly speaking, the law must serve a compelling government interest and must be narrowly tailored as the least restrictive means of curtailing the specific speech. Per the Overbreadth Doctrine: if the law punishes protected speech, it is void, and if it the law is too vague, it shall also be invalidated because people of common intelligence would be unsure what speech is actually prohibited, theoretically resulting in all speech being chilled.

Content-neutral laws, on the other hand, are unrelated to the content of the speech and do not favor one viewpoint over another. This type of regulation is notably subject to the O'Brien test from Chief Justice Warren's opinion in *United States v. O'Brien* (391 US 367 [1968]). Under the O'Brien test, content-neutral laws are subject to intermediate scrutiny rather than strict scrutiny. The law must serve a substantial government interest, the law must be unrelated to the content of the speech, and the law must be narrowly tailored but not necessarily as the least restrictive means of curtailing the speech. Lastly, the law must leave alternative channels for communication.

In which category would you place lobbying? The question, of course, is a red herring of sorts because it is important to note that the level of scrutiny required in judicial review of lobbying depends not on the act of lobbying itself, but rather upon the language of the law and how that statute aims to restrain lobbying.

In *Buckley v. Valeo* (424 US 1 [1976]) the Supreme Court laid down precedent that continues to resonate in the halls of justice and the chambers of Congress today. "Some forms of communication made possible by the giving and spending of money involve speech alone, some involve conduct primarily, and some involve a combination of the two," the court wrote, "Yet this Court has never suggested that the dependence of a communication on the expenditure of money operates itself to introduce a non-speech element or to reduce the exacting scrutiny required of the First Amendment."

The court in *Buckley* went on to distinguish *O'Brien* from the case before it as it considered the appeal to key provisions of the Federal Election Campaign Act of 1971 (FECA). Where *O'Brien* dealt with clearly content-neutral regulation (administrative interest in the preservation of draft cards), the court argued that it was "beyond dispute that the interest in regulating the alleged 'conduct' of giving or spending money arises in some measure because the communication allegedly integral to the conduct itself is thought to be harmful."

The court distinguished limitations on expenditures from limitations on the amount any one person or group may contribute to a candidate or political committee, upholding the latter and invalidating the former.

The argument was this: "A restriction on the amount of money a person or group can spend on a political communication during a campaign necessarily reduces the quantity of expression by restricting the number of issues discussed, the depth of their exploration, and the size of the audience reached." Whereas, a limitation on political contributions "entails only a marginal restriction upon the contributor's ability to engage in free communication, for it permits the symbolic expression of support evidenced by a contribution but does not in any way infringe the contributor's freedom to discuss candidates and issues."

The court found that FECA's limitations on contributions were constitutionally valid because they served a legitimate administrative interest in preserving the integrity of the democratic process without directly infringing upon the candidate or individual's rights to engage in political discussion. In contrast, the court invalidated the Act's expenditure ceilings because they felt that the provisions placed direct restrictions on the ability of candidates, citizens, and associations to engage in political expression, altogether in violation of the First Amendment.

**Pop Quiz:**

Which do you believe is the proper role of government in relation to the First Amendment?

1. The government should remain neutral as people in the private sector compete in the political marketplace. If some people have more money than others, and if their greater resources permit greater access to the public officials, the result is not something the government should or can remedy consistent with the First Amendment.

2. A system of free expression is one in which there is fair deliberation on what the public good requires, and inequality of resources can seriously distort that deliberation by heightening the level of one voice and diminishing another. The government should enact legislation to promote a more equal and fair public debate.

Answer: Both! Allow me to explain.

Consider James Skelly Wright's argument in his 1976 Yale Law Journal Article, *Politics and the Constitution: Is Money Speech.* In it, the chief judge of the United States Court of Appeals for the District of Columbia started with the "pluralist" belief that the First Amendment's highest function is to let group pressure run its course unimpeded, for to interfere would skew the process that determines the public interest. I happen to agree with this philosophy; however, I also agree with Judge Wright's assertion that the pluralist model "gives undeserved weight to highly organized and wealthy groups and drains politics of its moral and intellectual content." He went on further to argue, "What the pluralist rhetoric obscures is that *ideas,* and not intensities, form the heart of the expression which the First Amendment is designed to protect."

The simple fact remains that lobbying in the United States has spiraled out of control. John Smith, who owns a small business on Main Street, simply cannot compete with the money Wall Street firms or energy conglomerates can throw at lobbyists to wine and dine our elected officials. The result is not, as many politicians, and even our Supreme Court justices, have oft argued, "theoretical," and it certainly is more than an unsubstantiated, undue influence to the detriment of the common constituent. The result is the sub-prime lending scandal, forty years of inaction as it relates to our energy independence, immigration, education reform, and the list of inaction/biased exploits goes on and on. The impact is real; it is significant; and it is destroying our republic!

But, given the constitutional constraints of the First Amendment protection of free speech and petition, how do we reform lobbying in America without trampling on the rights of the lobbies in favor of the common man?

I would argue that any restriction aimed at limiting a lobby's access to politicians, such as by way of enacting ceilings on the amount of money the lobby can spend on a dinner party for a congressman or woman, would be a direct and substantial restriction on the ability of candidates and citizens (or a group of citizens represented by that lobby) to engage in protected political expression. As such, no law abridging such rights should stand.

Therefore, the only way to regulate lobbying properly, as I see it, without running afoul of the First Amendment, is to require more transparency than is currently mandated in the system. Each dollar spent by a lobbyist to reach the ear of a member of Congress or candidate, to include the entire gamut of lobbying tactics commonly employed, from one dollar and above, must be accounted for and reported by the lobbyist and his or her firm to a commissioner of accounts in the judicial branch. When a lobbyist advises a member of Congress or their staffers on proposed legislation, their hourly rate must be accounted for, the bill they were advising on and any specific language proffered must be catalogued, and the judiciary shall have jurisdiction of review and penalization for abuses and undue influence.

It seems clear to me that the judicial branch should have the authority to oversee the proprieties of lobbying and congressional action; as such an oversight power would constitute a check and balance in conformity with constitutional spirit.

This burden of full disclosure and transparency must be placed on the lobbying firm, and it must also be placed on the individual congressman or woman to report exactly what fundraisers, galas, etc. they attend and who hosted/financed the event.

Because no speech or petition is restricted (albeit hopefully discouraged) by such regulation, the judicial mandate of strict scrutiny need not apply in review of its legality. That having been said, such regulation, clearly, would serve the legitimate government purpose of avoiding corruption or the appearance of corruption by affording everyone clear, digestible access to information linking the efforts of lobbies to the actions of Congress. This would be accomplished by placing a relatively minute, ministerial task on Congress and lobbies— hardly too burdensome considering the magnitude of the corruption it stands to bring to light. Finally, the task to the judiciary would be similar to that of a commissioner of accounts' responsibility to audit accounts for decedent's estates—a function they already perform.

**Campaign Finance Reform:**

> *The polluting effect of money in election campaigns...[c]oncentrated wealth...threaten to distort political campaigns and referenda...[t]he voices of individual citizens are being drowned out [by the] unholy alliance of big spending, special interests, and election victory.*

> **– Skelly Wright, "Money and the Pollution of Politics: Is the First Amendment an Obstacle to Political Equality?"**
> ***Columbia Law Review 82* (1982): 614, 622.**

The deluge of corporate and union money into federal, state, and local campaigns is a very real impediment to the individual's ability to voice his or her concerns within America's existing political construct. An ordinary individual—not rich beyond description or backed by corporate treasury, simply cannot voice their outlook on any given issue via the endorsement of an elected official when their meager contributions are stacked against the piles of capital contributed by corporations and unions. Yet, while this inequity seems so clear prima facie, it actually proves nauseatingly difficult to regulate for the same reason it is difficult to curtail the influence of lobbies.

Let me first begin by discussing two of the oft-proposed legislative reforms aimed at reforming campaign finance: (1) Political Action Committee (PAC) expenditure bans; and (2) Soft Money limits.

Unfortunately, these, and many other proposed reforms, tend to run afoul of the protections afforded individuals and corporations/unions (groups of individuals) by the First Amendment.

A Political Action Committee (PAC) is an organization formed by business, labor, or other special-interest groups to raise money and contribute to the campaigns of political candidates or parties whom they support.

The reforms regarding PAC expenditure bans typically center around banning all expenditures by and contributions to PACs for the specific purpose of influencing elections for federal office.

Remember that in *Buckley*, though, the Supreme Court held that the only legitimate and compelling government interest in restricting campaign contributions and expenditures sufficient to satisfy the test of strict scrutiny is the government's concern in preventing corruption or the appearance of corruption. The Court further defined corruption narrowly as entailing a financial quid pro quo (dollars for political favors).

Despite their laudable goals, advocates for PAC expenditure bans can really only offer vague justifications for the proposed reforms. Understandably, they complain of an unresponsive government and a political process that has grown increasingly mean-spirited and decry elected officials who listen more to lobbyists than to their own constituents. While this criticized "influence" is conspicuous, constitutionally speaking, it does not pass as a justification for the proposed reform in that it falls short of the Supreme Court's test of strict scrutiny in failing to allege the existence or appearance of any specific corruption.

Knowing deep down in the pit of my stomach the corrupting influence the infusion of money has, I wish it were not the case that the list of grievances cited by the advocates of PAC expenditure bans simply do not amount to corruption as the Supreme Court has defined it. Yet, we must always be deliberative in our process and step back in this instance to realize that we cannot advocate the infringement of one group's right to speech by dint of a perceived or vague inequity any more than we would desire our own freedoms curtailed without concrete justification.

What of reducing the PAC contribution limit to $1,000, rather than banning it altogether? First off, I doubt that any politician would be corrupted by a single contribution of $5,000 (current maximum). As such, the interest that the contribution reduction would serve is merely curtailing the perceived dominance and influence of PACs in the political process. Once again, then, the First Amendment will not allow for such a restriction as it serves a government interest that has never been adjudicated as either legitimate or compelling.

Second, I would also add that a similar unintended consequence would arise if PAC contributions were limited just as did arise as a result of the Federal Election Campaign Act's ceilings on individual contributions to specific candidates. What interest would be served by rendering it that much more difficult than it presently is for candidates to raise money? In this age where candidates are forced to raise funds day in and day out, candidates would hardly be less distracted by fundraising if they had to raise money from an even greater array of people as a result of the smaller amounts that any one PAC may contribute.

What of soft money reform?

Hard money is contributed directly to a candidate and is there-fore regulated by law in both source and amount, and monitored by the Federal Election Commission. Soft money, on the other hand, is contributed to the political party as a whole, supposedly for the purposes of party building and other grassroots activities not directly related to the election of specific candidates. As soft money is not supposed to be used for specific candidate advocacy, it is not regulated by FECA. However, the Bipartisan Campaign Reform Act of 2002 (also known as the McCain-Feingold Act) pro-hibited unregulated contributions to national party committees.

Advocates of campaign finance reform often assert that soft money is the most corrosive in American politics today and typi-cally push for barring federal officeholders, candidates, and national political parties from accepting unregulated soft contri-butions. They also advocate subjecting all election-year expendi-tures and disbursements by political parties, including state and local parties that could affect the outcome of a federal election and also including expenditures for voter registration, get-out-the-vote drives, and any communication that identifies a federal can-didate, to the full range of federal regulations.

Reformers want to ban soft money because it undeniably invites the wholesale evasion of the contribution limits now in place by allowing corporations that would not otherwise be permitted to contribute to candidates' campaigns to make large soft-money donations to political parties. Yet, given that soft money cannot be used to advocate the election or removal of any particular can-didate from office, it is again difficult to establish a link between soft-money contributions and the appearance or reality of quid pro quo candidate corruption that alone provides a constitutional predicate for regulation.

Again, this issue comes back to *Buckely*. Regulating speech other than express advocacy of the election of particular candidates, the Supreme Court said "would create intractable vagueness problems and cause unacceptable chilling of protected, issue-oriented polit-ical speech." In other words, such an overreaching ban on soft money contributions would stifle speech regarding controversial political issues and the qualities of government policies, resulting in an abridging of the exact type of speech the First Amendment is meant to protect.

Enter the Supreme Court's 1996 decision in *Colorado Republican Federal Campaign Committee v. FEC*, which held limits on independent expenditures by political parties (expenditures not coordinated with any candidate) to be unconstitutional. Well, if individuals are not capped in their expenditures, it follows logically that the Court will eventually determinate that party spending on political activity cannot be limited, and also that contributions to the party by PACs or otherwise, will also be immune from regulation.

And then came the starkest example of the Supreme Court's determination to defend the principles of the First Amendment as it pertains to campaign finance reform. In its January, 2010 decision in *Citizens United v. FEC*, the Supreme Court struck down sections of the McCain-Feingold Act and overturned a 20-year-old ruling that had previously prohibited corporations and unions from using money from their general treasuries to produce and run their own campaign ads.

The Bipartisan Campaign Reform Act of 2002, (BCRA/McCain-Feingold Act), amended FECA to ban national political party committees from accepting or spending soft money contributions. While the legislation was challenged in *McConnell v. Federal Election Commission* (2003), and again in *Federal Election Commission v. Wisconsin Right to Life, Inc.* (2007), most of the act remained unscathed with only parts being effectively, though not formally, invalidated. The particular provision at issue in *Citizens United*, however, was Section 203 of the BCRA, which prohibited corporations and unions from using their general treasury funds to make independent expenditures for speech that is an "electioneering communication" or for speech that expressly advocates the election or defeat of a candidate.

By the terms of the Act, an electioneering communication was defined as "any broadcast, cable, or satellite communication" that "refers to a clearly identified candidate for Federal office" and is made within 30 days of a primary election, and that is "publicly distributed," which in "the case of a candidate for nomination for President...means" that the communication "[c]an be received by 50,000 or more persons in a State where a primary election...is being held within 30 days."

The facts in *Citizens United* were as follows: Citizens United, a nonprofit corporation, released a documentary critical of then-Senator Hillary Clinton, as she sought presidential nomination as candidate for the Democratic National Party. Anticipating that it would make the documentary available on cable television through video-on-demand within 30 days of primary elections, Citizens United produced television ads but was concerned about possible civil and criminal penalties for violating the BCRA should they air them. As such, Citizens United sought declaratory and injunctive relief, which they appealed all the way to the Supreme Court, arguing that that the BCRA was unconstitutional as applied to the documentary.

In its decision, the Court pointed out that it had previously recognized that the First Amendment applies to corporations, (*First Nat. Bank of Boston v. Bellotti*, 435 US 765), and extended the protection to the context of political speech, (*NAACP v. Button*, 371 US 415). The Court remembered that it had invalidated FECA's expenditure ban, which applied to individuals, corporations, and unions, because it failed to serve any substantial governmental interest in stemming the reality or appearance of corruption in the electoral process. However, the Court also had to contend with its 1990 decision in *Austin v. Michigan Chamber of Commerce*, 494 US 652, where it upheld a corporate independent expenditure restriction, bypassing *Buckley* by recognizing a new government interest in preventing "the corrosive and distorting effects of immense aggregations of [corporate] wealth...that have little or no correlation to the public's support for the corporation's political ideas."

The Court overruled its previous decision in *Austin*, stating as follows: "The First Amendment prohibits Congress from fining or jailing citizens, or associations of citizens, for engaging in political speech, but Austin's antidistortion rationale would permit the Government to ban political speech because the speaker is an association with a corporate form...Political speech is indispensable to decision-making in a democracy, and this is no less true because the speech comes from a corporation...This protection is inconsistent with *Austin's* rationale...First Amendment protections do not depend on the speaker's financial ability to engage in public discussion... Distinguishing wealthy individuals from corporations based on the latter's special advantages of, e.g., limited liability, does not suffice to allow laws prohibiting speech...Under the antidistortion rationale, Congress could also ban political speech of media corporations."

As result of this constitutional rubric, it is quite clear that any restriction aimed at limiting access to politicians, such as by way of enacting ceilings on the amount of money the national parties, PACs, or even corporations can spend on a campaign ad, for instance, would likely be considered by the court as a direct and substantial restriction on the ability of candidates and citizens (or a group of citizens represented by that PAC or corporation) to engage in protected political expression. As such, no law abridging such rights will likely stand.

With this matrix in mind, some have proffered the following as a means to accomplish campaign finance reform at the federal level without running afoul of the First Amendment:

```
All elections at the federal level shall be
publicly funded by taxpayer's dollars. Each
candidate will be entitled to a pre-determined
level of capital with which to run their cam-
paign. Each candidate shall be required to,
among other things, obtain a target number of
signatures to qualify for the funds.
```

Admittedly, this general construct is intriguing. Unfortunately, it won't work. To start, it is worth pointing out that any such system of campaign finance would have to be crafted with extreme care to guard against unintended consequences. For instance, we could easily create a slippery slope in the process of determining who is and is not eligible for the public funds. By making it too hard to qualify for the funds, we likely would disenfranchise some and by making it too easy to qualify for the funds, we could bankrupt the system.

Such a publicly funded system would arguably address the <u>directly</u> corrosive effect lobbying and campaign fundraising is allowed to have on the political process. Nevertheless, I posit that such a system is constitutionally obtrusive and would, in reality, do little to remedy the iniquity.

While public funding of campaigns would not place any restriction on individual and corporate expenditures in violation of constitutional precedent, it would place that very same restriction on the candidate. This already runs afoul of case law.

More importantly, establishing public funding of campaigns in an effort to skirt the rigors of strict scrutiny would do absolutely nothing to stop individuals, corporations, PACs, etc., from spending as they desire, in any amount, advocating issues and party platforms. The result would be one where a candidate is allotted a pittance via public funding of his or her campaign and then would be at the mercy of their party to back them. Why? Because if the party did not back them, they'd back another candidate and flood the airwaves with millions of dollars' worth of "propaganda" carefully designed to walk that fuzzy line between issue and candidate advocacy. The natural result: every candidate will pine for the backing of their political party, Democrat or Republican alike.

All such all a system will do is make the national parties that much more powerful by making them the bankrollers of campaigns and putting candidates squarely in their pockets. Whatever deals the party has made with the lobbies, corporations, or PACs would have to be abided by the candidate if he or she were to have any hope of obtaining the candidacy, much less win reelection.

So, where do we go from here?

It is important to note that in the wake of the *Buckley* decision, where campaign contributions have ceilings, candidates can no longer raise money in the traditional, relatively efficient way of attracting large donations from a small number of donors. As an unforeseen consequence, candidates are now forced to campaign day in and day out, year after year, in order to amass disorienting numbers of small contributions. It's no wonder nothing gets done in government!

Campaign spending must then be regulated with the aim of reducing candidate fundraising chores in lieu of the goal of restricting political expression. Regulation with fundraising control as a rationale for spending limits is constitutionally defendable because the harm remedied by curtailment is not the speech itself, but the effect the necessitated campaigning has on the candidate and the candidate's ability to perform his or her elected duties.

With this reasoning in mind, and remaining fully aware of the corrupting influence money is having on our body politic, I proffer the following as a means to accomplish campaign finance reform at the federal level without running afoul of the First Amendment:

By doing two things: 1) placing a relatively high cap, but a cap nonetheless, on the amount candidates can raise and spend per election; and 2) requiring full disclosure of the source of those funds, we can force candidates to choose wisely among their donors and the "strings" attached to those dollars.

Admittedly, this restriction on the amount of money a candidate can spend on a political communication during a campaign would reduce the quantity of any particular candidate's expression. However, such a spending cap would entail only a marginal restriction upon the candidate's ability to engage in free communication for it would permit them to raise and spend a relatively large amount and would not regulate the content of the candidate's speech.

This form of regulation, then, would be content-neutral and, as such, only intermediate scrutiny would be necessary in the review of its constitutionality. Applying the O'Brien test, the law would serve the substantial government interest of preserving the integrity of the democratic process. Though intermediate scrutiny does not require the law to be the least restrictive means of curtailing the content-neutral speech, this law would be narrowly tailored to govern the actions of a finite group: candidates.

Candidates, I would argue, are vying for the opportunity to serve the republic, and as incumbent or hopeful public officials, such a spending cap restriction is no less reasonable than the fiduciary duties imposed on professionals in the prosecution of their vocation. Lastly, the law would leave open alternative means of communication in that the candidates would in no way be forbidden to attend any further galas or fundraisers where they may be given an opportunity to speak to the public at large once their "cap" is met, so long as it is not for the narrow purpose of raising money for their campaign. The law also would not curtail the public's (individuals, corporations, PACs) ability to expend moneys and invite the candidate as, perhaps, an honorary keynote speaker with a platform to speak publicly.

Because campaign finance reform and lobbying reform, as above described, are so fundamentally complex and constitutionally problematic, I believe only small and incremental reforms are possible with respect to either one—that is, barring an amendment to the Constitution. Given the dire need for reform, I wish this were not the case, but even facing the corrosive effects money is having on our body politic, I can see no legitimate government interest sufficient to amend the First Amendment. Therefore, each reform must be carefully drafted to anticipate strict scrutiny under the law with case precedent always in mind.

**Term Limits:**

*Nothing is so essential to the preservation of a Republican government as a periodic rotation.*

**– James Madison**

*There is no provision for a rotation, nor anything to prevent the perpetuity of office in the same hands for life; which by a little well timed bribery, will probably be done....*

**– Mercy Otis Warren**

Constitutionally speaking, term limits for Congress may ironically prove the least difficult battle in the war to alleviate our republic from the crushing influence money has on today's political environment. This isn't to say it would not be difficult, for the establishment of term limits for Congress would likely require an amendment to the Constitution.

Let me first begin with the difficulty of passing an amendment to the Constitution, especially in regard to the institution of term limits in the legislative branch of our government. First, it would require two-thirds of both houses of Congress to vote to propose the amendment. This, in and of itself, poses a huge problem in that a supermajority of congress would literally have to vote to truncate the extent of their own power. Next, three-fourths of all state legislatures (also congressional bodies) would have to approve the proposed amendment to make it law.

Despite this glaring obstacle, I remain confident that such an amendment is feasible. While congressional officeholders are, for obvious reasons, most interested in shooting down any term limit referenda, the bicameral legislature, I would argue, is most susceptible to the popular demand of its constituents. With enough pressure, any candidate vying for the seat held by any incumbent will find it necessary to promise term limits. Incumbents, to keep their seats, will be pressured to promise the same. And if they don't deliver, well, then it is up to the common voter to vote that person out of office.

This has been done before!

George Washington set a precedent in his farewell address published in David Claypoole's *American Daily Advertiser*, on September 19, 1796. Just as he'd resigned his commission as general of the

Continental Army years before, he again relinquished his power for the good of our Republic and declined to run for a third term as president of the United States. Thomas Jefferson also adhered to the, then new, convention of a two-term limit. In 1807 Jefferson wrote in a reply to the legislature of Vermont, "If some termination to the services of the chief Magistrate be not fixed by the Constitution, or supplied by practice, his office, nominally four years, will in fact become for life."

Then came Franklin Delano Roosevelt. In 1940, FDR became the first and only president to be elected to a third term. His supporters cited the war in Europe as a reason for breaking with precedent. FDR won a fourth term in office in 1944 primarily out of strong concerns with changing the chief executive during the ongoing World War. However, when the war ended, many people across America felt that FDR had altered the presidency to become a more powerful office than the Constitution intended, representing a clear threat to the balance of power between the branches of government.

Due to this popular sentiment, President Truman ordered the Hoover Commission, which, among other things, proposed that Congress amend the Constitution to limit the number of terms a president may serve.

The result: our 22nd Amendment, which reads as follows:

**No person shall be elected to the office of the President more than twice, and no person who has held the office of President, or acted as President, for more than two years of a term to which some other person was elected President shall be elected to the office of the President more than once. But this article shall not apply to any person holding the office of President when this article was proposed by the Congress, and shall not prevent any person who may be holding the office of President, or acting as President, during the term within which this article becomes operative from holding the office of President or acting as President during the remainder of such term. (second section omitted)**

The legislative intent behind the adoption of the 22nd Amendment limiting the terms of a president is extremely important to note as it forms the exact same foundation for why another amendment must be made to limit the terms in Congress.

There can be little doubt that Congress currently holds significantly more power than does the executive branch. I would posit that the same is true in relation to the judicial branch, though perhaps less so as it pertains to the finality of the law.

While we are quick to praise a president for what he has done and crucify him for what he has left undone, the American public fails to realize that the president can actually do very little, especially domestically, without Congress' seal of approval. In fact, much of the gridlock in Washington begins and ends in Congress and it is why so much has been left undone for so long. Yet, we do not hold our senators and representatives to the same level of expected performance. In the 2000 election cycle, for instance, over 98% of incumbent Congressmen and women were re-elected, despite the ongoing political turmoil of the day and a shift from a Democrat to a Republican in the White House.

The fact is that Congress holds a vast amount of power and further it is evident that the longer our elected officials remain in power, the more likely they are to win reelection and the more powerful they become. As congressmen and women sit on commissions and rise through the ranks through tenure, they become increasingly capable of directing pork barrel spending, for instance. This one example, by the way, is a major contributor to our budget deficit and it has, to date, proven "uncheckable."

The very fact that Congress wields so much power and oversight is reason enough for considering term limits to guard against the corruption of power indefinitely held. More importantly, though, term limits are a means to establish rotation in the body politic and thereby reduce the ongoing (and necessarily hidden) stigma of financial quid pro quo as it pertains to any particular candidate. Allow me to explain.

Many argue that term limits in Congress would actually result in more candidates being in need of more money, thereby increasing the odds of financial quid pro quo deals with corporate money to purchase elections. I do not disagree with this notion, per se; however, the point is being missed. The purpose of term limits for Congress is not to stop the practice of financial quid pro quo, for that ought properly to be the goal of campaign finance reform and lobby reform as above described. Rather, the function of term limits is to reduce the effect financial quid pro quo arrangements have on our bicameral legislature as a whole and the independent judgment of our elected officials.

All things being equal, all candidates face the same dilemma: raise a lot of money from whomever you think might support you or loose to the other candidate willing and/or able to raise more money than you. This dilemma rings equally as true for incumbent as well as challengers. Therefore, it follows that the risk of financial quid pro quo is not affected by term limits since the type of candidate, incumbent or challenger, is irrelevant. However, the existence of a financial quid pro quo, as it pertains to the independent judgment of our elected officials, is in fact more and more destructive the longer that particular elected official remains in office. Why?

Say Joe Smith is elected to his first term in the Senate with enormous financial support from the tobacco industry. Basically, he is told that the money will continue to flow so long as he does not vote to make cigarettes illegal or raise the sales tax imposed on their products—a financial quid pro quo. He can never admit to accepting the money under these terms, less face public humiliation, reprimand, and possible impeachment. So, he keeps quiet. Next election cycle, the tobacco industry can now basically blackmail him by 1) threatening to pull their financial support; or 2) releasing somehow to the public his accepting of a bribe. Senator Smith keeps quiet. Third election cycle, then the fourth, fifth, sixth, and so on, and the financial quid pro quo line has gotten longer and the noose around the senator's neck tighter. As a result, the special interests of the tobacco industry are held higher than Senator Smith's constituents. As are the special interests of a growing legion of lobbies that expands the longer he stays in power.

Whereas, should term limits be imposed on Congress, Senator Smith, in the above example, could not be held under the thumb of any particular lobby for an indefinite timeframe. With a continuous rotation of Congress, lobbies would be forced to continuously fight for the attention and support of our elected officials—a reality which would foster competition between the special interests (Capitalism 101) and would also curtail any particular industry's ability to have an "inside man" ad infinitum by climbing into the pockets of any individual representative and simply staying there. Lastly, as for Senator Smith, he would be more likely to vote on principle than on special interests if he was barred from being a career politician.

There are a number of arguments commonly posited in opposition to term limits in Congress. Summarized, they are as follows:

1.  Term limits remove the "good" politicians along with the "bad."
2.  Term limits reduce voter choice.
3.  Term limits result in a loss of experience in Congress.
4.  Term limits will increase the power and influence of staff and lobbies.

In specific regard to the loss of "good" politicians. Admittedly, this would be a side effect of term limits. However, I'd argue that any such loss would be fully offset by the fact that incumbency would be removed as an obstacle for countless motivated, intelligent candidates to add to the value of our government.

Still, some will argue as follows: If Ted Kennedy is my senator, and he has been in office for as long as I can remember, and I am happy with his performance, why should I be limited in my choice to vote for him again? Also, Mr. Kennedy is extremely powerful and therefore able to bring home the pork—I don't want him gone!

In regard to any particular voter, such as the above hypothetical constituent of the late Senator Kennedy—he has a valid interest in continuing to vote Kennedy into office. Why would he vote Kennedy out of office if he's bringing home the public works projects, government contracts, etc. that provide jobs for himself and his neighbors?

The problem is this: representatives and senators in Congress are there to represent the interests of their constituents. However, as is evidenced by the ever-expanding use of the Commerce Clause, Congress is also charged with regulating the nation as a whole. That second charge is unduly influenced by an entrenched seniority with the power to appropriate pork barrel funding of special interest projects to regions without proper regard for the needs of the entire national constituency actually paying for the proposed project. It is beneficial to the state for their official to have tenure, but it is equally as, if not more, detrimental to the nation as a whole.

As to term limits reducing voter choice: while term limits will, in fact, remove the ability to vote for an incumbent who has maxed out his or her terms, voters will actually benefit from increased choice. The fact is that most voters are being deprived of real choice when over 98% of incumbents win against voter apathy. By infusing new blood into the system, voters will have new candidates, not career politicians to vote for and, hopefully, will be galvanized by new candidates in touch with the real world.

Will term limits result in a dearth of knowledge and experience in Congress and increase the power of staff, bureaucracy, and lobbyists? To the contrary, it would remove entrenched staff, bureaucracy, and lobbyists as above discussed, and would encourage the influx into Congress of a multitude of untainted and eager Americans as legislators, staff or lobby, alike—all probably less likely to be bowled over by special interests and embedded staffs, bureaucracies and lobbies.

The small business owners of America, the employers of over 50% of the population, having endured through the inefficiencies, opportunities and disadvantages inherent in today's global market competition, and how government over-regulation or under-regulation effects the bottom line, would suddenly throw their hats into the ring. These new, intelligent minds could renew our democracy, reinvigorate us to vote, and usher in a new era in government where we hold true to our Constitution and the sage foresight of our founding fathers to pursue the promise of our freedom in the face of today's adversities.

And, if necessary, these new representatives could always call on the sage advice, knowledge, and experience of any faithful and former colleague, staff member, or lobby. After all, what are the dethroned incumbents going to do, hang up when a "newbie" comes to Congress? I suppose if they did, that might tell us a little something about their true desires for power. Concomitantly, new politicians are less likely to have the knowledge necessary to exploit the system for personal gain and are more skeptical of lobbyists and special interests.

That is not to say that the experience of those in today's Congress is not substantial and often of critical importance. Certain levels of tenure, I believe, are in fact healthy and necessary to the proper function of a bicameral legislature operating within the complexities of the twenty-first century. Certain levels of clearance and closely held government secrets are perhaps not best for freshmen representatives to hold, for example. In many respects, such as is in the case in foreign policy, it takes multiple terms to gain proficiency as a true leader on any given subject matter properly under their jurisdiction.

As such, I believe it is proper that any term limits imposed on Congress should not reduce terms in the House of Representatives at all, but should be reduced to two terms (12 years) in the Senate.

As the nauseating battle over the debt ceiling unfolded this last year, we were once again witness to the ostensible veto power the Senate has over the president's agenda, and more importantly, over the House of Representatives. Bill after proposed bill has been dead on arrival, why? Because the bills proposed in the

House of Representatives by congressmen and women taking the interests of their individual state constituents into foremost consideration are killed by the Senate—a body comprising of only two senators from each state and thereby less capable of representing the regional interests of the state and more concerned with the effect any given decision has on the whole on the United States.

A two-term restriction on senators will alleviate the corrupting influence special interests have on the regional interests of individual states. Many corporations, unions, (factions) operate in multiple states, not to mention globally, and their interests often are not aligned with the desires of any particular state or region. But when they control the re-election of a Senator, one of only two from each state—we soon find that the senators are voting in favor of the faction's special interest, despite the effect it may have on a particular region, even the senator's own state. However, loosen the length of that financial string tied into the Senator's pocket by implementing a two-term restriction, and that senator will be more likely to vote his conscience and not to the detriment of his state. More importantly, that Senator, again, only one of two from his state, will not be drowned out by Senators from across the nation with divergent special interests tied with twenty yearlong strings to wallets thick with money.

Whereas, maintaining the status quo of no term limits in the House of Representatives will ensure that the level of expertise needed in Congress remains. Further, each state will have a greater voice in what happens in their state, as the Senators will not be bought and told to vote contrary to their state's interests for sake of the "interests of the multi-state faction." Representatives will find a more receptive floor in the Senate, and by reducing the influence special interests can have on the Senate, the individual states can enact regulation at a local, state, and national level, with far less restriction.

The result—a bicameral legislature that is in greater tune with the concerns of the constituents it represents. The voices from main street will be louder, and the problems of one region will

be dealt with by that region, more efficiently, and with less deliberation and less red tape. The result will be to reduce the size of
government!

For let me be clear—the best way to guard against corruption in the Federal Government is to REDUCE THE POWER OF
THE GOVERNMENT. Returning power to the individual states, as
intended by the Constitution, is the answer to how we cripple corruption in Congress. As James Madison himself wrote in *Federalist
Paper No. 10,* the key to guarding against the insidious nature of
factions is not in eliminating the causes of faction, for that would
require the destruction of liberty. The key to removing the corrosive vice grip lobbying has on our current body politic is found
in reducing the size of government and implementing term limits
in the Senate—thereby controlling the affect factions have on the
decisions made in the United States Congress.

CHAPTER FOUR:

# RELIGION IN POLITICS

*Whereas Almighty God hath created the mind free; that all attempts to influence it by temporal punishment or burthens, or by civil incapacitations, tend only to beget habits of hypocrisy and meanness, and are a departure from the plan of the Holy author of our religion, who being Lord both of body and mind, yet chose not to propagate it by coercions on either, as was his Almighty power to do.*

*Be it enacted by the General Assembly, that no man shall be compelled to frequent or support any religious worship, place, or ministry whatsoever, nor shall be enforced, restrained, molested, or burthened in his body or goods, nor shall otherwise suffer on account of his religious opinions or belief; but that all men shall be free to profess, and by argument to maintain, their opinion in matters of religion, and that the same shall in no wise diminish, enlarge, or affect their civil capacities.*

*And though we well know that this assembly elected by the people for the ordinary purposes of legislation only, have no power to restrain the act of succeeding assemblies, constituted with powers equal to our own, and that therefore to declare this act to be irrevocable would be of no effect in law; yet we are free to declare, and do declare, that the rights hereby asserted are of the natural rights of mankind, and that if any act shall be hereafter passed to repeal the present, or to narrow its operation, such as would be an infringement of natural right.*

**- "The Virginia Statute of Religious Freedom," drafted by Thomas Jefferson in 1777 and enacted by the Virginia General Assembly in 1786.**

A DECLARATION OF BELIEF:

I have no definitive proof, other than in my heart's faith, that my religion is more right or any less correct than any other religion, creed, or scientific theory of the cosmos, its origin, or the existence of parallel realities and God. It is evident that there is a vast, perhaps endless existence of ever-expanding galaxies, and, if superstring theory proves to be the true "theory of everything," not three, but perhaps eleven mindboggling dimensions of space and time.

In many regards, it seems that science is ironically proving the possibility of a higher being and that, regardless of whether or not that entity is the highest dimensional entity of all, we are all simply the energized realities of his mentally projected thoughts. It makes perfect sense if you really think about it from both a quantum mechanics and general relativity perspective. When you break it all down, atoms are comprised of protons, neutrons, and electrons, which are comprised of quarks, and on down until the smallest of particles are nothing more than vibrating energy oscillating at a particular frequency. Conscious thought is also nothing more than a wavelength of vibrating energy. I digress... but my point is this: because I, nor anyone else on this planet, can definitively say that there is or is not a God, I cannot and should not be permitted to convert any man by the sword against his free will. Nor shall any man be right in converting me by the sword against my will.

I was raised as a Christian and I do believe with the deepest of faith that Jesus Christ is my Lord and Savior. However, I realize that had I been born in India, I might be Hindi, or if born in Pakistan, likely Muslim. Further, I would likely believe as strongly in those creeds as I do Christianity. It seems to me that the randomness of one's regional upbringing is very important to consider. All generations, regardless of race, wealth, or religion, inherit the consequences of their parents' deeds and beliefs. It is the natural ebb and flow of civilization.

One could tumble down the dichotomist rabbit hole of free will versus predeterminism, but it is prudent to at least consider this: where we were born does not make us right. Perhaps religion is much like the game of telephone, where the message has been skewed over time and territory, but regardless of origin, the lesson, metaphorical or not, and when properly interpreted is always one of benevolence, morality, and philanthropy.

No matter the source, benevolence, morality, and a culture of selflessness must prevail in society, for without it, our nation, and all civilization, will crumble. The sources of morality, religion, family upbringing, etc., are extremely important to cultivate—but taken singularly, each is irrelevant so long as the end is one of a predisposition toward compassion. For me it was Jesus, my mother, and father that taught me the power of compassion, while for others it may be friends, Buddha, Allah—it matters not to the point of justifying conversion by the sword.

I believe that God has created the mind free, and that if he did not create it so, it nevertheless remains a fact that man's mind exists free. And history proves that all attempts to convert by the sword lead only to revolution and bloodshed. We must be continuously mindful of the fact that although we have the power to decree it otherwise, we should not interfere, regulate, or punish the deeds of others whether it comes to one's religion or otherwise. That is, unless the deeds of those we would seek to regulate or punish consist of deeds that interfere with the rights of others in their life, liberty, and pursuit of happiness.

If we are all really just energized embodiments of God's self-awareness, and with his infinite knowledge of good and evil came ours, perhaps the reason why he needs us to have faith in the good and just is because he, having created us in his own stardust image, must fight the same struggle against the cancerous erosion from within that we ourselves must face from within ourselves and our societies. Who's to say...but one fact does remain: man exists with free will and the knowledge of good and evil. Therefore, if there is a God, he has chosen not to exert his influence and convert us by the sword, and we should follow his lead—and if there is no God, the question still remains, should the laws of man permit conversion by the sword as just? The answer, absolutely, is no.

--------------------

Penned in 1776, the Declaration of Independence is Thomas Jefferson's greatest known work. However, his subsequent drafting of the Virginia Statute of Religious Freedom in 1779, to me, rivals his earlier work through its clarity of faithful thought and intellectual acuity. In fact, our third president was thought to have been most proud of the statute.

A precursor to the First Amendment, the Virginia Statute of Religious Freedom is a statement concerning freedom of conscience and the principle of partition between church and state. In it, Jefferson begins with a statement of natural right, a decree of his Deism—that is, the belief that God created the world and along with it, man's capacity to govern himself. Jefferson believed that God, as creator, granted us freedom of choice, including liberty of conscience in religious matters and that any attempt to restrict it is misguided. Building from that foundation, the act itself states that no person can be compelled to attend any church or support it with his or her taxes, and that all shall be free to worship or not worship as he or she pleases with no discrimination at law.

As governors of men, we are to do as God does: allow *freedom* to reign supreme, regardless of whether we have the power to force others to believe as we do. Freedom of thought, freedom of religion, freedom to fail—**Freedom**!

Jefferson could have stopped there, but his genius propelled him to address the dangers that could arise as a result of the people's right to change the law through their elected assemblies. Jefferson realized that the statute is not irrevocable because no law is, or ought to be. Because future assemblies are free to repeal or circumscribe the statute, Jefferson warned, appropriately, that any such circumscribing assembly would do so at their own peril, as to do so would be "an infringement of natural right."

Today in America, we unfortunately find that Jefferson's concern is coming to fruition. Americans of all religions suddenly now find themselves well down that slippery slope to no longer being religiously free, and by dint thereof, free at all.

The infringement upon each American's natural right to be free in his religious practice is not being caused by the outright repeal of the First Amendment, but rather a circumscription of that freedom is rising from a chronic misapplication and material misunderstanding of the amendment's true edict. As a result, we are witnessing a nationwide deterioration of the **morality** that served as the guiding principles in the formulation of our Constitution and which virtues are necessary to our nation's survival.

More so now than ever, we are faced with a new type of religious America. "We the people" has an entirely different scope than it did when our founding fathers wrote the Constitution. Spurred by the Immigration and Nationality Act of 1965, people from all over the world, not just Europe, have come to our shores, bringing with them their traditions and faiths. The religious creeds of the world—Islam, Hindu, Buddhist, Jain, Sikh, etc.—all now call America home and the United States now exists as the most religiously diverse society since the dawn of civilization. The percentage of foreign-born Americans has doubled from the 1970s to over 10.5% of the population, with the Hispanic and Asian populations growing the fastest. It is truly a modern miracle.

It is our system of ordered liberty, commanding protection of the inalienable rights of those immigrants through ten fundamental rights, that has made this miracle possible on Earth. Men, women, and children of all faiths live in the same neighborhoods, attend the same schools—but in America, unlike all civilizations before us, we do so in relative peace.

The Bill of Rights begins with the First Amendment, a decree that man shall not be converted by the sword. And it is through an innate, if not subconscious understanding of the Amendment's true meaning, that Americans eagerly greet morally grounded faiths with open arms.

However, our selfless attempts to embrace these faiths and traditions with open arms have transformed into an over-zealous and often imprudent passion to always be "politically correct." It is going too far, and as a result, we are quickly losing what it means to be an American. Family values, self-worth, and motivation, even the very lines between right and wrong are blurring, drowned out by the hustle and bustle of an increasingly frantic society too strained to stop and realize what we are losing, a government injudicious as to religious purpose, and to a large extent—it all comes at the misguided behest of our nation's "over-political correctness."

The idea of religious freedom is central to the very idea of America. Religious freedom has always given rise to religious diversity, and never, in any nation on this planet, has there been such religious diversity as there currently is in the United States. We lead the rest of the world by this example, as a living, breathing testament to the power of ordered liberty. We should see that we are therefore in a unique position to create a truly pluralist society in which this grand diversity is not merely tolerated but embraced as the very source of our strength.

In order to do so—in order to avoid a collapse from within, though, we must understand the deepest meaning of our founding principles, with full acknowledgment that our system of ordered liberty is steeply grounded in faith, particularly Judeo-Christian morality. Instead, an errant, liberal ideology has permeated academia and deceived our judicial system. We are erroneously being taught that the First Amendment's establishment clause means that the United States must purge all signs of religion from the public square.

Lawsuits to enjoin the local public library from displaying the Ten Commandments bombard the airwaves. In 2002 the United States Circuit Court of Appeals for the Ninth Circuit declared the phrase "under God" in the Pledge of Allegiance to be unconstitutional. An agenda that includes tearing down crosses and prohibiting crèches and menorahs on public property; indeed, the absolute removal of God and faith from the public square is sweeping our land.

Many argue that it is a secular socialist machine that's waging this war on religion because they see any religious worldview as the single greatest threat to their realization of a utopia where government is all-powerful. Certainly some may fit that mold, but I believe the problem has a less insidious root.

A very real affront to religion, particularly the practice of Christianity in the public square, is growing out of most people's desire to be politically correct, and despite the fact that they themselves are often religious. Why the particular assault on Christianity? Because Christianity was here first—it is the "establishment." Those desirous of being politically correct tend to admonish the majority representing the establishment. Unfortunately, this lends to <u>reverse-political incorrectness</u>, where the majority is discriminated against and, ironically, they fail to speak up for fear of being seen as politically incorrect themselves. This "catch-22" phenomenon is similar to Caucasians, representing the majority and "establishment," enduring reverse racism as a natural reaction to generations of long-overdue political correctness.

We can all relate to this situation: invariably a person at the table says they aren't religious, and you shouldn't impose your beliefs on him. Unfortunately, so many of us simply shy away from the subject, knowing there is no way to convince this man that there is a God, much less that our God is the correct one to worship. But what happens when that man's gripe begins to have the force of law, affirmatively denying us the right to respond? Must we not then stand up?

The problem is that this political correctness gone awry is creating a court-enforced wall of separation between the true historical spirit of America and a radically different, secular America without God, traditional values, or an understanding of its own history. In an attempt not to discriminate, or show favoritism toward one religion, we find ourselves removing all faiths from the public sphere. This none or all approach, where no religion is allowed for fear of retribution from others, is catastrophic to the future of America and her system of ordered liberty.

We must take a stand, and do so with an understanding of our history and the importance of maintaining religion in the public sphere!

Therefore, let me begin with a rhetorical quiz:

Question: Why is it difficult to draft a regulation that envisions every possible scenario and clearly addresses them in black and white?
   A. *Because someone always finds or creates a loophole, effectively skirting the*

> *law by hiding in creative gray areas;*
> *or*
>
> B. *Because humans are stupid.*

The answer, unfortunately, is A.

The truth results from the ironic paradox created by man's natural drive to aspire for a better future. It is our basic instinct to out-maneuver each other and gain the tactical advantage in our struggles for survival. These desires, combined with phenomenal intellect, form the backbone of innovation, indeed American capitalism. A desire to build a better home and future for our family drives us, and the freedom to do so is protected by our Constitution. The result is the most industrious nation on the planet.

Unfortunately, those same animalistic instincts can, and too often are, utilized to subvert the law. Hypothetically, let's say that in response to the outcries for campaign finance reform, a regulation passes through Congress mandating that no single candidate can receive more than 2% of their campaign spending money from any single donor, political action committee, or corporation. The regulation is even concise as to the definition of "corporation," setting out subsets to include LLCs, S-Corps, charitable organizations, subsidiaries, affiliates, etc.

It is only a matter of time before some of those organizations, desirous for whatever reason to circumvent that law, team up with others to form a faction designed to exert more influence than their competitor. They will form the next version of a political action committee if necessary, binding together to further their special interests. At first, they will weasel into gray areas. Eventually, they will break the law outright and have either convinced Congress to rescind or simply not enforce the law. This necessitates more regulation, further restriction of freedom, and so goes the vicious downward cycle.

The point I am making is this:

*We have no government armed with power capable of contending with human passions unbridled by morality and religion...Our Constitution was made only for a moral and religious people. It is wholly inadequate to the government of any other.*

**– John Adams, Second President, Signor of the Declaration of Independence and Bill of Rights.**

As a consequence of liberty, man must be responsible to govern himself. An immoral man will not abide by any regulation no matter how brilliantly crafted, for he is motivated by his very nature to circumvent that law's application. A moral man, however, will stop at the temptation to evade the legislation if it means infringing upon the rights of others or unjustly taking advantage.

Today, though, we have lost sight of the need for morality in our people as a whole. We've all noticed it, and it is frightening. It's not just that people are too busy or rude to acknowledge you as they pass on the street anymore; it's that they are often isolated and afraid. And in this isolation, immorality finds its breading ground.

Honorable people ask what they can do for their country, not what their country can do for them. Ethical people work hard for what they have, and do not expect or feel entitled to receive welfare, but are grateful when they receive it. And while it is a just and altruistic goal to provide welfare for those in need, it is an immoral, unmotivated person that will game those programs to take advantage. Multiply this dishonest individual into millions, and they will bankrupt the system. This is what we face today in America, and the dearth in morality is cracking the foundation upon which the pillars of our civilization are built.

The cultural history of Western Civilization enlightens us as to the true meaning of what it is to be an American and what America must remember to stand for as the last best hope for humanity. This historical journey illuminates the legislative intent behind the

First Amendment and equips us with the knowledge and power to forge a more perfect union for us all—a safer, cleaner, more affluent and more virtuous America.

The First Amendment to the United States Constitution reads as follows:

**Congress <u>shall make no law respecting an establishment of religion</u>, or prohibiting the free exercise thereof; or abridging the freedom of speech, or of the press; or the right of the people peaceably to assemble, and to petition the Government for a redress of grievances.**

By the black letter of this law, it is facially clear that nothing has been laid down in our Constitution to prohibit the free exercise of speech in regard to religion in the public sector. So then, what does it mean?

The Virginia Statute of Religious Freedom demonstrates our founding fathers' very clear understanding that government must not have the power over the conscience of the governed to force them to worship God. However, the founding fathers also believed that government and its institutions derive their power to command from God and do so under God in that, through his own free will, he has chosen to allow us the freedom to govern ourselves without his interference.

It is this second tenement as to the role of God in our government that is too often swept under the rug by those that do not consider themselves religious. The exact freedom that protects the non-religious from legal injustices is the same freedom that protects the religious right to proclaim and celebrate faith in public without persecution.

Predominantly, if not entirely Christian, our founding fathers formed their view of God's role in government, in part, from the Bible. Romans 13:1–6 state as follows:

Let everyone be subject to the governing authorities, for there is no authority except that which God has established. The authorities that exist have been established by God. Consequently, whoever rebels against the authority is rebelling against what God has instituted, and those who do so will bring judgment on themselves. For rulers hold no terror for those who do right, but for those who do wrong. Do you want to be free from fear of the one in authority? Then do what is right and you will be commended. For the one in authority is God's servant for your good. But if you do wrong, be afraid, for rulers do not bear the sword for no reason. They are God's servants, agents of wrath to bring punishment on the wrongdoer. Therefore, it is necessary to submit to the authorities, not only because of possible punishment but also as a matter of conscience. This is also why you pay taxes, for the authorities are God's servants, who give their full time to governing.

The Bible enlightened our founding fathers to the truth that government and its institutions derive their power to command from God and do so under God. Inspired by their creed's very cannon, they declared the self-evident truth that all men are created equal; that they are endowed by their Creator with certain unalienable rights; and that among these are life, liberty, and the pursuit of happiness. It is by this faith that our dollar bill states, "In God we trust."

Our founding fathers also realized that liberty was the true purpose of man's government over man, but that maintenance of liberty and justice over a free people requires virtue:

- ❖ "It is impossible to rightly govern the world without God and the Bible" – George Washington.
- ❖ "So great is my veneration for the Bible that the earlier my children begin to read it the more confident will be my

98

hope that they will prove useful citizens of their country and respectable members of society..." – John Quincy Adams.

❖ "That book, sir, is the rock on which our republic rests" – Andrew Jackson.

❖ "We have staked the whole future of American civilization not on the power of government...not in the Constitution... (but) upon the capacity of each and every one of us to govern ourselves according to the Ten Commandments" – James Madison.

Our American way of thinking, though born of faith, evolved out of Western Civilization. Studying the cultures, their politics and struggles, helps us understand the majesty of Judeo-Christian morality and what it must mean for us today.

The original settlers came to America to practice their religious beliefs free from the dogma of the established churches. The Puritans came to create a "city on the hill" to shine as a beacon of religious piety. The Pilgrims and Quakers, too, came to found new religious communities.

The Europe they fled, and from which they gleaned centuries of unique insight, had a long tradition of religious persecution. The ebb and flow of Western Civilization from the Dark Ages of religious absolutism to the humanism and self-awareness of the Renaissance, for example, steeped our American settlers in a rich and tumultuous history out of which our founding fathers were enlightened. Their forefathers had lived through the Crusades, the Papal Schism, the Protestant Reformation, and the ecclesiastical and structural reconfigurations of the Catholic Church in the Counter-Reformation that culminated in the Thirty Years War. They'd endured the combination of higher taxes, unsuccessful wars, and conflicts with the Pope that led to the Barons forcing King John of England to agree to the Magna Carta.

Braving the icy clutches of the Atlantic, our forefathers left Europe with a very clear understanding that the Ten Commandments, moral mandates they so fervently believed in, were paramount and critical not only to self-governance, but to the operation of a just government. Europe's war torn history also taught them that religious intolerance, blind dogma and conversion by the sword are the greatest enemies of liberty.

The unique condition of Western Civilization, properly studied, enlightened our forefathers as to the greatest dichotomy of all. Religion, faith, morality, and virtues are indispensable to the operation of government over a free people, while governments must not establish any law to require the practice of or abolishment of any religion—for to do so risks sectarian violence and the very destruction of liberty.

This mindset is wholly in accord with the Bible. Romans 13:8, which immediately precedes the declaration that governments derive their right to command men through God, states as follows:

> **Let no debt remain outstanding, except the continuing debt to love one another, for whoever loves others has fulfilled the law. The commandments, "You shall not commit adultery," "You shall not murder," "You shall not steal," "You shall not covet," and whatever other command there may be, are summed up in this one command: "Love your neighbor as yourself." Love does no harm to a neighbor. Therefore, love is the fulfillment of the law.**

Being that love is the fulfillment of the law because it does no harm to your neighbor, it follows logically that one man must not take up the sword to convert his fellow man in the name of the Lord and certainly not in the name of the law. Truly, as Thomas Helwys wrote in *A Short Declaration of the Mystery of Iniquity*: "For men's religion to God is between God and themselves. The king shall not answer for it. Let them be heretics, Turks, Jews, or whatsoever, it appertains not to the earthly power to punish them in the least measure."

The principles learned from the Ten Commandments and studied by our forefathers—those virtues are the foundation of

Judeo-Christian morality. This religious background, a centering of the Lord's teaching that one is not to convert by the sword, that one is to respect the law, against the historical backdrop of Western Civilization, from the Middle Ages to our Revolutionary War, educated our founding fathers as to the need for the First Amendment. Learning from history, they did not, and would not have written God from the public sector. To do so would run contrary to the lessons of history from which they gleaned, and run afoul of their true belief that liberty must be ordered and that order hinges upon virtue.

It was a religious revival in the 1730s known as the Great Awakening that stirred our founding fathers to fight for their God-given inalienable rights. It was also a spiritual resurgence in the nineteenth century that inspired the abolitionists' drive to end slavery.

Remember that the marching song of the Union Army during the Civil War, "The Battle Hymn of the Republic," included the line, "As Christ died to make men holy, let us die to make men free."

It was also a religious revival that led to a seventy-year women's suffrage struggle culminating in the ratification of the Nineteenth Amendment to our Constitution, prohibiting state and federal agencies from adopting gender-based restrictions on voting. And it was a Baptist minister, Dr. Martin Luther King Jr., who led the 1955 Montgomery Bus Boycott, founded the Southern Christian Leadership Conference, and delivered his "I Have a Dream" speech that led to civil rights being extended to African Americans.

The impetuses behind these virtuous movements throughout the history of America are all found in an underlying Judeo-Christian morality. It is from the Ten Commandments that our system of ordered liberty pulls most strongly, and to turn our backs on that is tantamount to denouncing who we are as a nation.

Now, I am not saying that one must be Christian or Jewish to be an American. Not at all. And I'm also not arguing that there is no morality aside from religious derivation. Rather, I am pointing out the importance of these faiths as they were of paramount inspiration to the declaration of our independence and the penning of our Constitution. In our history lies the answers to addressing our present and future obstacles as a free and ordered people—as moral Americans.

It is clear that morality has very strong roots in religion: Islam, Christianity, Judaism, etc. These faiths are centered on virtues; teach morality and compassion, the rule of law, and deference to a benevolent, higher power. But the growing intolerance toward the free expression of religious beliefs in the public square, in order to protect the sensibilities of the non-religious, presents a very clear and present danger to the continuation of our society's moral compass.

Freedom *of* religion does not mean freedom *from* religion. "Political correctness" has run afoul of this understanding, and it has reached a boiling point where attempts to appease those with different or no religious beliefs are now met with an intolerance at law toward the practice of Christianity and Judaism, the religions that serve as the cornerstone of traditional American liberty. That same intolerance is now turned to Islam in the aftermath of 9/11.

We must understand, and understand clearly, that this nation of ours, our system of ordered liberty, the right of every American to live free to pursue happiness, would not have been possible without the lessons of Western Civilization's history. Their faith in the Ten Commandments and their enduring through religious crusades and tyranny, resulting in a patent understanding of the Lord's word, form the Judeo-Christian morality out of which our Constitution was written. The United States of America is a nation able to host all the world's religions, peacefully, where each is free to practice their creed without interference at law or bloodshed, because of the founding father's historical, cultural, and religious wisdom—that, my fellow Americans, is God's Manifest Destiny!

And so, while it is not necessary that you be Christian or Jewish to be an American, to be an American, you and your neighbors must be morally grounded. Therefore, it is requisite for our generation to stand up and fight for the true protections our First Amendment was drafted to afford each and every one of us. We must fight to win back our God-given right to practice our religion and pronounce our faith in the public square, pushing back every judicial decision and public outcry to circumscribe that most American and first-affirmed liberty. Christianity, Judaism, Islam, Buddhism—all morally grounded faiths—are rightfully declared in the public square. The future of our nation depends on it!

The above described understanding as to the role of Judeo-Christian morality pertaining to our American sense of freedom, and the extent to which we as Americans stay true to those ideals will be critical in determining the outcome of a number of contemporary political issues facing our nation. This is because the key to prevailing in each exists in our American virtues. While this could be said of almost any topic, I am in particular talking about abortion and the War on Terrorism.

# CHAPTER FIVE

# ABORTION

*Before I formed you in the womb I knew you, and before you were born, I consecrated you; I have appointed you a prophet to the nations.*

**- Jeremiah 1:5**

T
he controversy surrounding abortion law is as dividing as the rift between Civil War North and South regarding the issue of slavery in America. The legal nuances inherent in the matter often dominate the decision process in the appointment of justices to our highest court, and therefore, the election of our representatives in government.

Before I delve into my position on the matter of abortion, though, I feel it is important to point out that the amount of influence the issue of abortion has on our decisions to back candidates is often destructive, and in my opinion, distracting. Particularly, in the Republican Party, I have found that far too many members absolutely will not even consider voting for a candidate that shares 99% of their virtuous beliefs and political foresight if they are not 100% pro-life. Quite literally, stating that you are pro-choice in the Republican Party is political suicide.

On the one hand, this steadfast adherence to an issue such as abortion is commendable, and I hope that the fight continues to further restrict abortions across our great nation. On the other hand, as a result of this issue, the Republican Party has become entirely too one-issue oriented. This is an impediment to the

Republican Party's ability to implement its proper platform on all other issues as we are losing the vote of the common constituent understandably more concerned with the economy, education, and the environment.

Here is a perfect example: I sat down to lunch with a client and friend of mine recently. He is a 92-year-old Republican who ran his own dental office for almost as many years and co-founded the McLean Bible Church in Vienna, Virginia. Extremely devout, I often tease him that he should have been a preacher.

We got to talking about politics and religion, as we always do, and the issue of abortion came up. His view on abortion is that it is always, unequivocally, a sin to abort a child unless there is extreme danger to the mother. Every single time the subject comes up, he falls back on the Bible passage of Jeremiah 1:5:

**Before I formed you in the womb, I knew you. And before you were born, I consecrated you; I have appointed you a prophet to the nations.**

His argument, ostensibly, is that a human being exists at the very point of conception, and therefore its abortion is tantamount to murder if there is not extreme justification.

Playing devil's advocate, I asked the following hypothetical: If you were a senator, would you vote for legislation that does allow abortions, but further restricts abortions by requiring all women over the age of 18 to prove risk to their health for their abortion to be legal?

He responded as anticipated—Absolutely not! I countered, arguing that at least it would be a step in the right direction. To that I was satisfied to gain his concurrence.

So, what am I? Am I pro-life or pro-choice? Here's the problem—too many Republicans won't even listen to a candidate who says he is pro-life but believes abortions are proper under some circumstances. Upon a further elucidation of the facts and moral considerations, however, I believe most Republicans would actually agree that there is a proper, <u>LEGAL</u>, threshold.

Therefore, I am bold to say that I am absolutely pro-life, however, I do believe that abortions are sometimes an unfortunate necessity and our government does not and ought not have the authority to regulate it to the level of abolishing the practice altogether. Allow me to explain:

The paramount case concerning abortion law, unquestionably, is *Roe v. Wade*, 410 US 113 (1973). The Supreme Court determined that a right to privacy afforded by the due process clause in the 14th Amendment extends to a woman's choice to have an abortion. However, the court maintained that the mother's right to privacy must be balanced against the state's two legitimate interests for regulating abortions: protecting prenatal life and protecting the mother's health.

Arguing that the state interests mature over the course of a pregnancy, the Court resolved this balancing test by tying state regulation of abortion to the mother's trimester of pregnancy. The Court later rejected *Roe*'s trimester framework, but continues to affirm its central holding that one has a right to abortion up until viability, which the court defined as being "potentially able to live outside the mother's womb, albeit with artificial aid," adding that viability "is usually placed at about seven months (28 weeks) but may occur earlier."

Defenders of *Roe* argue that case precedent prior to the decision delineated a sphere of private interests and that at the core of that sphere is the right of the individual to make the fundamental decisions that shape family life: with whom to marry; whether and when to have children, etc. However, I would argue regulation of abortion would not be virtually impossible without the most outrageous sort of government prying into the privacy of the home—which was the sole rationale in *Roe*'s antecedent case of *Griswold v. Connecticut*, 181 US 479 (1965) where the Supreme Court invalidated only a certain portion of Connecticut law that proscribed the use, as opposed to the manufacture, sale, or other distribution of contraceptives.

It is clear that the government would have to sneak into the privacy of the bedroom to determine whether contraceptives were being used, and it is equally as clear that such privacies must not be invaded without extreme exception. Abortion, on the other hand, is something that can and is "monitored" outside the bedroom and instead in the doctor's office. Clearly, the level of privacy is much less intimate, though arguably, not necessarily less personal.

However, I believe the debate surrounding the right to privacy as it pertains to abortion law is acutely misguided. To begin, one might argue that the protection of a woman's right to privately abort her child is synonymous to the protection of a woman's right to murder her spouse in the privacy of her basement. Clearly, the government has the right, in fact the mandate, to intervene in the latter. What is the difference between the two? It comes down to the true issue at the center of the abortion debate—at what point should the law consider abortion as tantamount to unjustifiable homicide? In other words, when are you committing the murder of a living person?

The decision in *Roe* was fundamentally flawed. In reaching their decision, the Supreme Court skirted the issue of unjustifiable homicide, writing, "We need not resolve the difficult question of when life begins. When those trained in medicine, philosophy, and theology are unable to arrive at any consensus, the judiciary, at this point in the development of man's knowledge, in not in a position to speculate as to the answer."

That "difficult" question, though, is central to the state's compelling interest of protecting prenatal life, and it is fundamental to the debate surrounding the issue of abortion altogether. Therefore, the Supreme Court erred in ignoring the question.

By ignoring the issue of life and when a fetus becomes a person, the court was able to shift the debate toward a red herring—privacy. They focused on the privacy of the pregnant woman and her right to choose whether to carry the child to term or terminate. The harm that the state would impose upon the pregnant woman by denying the choice altogether, the court argued, is evident. Maternity or additional offspring might force upon the woman a distressful life and future, mental and physical health might be taxed in childcare, and there is also the problem of bringing an unwanted child into the world, among others.

To be clear, I believe that these are compelling concerns. In fact, I cannot even begin to put a value on saving a child from the horrors of growing up unwanted and unloved. One could even argue that it is more immoral to force a child's birth into an unloving and destitute home than it is to abort the unwanted child. And it is unfortunate when a woman becomes pregnant, is abandoned by the father, and her life is ruined financially, socially and often times, spiritually. Further, proponents of abortion will rely on the sudden decrease in crime as a result of abortions, pointing out that since less unwanted children were born, less crack dealers, murderers, etc. were roaming the streets twenty years after the decision in *Roe*. A popular book, *Freakonomics*, has an entire chapter dedicated to that very phenomenon.

What it boils down to, in my opinion, is this: *Roe*'s notion that the state's interest in protecting prenatal life is trumped by a woman's constitutional right to privacy in deciding whether or not to terminate a pregnancy, is not only erroneous, but it runs utterly afoul of basic morality and the most fundamental of constitutional guarantees—the right to life.

Does the right to privacy exist? Yes, and I believe, undeniably. Also, I ardently believe that the state must not have the right to interfere in one's privacy. That is, unless the state has a compelling interest and the regulation is narrowly tailored to address that legitimate interest. In regard to abortion, the state has a compelling interest, and that is the protection of life. Yet the states have been injudiciously deprived of their sovereign right to police that compelling interest as each state sees fit.

Morality is the real issue. Abortion may in fact be "good" for the economy insofar as unwanted children are not brought up in ghettos, crime is proximately curtailed, and the population is controlled, but to champion the right to abort a child in the name of these economic windfalls is disingenuous to who we must be as Americans. Should we legalize crack cocaine and LSD because it would cost us less not to police it? Clearly not, because of the harm these drugs are known to have on the user, but more importantly, the harm it causes the user to voluntarily or otherwise inflict on those around them. Why then should we allow a woman to kill a human being purely for economic concern? We should not.

It is obvious that the state has a compelling interest in making it illegal for me to kill my next-door neighbor for slandering me, despite the fact that his defamation of my character is causing me extreme mental anguish and possible economic hardship. So why is it that the state cannot regulate the killing of a fetus? Because it is not a person?!

Despite first declining to resolve the question of when life begins in reaching its decision, the court in *Roe* spent considerable time persuading itself that a fetus is in fact not a person as defined in the Constitution and therefore is not protected as to its right to life. In their analysis of all the contexts in the Constitution in which the word "person" was used, the court was correct in finding no indication that it had any possible pre-natal application. They wrote, "all this, together with our observation that throughout the major portion of the nineteenth century prevailing legal abortion practices were far freer than they are today (in 1973) persuades us that the word "person," as used in the 14th Amendment, does not include the unborn."

The court erred here as well. To begin, while the word "person" is never defined to include the unborn within the four corners of the Constitution, the converse is equally as true—the Constitution does not expressly remove the unborn from the definition. And as to abortion laws being "freer" at the time of ratification—are not the protections of personhood afforded African Americans despite the fact that slavery was rampant when the Constitution was drafted? Could it be, that despite all their collective genius, the founding fathers simply did not think to define person?

Next, the court turned to legal precedent, arguing that the law of torts and inheritance, for instance, has been reluctant to endorse any theory that life begins before live birth or to accord legal rights to the unborn except in narrowly defined situations and except when the rights are contingent upon live birth. However, consider this: aside from natural miscarriage, wouldn't the fetus live and be born but for the intervening abortion? To terminate the pregnancy, you must kill the fetus. Logically, does this not mean that there is life being terminated?

So, an abortion, boiled down to its logical absurdum, is the intentional killing of a living organism that, without intervention, will become a human being. Who, then, is the court to decide that a human being, which the state has a compelling interest in protecting, exists only upon viability? Scientifically speaking, yes, the fetus cannot survive as a human outside the womb prior to viability, albeit with artificial assistance, but abortion terminates the further development of that fetus when it naturally could have reached viability.

The question then, is not one of privacy, but rather one of a compelling interest in protecting life. It is not the place of the Supreme Court to decide when the compelling interest of protecting life begins or ends. Rather, this is a question that ought to be left to the individual states. The protection of the life is properly a decision that must be made by each state's moral majority through the branches of each state's independent representative government. Therefore, it is my opinion that the court's decision in *Roe* exceeded the judiciary's proper Constitutional reach.

Each state ought to be left to decide for themselves whether or not their interest is strong enough to regulate abortions prior to or after viability. Why? Because the constituents of each state can decide for themselves as to when life begins and when life should or should not be protected as pitted against the concerns of the mother. The moral majority, which I hope would adhere to the belief that life begins at conception, would determine the appropriate level of regulation propounded by their state legislatures. This is the true spirit of our democracy.

The Court itself said that it cannot determine when life begins. Therefore it must not be permitted to tell the states that their constituents' belief that life begins at conception is erroneous and therefore not compelling.

Pro-choice advocates argue that the right to privacy at issue is the woman's interest in having control over her own body and bodily integrity and, therefore, this privacy is one that is of even greater importance than the right to be left alone in the home. To be clear, I agree. But there is more to be considered. They are seeing only one side of the issue presented.

The state absolutely should not have the power to require a woman to have a child. However, the state does and ought to have the power to regulate against homicide. The question that then presents itself is whether or not the abortion is tantamount to homicide. Therefore, to skirt the question of when life begins, as the Supreme Court did in Roe, is judicial blunder.

There are situations, such as self-defense, where even homicide is justifiable at law. For similar reasons, I do believe that abortion is sometimes, though narrowly, justifiable.

First, and foremost, in the case of rape, I believe that the woman, having not made the conscious and voluntary decision to engage in intercourse, should not be required to carry a child to term. To do so would perpetuate a second wrong on the pregnant victim by requiring her to endure the physical, mental, and social consequences of a pregnancy not a corollary of her action.

Let us then look at the issue of abortion through another lens: **Sentience**.

When a woman makes the conscious decision to engage in intercourse, she voluntarily assumes the risk of pregnancy. Having assumed that risk, and having become pregnant, her decision to abort the unwanted child is one to kill a life in being, albeit one arguably without sentience. What we have, then, is a helpless life that has been brought into being without consent and killed by a sentient woman unable to own up to her mistake. I believe it is absolutely fair for a state to determine that they have an interest in protecting the helpless life over the privacy concerns of the imprudent mother.

In the case of rape, however, the mother has not been imprudent insofar as assuming the risk of pregnancy as a consequence of intercourse. What we have, then, is a matured, sentient woman in whom the family and also the state have already invested, pitted against an insentient fetus. It is proper for the state legislatures to determine that the matured woman's right to privacy outweighs the fetus' right to life.

This brings me to the very question I posed to my friend at lunch: If you were a senator, would you vote for legislation that does allow abortions, but further restricts abortions by requiring all women over the age of 18 to prove risk to their health for their abortion to be legal?

In one form or another, all states have statutory rape laws on their books. The theory behind statutory rape, with respect to a minor female, is that she is too young to give true, voluntary consent to intercourse because of her innocence and ignorance, among other factors, and therefore intercourse with her is without consent—statutorily defined as rape.

I ask you this then: What if a 16-year-old girl engages in intercourse with her boyfriend and gets pregnant? Logically, it follows that she did not give true, voluntary consent to the intercourse and that because of her naivety she did not truly assume the risk of pregnancy through her actions.

In this case—that is the case of a minor, as defined by state statute, becoming pregnant—I posit that it would be constitutionally impermissible for the state to ban the abortion altogether. Here, the innocence of the minor, no matter how unfortunate, mitigates against her culpability, and her decision to have or not to have a child, her right to privacy, could be argued to outweigh the compelling state interest of preserving prenatal life, just as in the case of rape.

Now, having said the above, it is important to note that there are instances when even minors are to be treated like an adult in the eyes of the law and the same should apply in the case of abortion. By way of example, a 16-year-old boy can be tried as an adult for murder. What of the pregnant 16-year-old: can she be treated as an adult and her abortion outlawed except to protect her health? Quite possibly, yes, but it is the individual state legislatures, not the Supreme Court that should make that determination for each state.

Lastly, pro-choice is now well ingrained in the American ethos. And the right to a woman's privacy as to what goes on in her own body is most intimate and sacred. I'll therefore end on analogy for consideration: All women, all persons for that matter, have the unfettered right to "abort" a virus nested within their own body. In fact, people have the right to end their own life, refuse treatment, and allow themselves to die. The state cannot regulate whether or not a woman uses a drug, herbs, or other remedy to alleviate herself of the unwanted bodily intruder. Now, obviously I would argue that a fetus is not akin to a virus, but the analogy is nonetheless powerful.

The decision that needs be made is at what stage the state's determination that life exists and shall therefore be protected trumps the woman's sacred right to privacy. At what point does the state's moral imperative to protect prenatal life simply become one faction's imposition of their morals over the entire constituency without regard for the immorality inherent in forcing a child to be born into destitution by a mother that does not want the child, will not or cannot care for the child, has been abandoned by the father, and who's life is ruined by the very birth of that child? Which is more immoral? These are extremely difficult questions, but it ought to be for each state to decide. The moral majority should prevail as the law of the land in each state, not the erroneous conclusion of the Supreme Court.

# CHAPTER SIX

# THE WAR ON TERRORISM

*War is an ugly thing, but not the ugliest of things. The decayed and degraded state of moral and patriotic feeling which thinks that nothing is worth war is much worse. The person who has nothing for which he is willing to fight, nothing which is more important than his own personal safety, is a miserable creature and has no chance of being free unless made and kept so by the exertions of better men than himself.*

**- John Stuart Mill**

Every American old enough at the time remembers where they were on 9/11. Some remember it as distinctly as the day President Kennedy was assassinated or the Space Shuttle Challenger exploded after liftoff. On that fateful September day, radical Islam declared a new religious crusade against Western Civilization. In an act of war, terrorists sounded their call for the destruction of our very way of life. Denouncing everything we say we stand for, truth, liberty, and justice, they took aim at what they believe our nation is founded upon. **Money!**

As the World Trade Center's Twin Towers buckled amidst plumes of smoke, hundreds of thousands, millions even, across the planet cheered for the destruction of America. Our hearts sank at the tragedy—they praised Allah. Over a decade later, and the nightmare has only deepened. The war in Iraq and the ongoing war in Afghanistan have collectively endured longer than both World Wars combined. The death toll is only rising with militant fundamentalists in Pakistan and Iran fueling the chaos.

Make no mistake about it. As September 11, 2001 proved—the threat is real. The wars in Afghanistan and Iraq, the bombings in Spain and England, the attacks on Mumbai, the genocide in Darfur, the fragile stability of Pakistan, the usurping of citizen revolutions in Egypt and Syria, and the belligerence of Iran's president, Mahmoud Ahmadinejad—all of these are testaments to the absolute malevolence we are facing.

Americans are constantly on terror alert, paranoid much the same as we were of Russian spies and nuclear holocaust during the Cold War. And every day that we are called on to put our sons and daughters in the line of fire we question our purpose and our resolve is tested. This dichotomy of good and evil in religion is not new to the history of man, but this time it is most insidious and horrifying.

Before we can address how we should wage the War on Terror, we must first understand the reality of what exact threat it is that we are facing. What every American needs to understand with absolute clarity is just how severe and pervasive the threat really is, because it is clear that so many of us are unaware of the profundity of this ideological menace.

Now, media pundits often make the case that our government is war mongering, striking fear into the hearts of American citizens for the tactical purpose of some ulterior motive. They will argue that the threat is nowhere near as terrible as President Bush made it out to be. I wish it were the case, but the unfortunate truth is that the media's conspiratorial claims are misguided and they do the American citizens a horrible injustice by sugarcoating the severity of the clear and present danger posed by Islamic fundamentalism.

The jihad being waged by radical Islam is not being fought by a mere band of scattered guerilla warriors hiding in far off deserts or the remote caves of Tora Bora, Afghanistan. Radical Islam does not consist only of Al Queda and the Taliban; it is a way of life, an extreme and fanatic mentality bread into the hearts and minds of millions across the globe.

We must remember that with the destruction of the World Trade Center, there was a general response within the radical Muslim world of jubilee. Two days before the attacks of September 11, the Mufti of Palestine, the senior religious figure in the Palestinian authority, and with millions of followers, openly prayed on radio for Allah to destroy Great Britain, Israel, and the United States. After the Twin Towers buckled, almost immediately, Palestinian airwaves were flooded with propaganda, boasting that a divine blow in the name of Allah had been dealt against the enemy [the United States] and that Israel is to follow.

We must understand further that this propaganda machine is not confined to remote villages or forgotten corners of the world. The machine is vast, spanning continents and infecting the minds of people in Africa, Asia, Europe, South and North America. There are the Pakistan-based Lashkar-e-Taiba and Jaish-e-Mohammed, who seek the Indian state of Jammu and Kashmir's accession to Pakistan; the Bangledeshi Jamaat-ul-Mujahideen; the Chechnyan separatist "Special Purpose Islamic Regiment", thought to have trained the older of the Boston Bombers; the Sunni Hezbollah of Turkey and the Shia Hezbollah of Lebanon. In Iraq there's the Abu Musab al-Zarqawi's al-Qaeda affiliate, and Al-Faruq Brigades, a militant wing of the Islamic Movement in Iraq (Al-Harakah al-Islamiyyah fi al-arak) to name only a few. There's the Israeli and Palestinian Al-Aqsa Martyrs' Brigades and Hamas, which calls for the destruction of Israel. Armed terrorist organizations are growing in Algeria, Yemen, the Philippines, the Sudan, Russia, Georgia, Spain, France, England, Germany—the list goes on and on as the cancer spreads—even into the United States!

The dangerous ideology these extremists preach is in fact more than simple dogmatic propaganda. It is a media of terrorism. And it is so prevalent, literally as ubiquitous as CNN and Fox News are to us Americans, that the fanaticism it preaches has become part of the way the populations of these regions see the world. The machine targets youth—often the most innocent, those that are lost, without shelter, food, medical care, a family. It pontificates a culture of hatred, a demonization of Western culture, appealing to those in extreme poverty, those with the least hope, by promising heaven in the afterlife if, and only if, an oath to wage jihad against America is taken.

The infiltration of radical Islam into our cultures is so deep and pervasive it is shocking. The frontlines aren't just in Iraq and Afghanistan, or even Pakistan, Israel, or India. Their ideology is spreading like a malignant tumor, feeding on human desperation with frightening speed. The front lines, my fellow Americans, are in Madrid, Paris, London, Berlin, Washington DC, New York, Boston, right down to Fort Hood, Texas. Their twisted worldview of unquestionable obedience to Allah and destruction of Judeo-Christian Civilization is in our very own backyards. Their war, their ideology of hatred, has come ashore our land of liberty, and they have sworn to take us down by any means.

Yet, in America, we tend to think of this extreme fundamentalist sect as being in the decided minority in the nation of Islam, small and distant. And while the terrorist acts on 911, in Madrid and London's train stations, in Germany, in Mumbai, now make us turn our heads, we still generally think of Muslims as good, law-abiding, faithful, loving people because we don't see the fanaticism in the Muslims that live among us.

In America, this belief in the goodness innate in Muslims as a religious people is accurate and right. We know that not all Muslims are part of radical Islam, we have faith in the moral compass of our Islamic neighbors, and rightfully so. But, the false logic is this: just because the majority of Muslim Americans are peaceful, virtuous, law-abiding people, it does not mean that all are. Not internationally and not domestically.

The Qur'an is a beautiful religious text, and in its purpose to the nations of Islam as the verbal divine guidance and moral direction for mankind, it stands as perhaps the finest piece of literature in the Arabic language. Just as the Bible teaches morality, compassion toward others, and the rule of law, so does the Qur'an. In fact, the Qur'an itself cites an intimate, reverential relationship with the earlier transcribed Torah and New Testament, attributing their similarities to their unique origin from having been revealed by the one God.

> *It is He Who sent down to thee in truth, the Book, confirming what went before it; and He sent down the Law (of Moses) and the Gospel (of Jesus) before this, as a guide to mankind, and He sent down the criterion (of judgment between right and wrong).*

— **Qur'an 3:3**

But our sense of security is false when we translate what we know of domestic Islam into a belief that extreme fundamentalist Islam is few in numbers and that, as "Muslims," they actually follow the Qur'an. Whereas our system or ordered liberty is founded upon the Judeo-Christian virtues that celebrate the sanctity of life and teach us the truth that love is the fulfillment of the law, radical Islam teaches their children to hate in life and die for the sake of Allah.

These radicals, we must understand, don't follow the Qur'an. They think they do, in fact they obstinately proselytize that they do. But in fact, many of them have not even read the Qur'an. Discounting the hundreds and thousands of these radicals that are illiterate, those that do read often don't read the Qur'an. While the Qur'an teaches compassion, love, and equal justice, they instead follow the teachings and writings of men like Mohammad Ibn Abdul-Wahhab, an eighteenth century zealot desert preacher who preached that all forms of adornment and modernity are blasphemous and that all non-believers in his version of Islam must be converted or destroyed.

Unlike traditional Islam, Wahhabism treats women as third-class citizens, imposes the veil on them, and denies them basic human rights such as the freedom of traveling within the country or leaving it without permission or Mahram (a relative male chaperon).

In addition, Wahhabism outlaws the celebration of Almoulid, the Prophet Mohammad's birthday, forbids religious freedom, outlaws political freedom, and forces the public to observe strictly regimented prayers. Wahhabist authorities intimidate the masses by publicly beheading convicted killers and hand-amputating alleged thieves. Perhaps most telling of this "theology's" absolute perversion is the fact that it considers itself to be the only correct way in all of Islam, and any Muslim who opposes it is a heretic who must be enslaved. Just imagine, by analogy, if all Catholics hunted and persecuted all other Christians for their differences in belief.

This is not Islam as learned from the Qur'an, rather it is a fundamentally savage, backward, and perverted form of preaching that is contrary to the Qur'an used to brainwash legions of extremist Muslims to become hell-bent on the destruction of America. It is not the Qur'an that has taught them to wage jihad and convert by the sword or die in martyrdom with the promise of virgins in the afterlife. Rather, it is an entirely different set of books, books of jihad written or orally passed down by Wahhabist-style preachers who follow and embellish upon Mohammad Ibn Abdul-Wahhab's teachings and "cherry pick" from the Qur'an out of context.

What we see all across the world is the utilization of these perverted teachings in order to preach Wahhabism through rote memorization to an illiterate or otherwise impoverished, desperate, and credulous set of Muslims. In Afghanistan, the Taliban employ this technique with horrifying efficiency through a network of Saudi Arabian funded schools called Madrasahs. In these Medrasahs no subjects are taught except for Wahhabism. The hopeless are brought in, given food and shelter, with the requirement of submitting to the teachings therein.

Medrasah literally means school, and historically they have not been anti-American, anti-Western, pro-terrorist centers having less to do with teaching basic literacy and more to do with political and theological indoctrination. And certainly not all are today. But, these Medrasahs of which I speak are widespread and they are effectively brainwashing a generation of desperate Muslims to hate America, to hate western civilization, and to covet the destruction of all that we stand for.

They brainwash their recruits and followers to believe that they've revived the Islamic jihad, dividing the world into two camps, the Muslim and the non-Muslim. They sermonize that Allah is happy when non-Muslims die, that the laws of Islam, the books of jihad, demand that non-Muslims are to be taken to the slaughter. To these radicals, any non-Wahhabist Muslim, to include American Muslims, are called Kafirs (infidels), cows to be taken to market, sold, and butchered. Quite literally, they are brainwashed to believe that no infidel is innocent, period.

Americans must understand that a countless horde has demonized us. It seems so odd and inconceivable to us that so many people have been brainwashed to this end. But, to fathom this mentality, again, we need only look to our own, relatively recent history. Recall that Christians, out of the desperation caused in the aftermath of the First World War, fell for the extreme Nazi propaganda machine calling for the eradication of the Jews. If we fell for it, why would the Muslims not when faced with similar extreme conditions?

A seed of anti-Semitism, just as it did in Nazi Germany, has burst, bringing Christianity and all other faiths into the crosshairs. Hitler committed a crime against the youth of Germany by stealing their innocence and brainwashing them with a message of hatred. Radical Islam is committing the same crime against non-radical Islam, stealing their youth and capitalizing on desperation and ignorance to instill a fundamental hatred of any non-radical, Muslim, Christian, Jew, and Hindi alike. In many regions of the world, hundreds of thousands of these radicals comprise the majority, and any non-radical Muslim living in the purview of these terrorist havens is treated like a cow, a target to be slaughtered on site.

One would think that drawing a similarity to Hitler's Nazi regime would be the most horrifying analogy possible. Yet, the circular dogma that led to fascism under the Nazi regime was actually less dangerous and sinister than radical Islam. In Hitler's Germany, Nazi's hated and killed in the name of the Fuhrer, while in radical

Islam, jihadists terrorize in the name of God. Their creed is the same: destroy all those that do not believe as they do. With the Aryan race, this hatred was primarily confined to the Jews, whereas radical Islam has widened its sights and taken aim at Christians, Buddhists, Hindi, and even Muslims that do not believe as they do.

America must wake up to this unfortunate reality. And we must be willing to appropriately and decidedly address any insight to violence against Western Civilization, regardless of whether the origin of the incantation is domestic or foreign.

A clear understanding of this threat, though, is only the first step to thwarting it. The next question is one that has to date eluded us on many fronts; how do we fight this terrorism?

As aforementioned, we must first look inward to see what we are made of. To be clear, I'm not talking of our strength and resolve, as I believe our endurance through the Iraq and Afghanistan Wars is proof of America's tenacity. Further, a proper understanding of the threat's pervasiveness should only fortify our steadfastness as a nation. Rather, I am talking about our morality. Perhaps more pointedly, I am talking about our priorities.

You see, these terrorists have made a calculated decision in the way they are waging their war. Presented with the dilemma of taking down a giant, a world superpower with a vastly superior military, they have hedged their bet. Strictly speaking, they have bet that we are consumed by money and that if they can take down our economy, they can win their war. Why do you think Osama bin Laden chose the World Trade Center as his first target on 9/11?

Radical Islam preys on the impoverished, brainwashing extremism into the minds of those living in extreme conditions. They promise something as simple as food and shelter to the hopeless, the desperate, and the forgotten souls of society, and then bombard them with fanaticism. It is a vicious cycle of impoverishment leading to fanaticism and extremism that inexorably results in violence.

Radical Islam is aiming to create the same impoverished and hopeless reality in western civilization. It starts with one street in

Detroit perhaps, where nobody has jobs, everyone has been evicted from their homes, crime and drugs are rampant. Then they offer their poisoned apple in this extreme reality, promising the fruits of a happier, sanctified life. Instead, they will give over strict fanaticism, breed extremism, and eventually demand violence. We are already witness to this reality.

They hope to do this, first, by bringing down our economies. Their design is to turn our collective societal wealth and comfort on its head, lead us into bankruptcy, and then allow what they perceive as our immorality to tear us apart from within. Much like how the Spanish Conquistadors divided and conquered the Incan civilization when they came ashore in South America, they aim to factionalize us, get us to fight amongst ourselves over a dwindling supply of money, and then convert us by the sword or murder us when our defenses are down.

We must understand that, to the terrorists, we are not a nation of moral, benevolent people. Instead, we are non-believers who are laden with greed. They see us as power hungry demons thirsting for global dominance and filthy riches. Their bet is that in bankruptcy we will turn our back on our own Constitution; that we will brush our Bill of Rights under the rug and denounce everything we say we believe in.

Of course, each one of us will unwaveringly respond to this gross characterization adamant that we are not what they perceive us to be. We believe it in our hearts—we know it! And I absolutely believe it to be the truth that we are not these greedy, filthy demons; rather we are a force for justice, for liberty, for morality, and peace.

That being said, and it utterly pains me to say, our greed and increasingly sedentary ways are of grave concern. Our economic crisis is beginning to shed light on some of our true, less flattering colors. And it is incumbent upon us, individually and as a nation, to take a long hard look at ourselves in the mirror. We must recognize our flaws, embrace the fact that we have a lot of work to do, understand that we are far from perfect, and move forward with our core ideals reaffirmed. If we can do that and only if we can do that—the War on Terror is already won and America will come back stronger than ever.

To start then, let us look in the mirror:

The economic collapse, exacerbated by the War on Terror, is testing the moral fabric of our society. Capitalism, our fundamental system of free commerce, is being impeached, our banks and industries are struggling, and our infrastructure is corroding in disrepair. Our homes, nearly ten million of our American Dreams, now stand vacant, devoid of families. Unemployment has reached as high as 10% nationwide, crimes of extreme moral turpitude, divorce, and domestic violence are rising sharply and our borders are being invaded by illegal aliens without respect for the law.

Unfortunately, while these trials and tribulations befall us, our government is failing us. As we look to our elected officials, too often the mirror they reflect of us is one in accord with radical Islam's disgusting critique of our society. I say this because Washington's answer to all our troubles seems to be one-dimensional: throw money at the problem and demonize the opposition. Mark my words—if this continues, we fail.

The question that presents itself in this pivotal moment in history is whether, in the face of deepening financial turmoil, we will continue with the materialistic, over-indulgent, sedentary mindset that set us up for our current economic collapse, or whether we will reaffirm our moral grounding as a nation and fight for all that is good in America by standing, rolling up our sleeves, and doing what is right, regardless of the difficulty.

Regrettably, our government is acting only to reinforce our materialism, exactly as they have for decades. Government policy has encouraged us to spend on credit and take on mounting debt to where by the end of 2009, total US consumer debt reached an astronomical $2.45 trillion, with total individual household debt, including credit cards, mortgage, home equity, and student loans, skyrocketing to nearly $17,000 per household. The mean average unpaid credit card balance jumped to $3,389 per person in America.

Believe it or not, this spelled disaster for the federal government, but not because the amount was too high, rather because the total US consumer debt had dropped sharply from $2.56 trillion at the end of 2008. The recession meant that people weren't spending. Something had to be done!

So, in shortsighted reaction to this fiscal meltdown, our government has responded with an economic stimulus plan centered on encouraging us to spend. First, we were given a measly couple hundred-dollar tax refund and encouraged to quickly go and spend it—God forbid save it. And, we spent it, plus some, just as the government wanted us to. Why? Because, we've been told that our economy is based upon consumer spending and that if we stop spending, the engines of our economy will grind to a halt. If Washington can just keep us spending our hard-earned money, as well as the money we have not yet earned, they believe the economy will continue to grow at a healthy rate.

Unfortunately, they are wrong! And they are wrong because our spending is no longer rationally linked to our production. Because income is being eclipsed by our expenses, we have for decades now been forced to live on credit. What happens when that credit runs out?

Washington governs itself with this same spendthrift state of mind that we have individually adopted, and as a result the United States public debt (the "Federal Debt"), which consists of two calculations: "Debt Held by the Public," defined as US Treasury securities held by institutions outside the United States government, and the "Gross Debt," which includes intra-government obligations such as securities held by the Social Security trust fund or the Federal Reserve, is absolutely staggering.

Note that the costs incurred in World War II, in addition to President Roosevelt's New Deal, and the social programs of the Truman presidency caused a sixteen-fold increase in the federal debt from approximately $16 billion in 1930 to $260 billion in

1950. As a Republican, it pains me to say that this debt more than quintupled during the Reagan and Bush presidencies from 1980 to 1992. Then came the War on Terror and during the administration of President George W. Bush, the debt increased from $5.6 trillion in January 2001 to $10.7 trillion by December 2008, rising from 58% of GDP to 70.2% of GDP. But now, under the Obama administration, the situation has deteriorated at a far more alarming rate.

As of September 2010, the federal debt of $13.56 trillion was approximately 94% of US annual GDP—now our debt of $15-plus trillion is more than 100% of our annual GDP. In simple terms, we are drowning. And this is what radical Islam wants. Because, with such unconscionable debt, more and more of our money must go to the purchase of government debt, rather than investing in productive capital goods such as factories and computers, leading to lower output and incomes than would otherwise occur, further exacerbating the situation. A downward spiral is begun much the same as an individual with too many credit cards fighting to pay even the minimum monthly balance, drowning in interest, and never saving for the future.

The federal debt is a phenomenal threat to our national security. Why? Because if higher marginal tax rates are used to pay the rising interest costs of this debt, individual and corporate savings will be reduced and work, industry, and innovation will be depressed. How then will we pay for the renovation, much less the re-engineering of our decaying infrastructure? We won't! We will continue to import 9,013,000 barrels of oil per day at a staggering cost of $297 billion per year. Over $50 billion of which goes to countries that harbor and arm terrorists bent on our absolute destruction.

In fact, the interest costs on our debts are already forcing reductions in government programs that the government actually ought to be administering. And, it's not just the federal government—nearly every state in the Union is facing a massive budget crisis. As a result, more and more Americans are out on the street with nobody to turn to. No help, no food, no hope. This growing crowd of people has already become malcontent and in many cases, outright enraged at the government. Occupy Wall Street is just the beginning. How much worse will it need to get before there are armed riots in the streets? How much worse will it need to get before plots the successful bombing at the Boston Marathon become the norm, rather than the exception?

It is upon the most impoverished, uneducated, enraged, and hopeless of this crowd that radical Islam will focus upon to recruit domestic terrorists. It is upon these people they are already successfully preying upon in Europe.

Unfortunately, the situation is only primed to worsen. As a result of our over-consumption, individual, corporate, and government alike, and the tremendous amounts of money we have spent bailing out Wall Street, we will eventually have to pay a price in terms of higher taxes to meet the interest on that debt. Higher taxes will unfortunately become requisite to meet the claims of our domestic foreign creditors. The tax hikes to afford the fiscal cliff of January 1, 2013, are evidence thereof.

How then can the government deal with this debt? First off, to date, they have not. For thirty-plus years, our government has kicked the can down the road for future generations to deal with the problem. That generation is us, now!

Historically, in an attempt to forego raising taxes, such debts have been met with the temptation to default by stealth. In other words, allowing the dollar's value to deflate.

But, the dollar's deflation means something equally as grave for Americans—inflation. Soon, we likely could see the cost of a gallon of milk rise to $15, an ear of corn to $5, cereal, butter, sugar, meats, our entire grocery bill could go up in cost by 20–30%. This inflation, coupled with an unemployment rate that continues to climb, and where salaries are frozen or slashed for those still employed, spells even further economic disaster. It is a recipe for civil unrest!

More and more people will fall into impoverishment. The middle class will become the poor and the poor will become the destitute. It is in this economic climate that radical Islam wants us to fester. We must wake up from this nightmare immediately because commodities have already skyrocketed in cost, and that expense is already being passed on to the American consumer. Across the board, everything from groceries to clothes, plastics, etc. have already increased in cost by 5–15% in the last few years. Inflation has already begun!

The first and most important thing we must do in order to intelligently combat terrorism, then, is to revamp our economy. I'm not speaking of turning our back on capitalism in favor of socialism as many of the disillusioned have proffered out of fear. Not at all. In fact, I believe passionately that the key to our economic salvation is capitalism, in its true, pure form.

We must unleash the power of American ingenuity; promote and foster intellectual investment in American business so that we may once again produce for export as well as domestic consumption. For Washington's belief that consumer spending is essential to keep the engines of our economy running is true, but it is only half of the equation.

Production is the necessary first half of the economic equation, for when a company produces something that people want to consume, the basic and elementary economic law of supply and demand is fulfilled. Yet, for decades, America has failed to produce at a level necessary to meet the demands of our own consumption and the result is nearly a trillion dollar a year trading deficit.

The US has held a trade deficit since late in the 1960s, but since 1997, our trade deficit has been increasing at a rapid rate. Between 2005 and 2006 for example, the US trade deficit increased by $49.8 billion to a worldwide record high of $817.3 billion. It is now over a trillion dollars per year.

*We must always take heed that we buy no more from strangers than we sell them, for so should we impoverish ourselves and enrich them.*

**– Fernand Braudel, *The Wheels of Commerce***

To be clear, the concern here is not necessarily with the size of the trade deficit. This is because the trade deficit can be affected by myriad factors such as the cost of production (land, labor, taxes) in the exporting economy vis-à-vis the importing, the cost, and availability of raw materials, exchange rates, trade restrictions, and the price of goods manufactured. In fact, as Milton Friedman, the Nobel Prize-winning economist and father of Monetarism contended, trade deficits are not necessarily, in and of themselves, omens of economic failure, because high export levels increase the value of the exporting currency, eventually reducing aforementioned exports, and vice versa for imports, thus naturally removing trade deficits not due to investment.

By reductio ad absurdum, nineteenth century economist and philosopher Frédéric Bastiat even argued that the national trade deficit was an indicator of a successful economy, rather than a failing one. Bastiat predicted that a successful, growing economy would result in greater trade deficits, and an unsuccessful, shrinking economy would result in lower trade deficits. And it seems these theories are being proven fundamentally sound given that since the Great Recession began, the annual US trade deficit has fallen by over $3 billion.

The real concern here is the fact that the trade deficit is mounting alongside a federal deficit—compounding the issue. Essentially, we are borrowing money to trade in the red. Or to play off of a syllogism: we are borrowing from China so we can rob Peter to pay Paul.

The reason for this phenomenon stems from America's continuing failure to produce goods for the marketplace, both domestic and international. The free system of enterprise, the liberties afforded us as a people, long left people like Andrew Carnegie to modernize the production of steel. Yet, for a number of reasons, America is no longer producing goods for sale. Instead, we consume and put the cost on our credit cards, individually, and as a nation.

Post-World War II, America was primed as the world's industrial superpower. The factories previously manned by "Rosie the Riveter" women in order to crank out the war machines were primed to build modern America. And when the Greatest

Generation returned from saving the world from fascism, they were ready to go to work in the only true remaining industrialized nation on the planet. All other industrialized nations sizeable enough to compete, after all, had been leveled in the war.

What came next were America's economic golden years. Through grit and hard work, we built the wealthiest, most industrialized, modern nation on the planet. The United States GDP grew to a record $482.7 billion by the end of the 1950s. In the 1960s our nation enjoyed the most sustained period of economic expansion we'd ever known, accompanied by rising productivity and low unemployment. With real income rising 50% during the decade, we were sitting pretty with more Americans enjoying the luxuries of the middle-class lifestyle than ever before.

But, then came the advent of deindustrialization in the late 1960s and early 1970s. Among other factors, increased free trade, globalization, and high corporate taxes resulted in US companies shifting their manufacturing and heavy industrial operations to second- and third-world countries with lower labor costs. It literally became more attractive to the American corporation's bottom lines to dismantle their industrial infrastructures in favor of producing elsewhere. While this meant a flood of cheaper imported goods into our economy for us to purchase at places like the Dollar Store and Walmart, these policies resulted in a massive reduction in the percent of the US labor force engaged in industry (from over 35% in the late 1960s to under 20% today).

Detroit and the auto industry are an unfortunate example of de-industrialization and the effect it has had on our nation. Once the world's largest center of automobile production and associated with a high standard of living, Detroit today is associated with a high concentration of poverty, unemployment and manifest racial isolation. The vast urban production complexes that once built the automobiles driving on our highways stand abandoned and over one-third of Detroit's residents now live below the poverty line. Similar fates have befallen the steel industry of Pittsburgh, the manufacturing and shipping industries of Baltimore, and so the list goes on.

The simple fact stands that the American economy has undergone a fundamental shift from a manufacturing and industrial based economy to a service-based economy.

After World War II service industries accounted for less than10% of non-farming employment, compared with 38% for manufacturing. But since the late 1960s, the American economy has moved away from producing goods to providing services at a disquieting rate.

In 1970, there were approximately 50 million service-providing workers in the United States and 23 million employed in the goods-producing sector, representing a service-to-goods ratio of about two-to-one. According to the Bureau of Labor Statistics, the ratio of service-to-goods workers soared to five-to-one with over a third of the US population employed in the service industry by 2005. The face of our economy has completely changed—and it is destroying us.

American consumption currently accounts for over 70% of our GDP. Of this 70%, half is spent on services, such as haircuts, car washes, and restaurants. The problem, then, is this: if we're just going out to restaurants, what are we selling to the rest of the world? With all that China is selling to us, what are we selling to them and the remainder of the world? Very little! And hence our enormous trade deficits.

Analogy time: Think of Jamaica, or almost any destination in the Caribbean archipelago. What is the common thread between the economies of these beautiful islands? All of their economies are primarily dependent on the tourism industry. They do not produce much of anything, rather, they provide services, and as a result, their economies are weak, unemployment is high, and those that do work earn low wages. Well, in America, the problem is much worse to scale.

While we provide services to ourselves, all we are doing is redistributing wealth amongst ourselves. But, in order to provide those services we are consuming products from overseas. The result: we are redistributing wealth among ourselves from a dwindling pot.

There has been a forty-year mass exodus in America from our time-honored tradition of rolling up our sleeves, working hard, and making products for sale in the marketplace. Instead of reversing this trend, however, the drift has been worsening in recent years. Post 9/11, the United States has shut down nearly 45,000 factories, equating to a loss of one-third of our manufacturing jobs in that timeframe. At the end of 2009, 12 million jobs in the US were geared toward the manufacture of goods. The last time so few jobs in the United States comprised the manufacturing sector was prior to World War II, before we climbed out of the Great Depression, and when our population was far fewer in numbers.

The result is a reality in America where overall capitalization in the stock market exceeds 100% of US GDP. Historically, the stock market's value has been approximately 58% of GDP with lows hovering at 37% in the early 1950s and 25% during the Great Depression. Highs in this measurement were around 75% of GDP, each occurring at all the significant market downturns in the last eighty years, including the 1929 and 1966 crashes.

As recently as 1991, the market was at the historic 58% level of GDP. Since then, however, we've completely lost sight of this economic indicator. By the fourth quarter of 1999, stock market capitalization increased to a confounding 185% of total GDP!

We've all seen this at play. Each day when we watch the news or check our phone apps, we see that the stock market is soaring or strong. But how can it be that the Dow Jones Industrial Average is doing so well when America is drowning in unemployment and debt? The answer, unfortunately, is that two economies have burgeoned. One for the rich, and one for the poor, with the middle class being torn in either direction, more often than not toward the poor.

America's economy now primarily consists of ones and zeros—digital currency for the rich to play with and the poor to sit out.

When we aren't producing anything, the only way to make money is to invest in others that do and maneuver around the market-place with snakelike craft. Wall Street is first-rate at this, but the result is the constant ebb and flow of boom and bust in the mar-ketplace. The dot.com and sub-prime lending bursts are just the most recent, and with each bubble, the rich are getting richer; with each burst, the poor are getting poorer.

This last crash has been the most telling of this wealth dispar-ity. Since the dawn of the Great Recession, Americans have lost an estimated average of more than a quarter of their collective net worth; housing prices, historically our largest nest egg, have dropped over 30% from their 2006 peak; total retirement assets, Americans' second-largest household asset, dropped by 22%; sav-ings and investment assets lost $1.2 trillion and pension assets lost $1.3 trillion across the board. Taken together, these losses approxi-mately total an unimaginable loss of $10 trillion from the pockets of hard working Americans.

Meanwhile, the number of millionaires living in the US has spiked. In 1928, one year before the Great Depression began, the wealthiest .001% of the US population owned about 892 times more than 90% of the nation's citizens. Today, the top .001% of the US population owns over 976 times more than the entire bot-tom 90%.

Then there's this fact which has Americans enraged: according to a study by the Institute for Policy Studies, in 2008, top execu-tives in the United States took home salaries that were 319 times greater than the average worker (about $10 million per CEO). We see reports of massive profits and obscene bonuses at the very firms who owe their continued existence to $700 billion in TARP funds—our tax dollars. No wonder we are exercising our First Amendment right to assemble in the streets and protest corporate greed.

Here is where we must be very careful however. Many have begun to argue that the financial crisis is merely a subset of a systemic crisis—capitalism itself. According to Samir Amin, an

Egyptian Marxist economist, for example, the constant decrease in GDP growth rates in Western Civilizations since the early 1970s created a growing surplus of capital which did not have sufficient profitable investment outlets in the real economy. The alternative was to place this surplus into the financial market, which became more profitable than capital investment, especially with subsequent deregulation. The result being the financial bubbles that keep on bursting. This, by the way, is exactly what radical Islam wants us to do—impeach our own economy.

But, capitalism is not to blame. I do agree that the decrease in GDP growth rates have led to insufficient profitable investment outlets in our real economy, leading to engorgement in the financial market. The problem, however, is failure to produce, not capitalism. Our economic policies must again be geared toward the promotion of capital investment, because socialism, history has shown us, will do just the opposite. Capitalism, then, is the answer!

Instead, our government is itching to intervene in corporate operations in order to cut CEO pay. But this is America. We don't disparage wealth. In fact, we always have and must continue to encourage it. This is precisely why President Obama's $500,000 cap on executive pay sets a bad precedent. Cutting executive pay simply is not the answer.

Instead, regulating corporate expenditures is a disincentive to innovate and produce. Government intervention in the free market, we must continue to recognize, is a very dangerous thing. Now, Obama's decision actually was palatable in that it applied only to executives of firms that we, as taxpayers, bailed out to the tune of $700 billion—but it must stop there.

CEOs making as much money as they do, we must understand, is a natural function of the free market. Understandably upset at our losses, we often forget that these people lead major multinational corporations with scores of employees and $50 billion in annual revenue. Performing properly, they create thousands of jobs, deliver a lifetime of wealth for innumerable investors, and drive life-changing innovation. While most chief executives are in fact compensated at a far lower rate than our NBA superstars and Hollywood celebrities, the criticisms thrown at them are far more relentless. Moreover, in the economics of large multinational corporations, $10 million is no more than a line item budget amount for office supplies such as pens and paper.

We are understandably upset at the chasm growing between the rich and the poor, and as such, it is only natural for the middle class to look up at the rich with disdain as they fall toward the lower class. However, it is my opinion that in criticizing CEO compensation, the government and the media are demonizing the wrong people. Out of anger, we are looking for a scapegoat: the rich. We've grown to hate those that are succeeding in their industries because our livelihoods are vanishing.

We must pause, take a step back, and realize just how un-American the abhorrence of the rich is and turn our attention back to the real problem facing our nation's economy.

America is the land where enterprise and the chance at becoming rich have always been encouraged. We must never discourage people from getting rich, lest we discourage innovation and progress. It is wrong of us to detest those that have gotten rich in their industries. What is proper is for every American worker to be upset at the fact that there are fewer and fewer opportunities for them to get rich or even sustain middle class status. We should also be mad that many of the rich are ostensibly hijacking Congress to ensure they remain rich despite the hurtful consequences to the remainder of the constituency.

The real problem in America, what is causing the growing rift between the rich and the poor in our nation, is not capitalism; it is how we are wielding the power of the free market. We built our nation through hard work and determination, but for decades we have been content to sit idle instead of continuing as the pioneers of industry.

Why? To an extent it is because of human nature. As I said before, man is much like water, instinctually inclined to take the path of least resistance. So, again, let us take a long hard look in the mirror. Individually, most of us would rather work in the services sector as white-collar workers rather than in a theoretically more difficult blue-collar vocation. It certainly is physically less demanding. As a nation, we worked so hard building modern America, generating massive amounts of wealth, and sometimes we feel entitled to kick back and relax. This is only human nature, and the wealth accumulated in our golden years afforded us the ability to utilize our mental talents toward innovation and pay others to do the backbreaking labor for us. Why fix your sink when you can pay a plumber to do it, right?

But we must awake from this apathy because, as a nation, we no longer have the money to pay the plumber. Unfortunately, though, we've been very slow to wake from our lethargy in part because our economic and tax policies have compounded the issue by encouraging our instinctual indolence and masking its effects.

Now, you are probably wondering why I am talking so much about the economy in a chapter purportedly aimed at the issue of international terrorism. The reason is simple. Our economic security is intrinsically linked to our national security, especially when it comes to the War on Terror. The insolvency of our nation will bankrupt our ability to fight terrorism abroad and lead to civil unrest within our borders. This must not happen because we absolutely must win this war. What we face in radical Islam is a clash of civilizations and they have made it very clear that it is either us or them. Failure, then, is not an option.

Here is what radical Islam thinks of us: we are succumbing to sloth. We are greedy, we want to consume everything, and we don't want to have to work for it. Radical Islam is betting that we are the next Rome and that we will implode, falling upon the sword of our own opulence. They forecast that globalization and the additional financial pressures their mounting campaigns of terror have on our bottom line will result in us becoming slaves to the third world. They believe that the third world, upon which we prey for all that we consume, will surpass us, that the balance of power will shift in their favor and we will grow weaker and weaker. Their hope is that our current economic crisis will snowball into a downward spiral, leaving us broken and powerless to stop the spread of their twisted creed.

<u>But they are dead wrong</u>! Americans work harder than the citizens of any other nation on this planet. We are the most innovative workforce on the globe and our collective talent eclipses all others. Laziness, while an exacerbating factor, is not to blame. Resting on our laurels is. This crisis is borne out of our societal ignorance and collective indifference to the direction we have allowed our government to steer the economy for the last forty years. We've all been playing ignorant to the effects of our service-based economy; our natural human instinct to take the easy road has blinded us as to the inevitable rise of Asia as an economic powerhouse with whom we must compete. But now, after decades of craftily avoiding the unavoidable through the stock market, we are finally learning the truth. The truth of the matter is this: we must get back to work producing for ourselves and the rest of the world. For the rest of the world also wants and is willing to compete for the standard of living we've shown them is possible.

This is precisely why educating America about the true threat facing us, the true crisis facing our economy, and how to transcend these challenges is of paramount importance. The silver lining in the Great Recession is the fact that it is opening our eyes. The extremes we are facing, massive unemployment, for instance, are shaking us from our apathy, forcing us to ask the tough questions. The key is to answer those questions intelligently and educate America as to just how far down the wrong path we have gone so that we may redirect.

I believe that in America, our privileges, the opportunities we have, our wealth, our power—this has not made us weak and lazy any more than it did the Greatest Generation before they left for World War II. We've had more opportunity than any civilization before us to venture down that road of lethargy, and in many respects, we have, but hopefully to realize the evils of excess. In fact, the liberties afforded us in our Constitution have afforded

Americans the ability to witness firsthand the pitfalls of material-ism run amuck. This experience, and the freedoms still afforded us, give us a unique perspective from which to correct our course, as well as the power. Perhaps the greatest majesty of our American tradition of ordered liberty is that we are all free, individually and institutionally, to look into the mirror and make the changes necessary. It is this power, properly wielded, that will win the war against terrorism as well as bring back our economy.

Having gained so much, we have so much to lose and American's will not let go easily. It is the same determination that led us to erect the Hoover Damn, the Empire State Building, and the interstate highway system that will empower us to overcome the current economic crisis, avoid future recessions, and win the War on Terror.

But first- back to the mirror. We are currently making a lot of mistakes, and unfortunately, money seems to be the governing fac-tor in our rash decisions. For starters, we are cutting education—an extremely shortsighted, reckless, and irresponsible response to our financial crisis. I will delve into that in a later chapter.

Here's an interesting example of money overriding our logic: California passed SB 1449 on October 1, 2010, reducing the posses-sion of less than an ounce of marijuana to a civil infraction where the person in possession is slapped with the equivalent of a mere parking ticket. The reasons cited by Governor Schwarzenegger were the cost to police the illegal drug and the possibility of raising tax revenue if it were to be fully legalized and regulated. Both of these are valid considerations, no question. However, the problem is this: the decision to ostensibly legalize the drug was made solely on fiscal grounds without proper consideration of the effects of the drug or why it was made illegal in the first place. Now, to be fair, marijuana is not cocaine or heroin, and its health effects argu-ably are not even as bad as alcohol. A valid argument for mari-juana's legalization on the basis of its effects versus alcohol can certainly be made, but the decision to legalize it in California was based solely on monetary concerns. This is wrong! If money is the only consideration, the same argument can be made for the legalization of all narcotics. The same reasoning has been utilized in California to justify the release of criminals convicted of assault with a deadly weapon, battery, domestic violence, and attacks on children.

It is unfortunately quite clear that the tactic being employed by radical Islam, namely to destroy our economy, is effective. In many respects, it is forcing us to turn on our own moral compass. Why? Because it is hard to stay moral when it comes down to dog eat dog. They know this to be human nature. We must not let this happen, because the more we allow this to occur, the more we are at risk of civil unrest, revolution, loss of freedom, and a continuous wave of crisis that will lead to us turning on ourselves and our institutions. Divide and conquer!

Radical Islam abhors our freedom above all else. It therefore aims to force us to erode the freedoms protected in our Constitution for the sake of our security, because it is in a tyrannical system where freedoms are forgotten and the individual is nothing that their fanatical worldview can take root.

Unfortunately, they have already begun to succeed. In reaction to their terror, our freedoms have been truncated under the Patriot Act and our personal boundaries are being invaded by humiliating pat downs and scans at the airport. The government has created a vast domestic spying network to collect information about Americans in the wake of 9/11 and subsequent terror plots. An immense network of over four thousand counter-terrorism organizations utilizing state and local law enforcement agencies to collect information about thousands of US residents has been created to feed information to Washington for analysis. Big Brother is upon us! Is it necessary? Yes, unfortunately. But we must not allow it to go too far—if we haven't already.

Daily they are forcing us to decide what freedoms we are willing to forego and where to draw the line. While many of us will say we don't mind giving up a little bit of our freedoms for the sake of security, the issue arises when we find ourselves on the slippery slope to foregoing too many of those freedoms to a government that becomes immune to habeas corpus. It is on this slippery slope that we already find ourselves, and we must be careful not to allow the protections our forefathers fought for to be swept away out of fear. That is what the terrorists want.

Our history from 9/11 on shows us that the longer the War on Terror continues, the more pervasive we allow it to become, the greater number of rights and personal freedoms the government will find it necessary to overwrite for the sake of our own security. This, in and of itself, makes the War on Terror one where time is very much of the essence. We must therefore act decisively and expeditiously to push radical Islam back and eradicate this threat.

Stage one to winning the War on Terror, as I have mentioned, is to revamp and revitalize our economy.

If you look at Lehman Brothers, Goldman Sachs, the sub-prime lending crisis, the collapse of the Celtic Tiger, Greek debt, all the way back to our very own dot.com burst, and even the savings and loan crisis, we must realize that what we are dealing with is far bigger than these individual crises themselves. We are dealing with a fundamental shift in the way the world economy operates. While for two hundred years America and Europe dominated world production, investment, manufacturing, and exports, Asia is now out-producing us. Instinctively, many have called for protectionist policies in reaction to this truth, but this is unwise.

As a result of production, Asia's economy, most notably China's economy, is growing leaps and bounds just as ours did post-World War II. Consequently, Asia's consumer market is estimated to be twice that of ours by 2020, and therein lies our opportunity.

The first step to dealing with the current financial crisis was to stop it from becoming another Great Depression. To that end, TARP, and all the subsequent bailouts have been aimed at stopping the bleeding. Arguably, they have succeeded, for now- but they are mere Band-Aids covering a massive laceration because they are propping up arcane business models and industries that now serve only as relics of America's past industrial strength. The proof in this assertion is the fact that despite all the government "stimulus" unemployment continues to rise.

Stage two to dealing with the current financial crisis is to get the global financial systems working properly, and in tandem with reality, a task that hinges on stage three—reducing unemployment and fostering growth through economic policy geared toward encouraging capital investment and production.

I have absolute faith that we can meet this challenge. We already have the brand names and the custom-built products recognized around the world, and when you combine that with the advantage of having the most innovative and technologically advanced economy in the world along with the most creative talent in the world, we absolutely have it within our power to rise to the occasion. The re-birth of the American Dream in this generation is possible and the way we do it is by tapping into our native genius and creative talent to produce high technology goods for the remainder of the world. We must ride out to meet the challenges presented by the growth of a middle class in India and Asia and capitalize on their consumer needs. Our salvation is in producing these high technology goods to satiate our own domestic consumption as well as for export to the remainder of the world, for doing so will satisfy the basic economic law of supply and demand.

Stage two in successfully fighting the War on Terror is stopping the spread of extreme poverty in the world. This, undeniably, is the most difficult task imaginable. No nation, no generation before us has ever come close to eliminating poverty. And while the task is beyond intimidating, it must be tackled head on for radical Islam takes root in these extreme living conditions. Additionally, it is the just and benevolent thing to do!

Living proof that radical Islam's grotesque characterization of us as greedy infidels being utterly erroneous is the fact that Americans are the most charitable people the world over. Time and time again, it is America that leads the efforts to bring prosperity to people less fortunate. When the 2004 tsunami obliterated Indonesia, more Americans came to the rescue than from any other nation on the planet, bringing with them more food, provisions, and financial assistance than all other countries combined. The same is true as to our response to nearly every major disaster worldwide for the last fifty years; to include the earthquake that has crippled Haiti, the floods that drowned the Khyber Pakhtunkhwa, Sindh, Punjab, and Balochistan regions of Pakistan in 2010, and in response the tsunami and nuclear crisis in Japan.

American charities dedicated to assisting those in need around the world far outnumber the charitable organizations of any other and the amount of money we have pumped into the United Nations and various NGOs is practically incalculable. Simply put, America is the most giving nation on this planet.

But, Americans are understandably growing weary and charitably drained. Every time we turn on the television there's another commercial asking that we pay one dollar a day to save a starving child in Latin America, another asking for contributions to save the rain forest or some animal welfare league. The news constantly reminds us of the tons of money we are wasting on defunct programs in Africa as AIDS and extreme poverty continues to smite them as a result of endless civil unrest. Meanwhile, we receive countless solicitation calls from the Salvation Army, the Lupus Foundation, the next canned food drive, the police and firefighters walk around with their boots—it seems that everyone has their hand out these days.

In this harsh economic climate, it is very difficult to remain charitable. If we can't even house and feed our domestic population, then why the hell are we spending so much money, money we don't have, to aid other countries? Where was their aid when Katrina hit... when Superstorm Sandy hit?

It is very easy to justify being covetous these days. But we must not be so.

The first prong to tackling terrorism is the restoration of our own economic strength, and for our Western allies to do the same, because our collective ability to execute stage two, that is to bring sustainable prosperity to those regions radical Islam aims to gain a footing, hinges upon our financial ability to be charitable, fund our military, and guard against injustice, both domestic and abroad.

Our reluctance to intervene in Libya and Syria, in part, is a testament to this truth. It is impossible to fight a war when you can't afford it.

The reason why radical Islam aims to bankrupt our economies is not only to disarm our ability to fight them and to cause domestic insurrection but also to stop us from spreading prosperity to other regions of the world. Their goal is to cause the spread of poverty and hopelessness, because in doing so they can placate to the starving and the angry, feed them their hatred, breed their fanaticism, and grow their legion.

Therefore, we must also demand assistance in this fight from our allies around the world. Assistance with funding, manpower, and gunpowder as necessary. Our partners around the world from Europe to Asia and South America—those who cherish life and liberty, must all stand up and follow our example, for we cannot police the world ourselves. Nor should we. But, as a coalition, with pooled resources and coordinated efforts, we can spread freedom and stamp out poverty faster than we could have ever imagined possible.

We must always remember just how lucky we are in America. Most of us take for granted the luxury of a daily hot shower, for instance. Meanwhile, over a billion people on this planet, even now, in the twenty-first century, don't have access to safe drinking water, and 2.5 billion people don't have access to basic sanitation. These deplorable living conditions, where every twenty seconds a child dies of water-related disease, most commonly diarrhea, where food is just as scarce, much less a roof, heat, or air-conditioning—this is the cesspool out of which blood-thirsty radicalism breeds. Somalia and Yemen are regrettable examples of this fact.

Yet, securing the financial means and collective aspiration to purvey freedom is not enough. We must also be smart about where we concentrate our foreign investments.

Without neglecting other regions of the world—Africa and South America most notably—I believe that the United States should concentrate heavily in assisting India to build its infrastructure. I make this suggestion for a number of reasons: First, India has a population of 1.18 billion people and is projected to become the world's most populous country by 2025, surpassing China. India's economy is the eleventh largest in the world by nominal GDP and the fourth largest by purchasing power parity. As of 2005, however, according to World Bank statistics, 75.6% of the population lives on less than $2 a day (PPP), while 41.6% of the population is living below the new international poverty line of $1.25 (PPP) per day. Likewise, some 600 million Indians have no means of electricity at all, with only 44% of rural households having access to electricity. Water supply is also a major problem even in urban India, with most cities getting water for only a few hours during the day. The United States, therefore, has an incredible opportunity to export high technology goods, alternative energy, and engineering expertise to India. We can literally get rich while helping to lift a billion people out of poverty.

Second, not only will lifting a billion people out of poverty in India create a vast market for our exports, it will also remove this vast population from the deplorable living conditions in which radical Islam breeds.

Third, India is a parliamentary democracy. When India gained its independence from British rule, they retained the parliamentary system of government based largely on that of the United Kingdom's Westminster system. Naturally, America shares many institutional ideologies and practices with India, basic concepts of human rights, for instance, that we do not share with China. We should be assisting the world's largest democracy to grow in a mutually beneficial economic and diplomatic relationship, rather than shoveling all of our money into China, supporting communism.

Fourth, India has a longer history than perhaps any nation on this planet in dealing with the terror of radical Islam. Most notably, they have been engaged in a bloody border dispute with

Pakistan over the northwestern Kashmir province since the partition of 1947, which created the Muslim nation of Pakistan. Having endured terrorism for so long, India has a perspective that could prove invaluable in the operative success of our military strategies in the combat of terrorist insurgencies.

Finally, India's geographical location provides the United States with an enormous ally wedged squarely between East Asia and the Middle East. And as India dominates the shoreline of the Indian Ocean, American and Indian naval cooperation naturally would lend to strategic military and economic maritime advantages in the region.

Yet, world hunger and extreme poverty is not confined to India. It is a staggering and far-reaching problem that America simply cannot tackle on its own. It is also a crisis that cannot be fixed over night as the fact remains that despite all of our concerted efforts to date, despite all of our charity so far, the problem persists like a resilient and entrenched tumor.

In order to expedite progress in pushing back extreme poverty worldwide, we must work long and hard with our allies to tackle the issue cooperatively. We must work through NATO, for instance, to promote security in regions where tensions are giving rise to security crisis, and rally member nations to step-up their financial contributions to the cause and willingness to stand up for what is just. In fact, we must demand that they stand up, for the survival of NATO, and to a large extent, Western Civilization, necessitates that they do.

And we must coordinate our aid more wisely and efficiently, for it is common knowledge that foreign aid given to any particular region is almost universally squandered by those holding power in the region. Their corruption is often the cause of their constituent's affliction, yet we continue to give them hundreds of millions of dollars with too few strings attached and only the hope that they will use it to better the lives of those they govern. In reality, we all know that these corrupt governments, dictators, warlords, etc. use the money first and foremost to further their own causes without consideration for the people starving under their dictatorial thumb.

Therefore, we must double our efforts in the diplomatic arena to bypass the corruption that hinders progress in these regions and work closely with our partners and NGOsto develop stricter accounting of the funds given as aid. Most importantly, we must work with the people of these regions as directly as possible so that they can bear witness to our good deeds. To begin with, this will result in the recipients of our charity becoming insensitive to radical Islam's malicious intimations regarding Americans as "evildoers".

Example: The common mechanism for delivery of aid to foreign nations is to wire funds to the government with use requirements rarely policed. The result—squandered aid. Instead, let's say that an American 501(c)(3) charitable organization partners with an American contractor to build houses in the African country of Liberia, a nation colonized and founded by the slaves who escaped from America and where the per capita GDP is equivalent to $379 per year. The American contractor company will go into Liberia, bringing with them managers with the knowhow to erect homes fitting for the needs of the people in the region. These managers, in turn, will hire from the local populace to perform the manual labor and pay them a salary for their hard work. The manager will also teach the local population how to continue to build these homes after the contractor leaves. The charity, backed by foreign aid, will assist in a stricter accounting for the funds used and coordinate with the regional government to make sure things run as smoothly as possible.

Though I have admittedly paired this method of foreign aid down to its most bare bones form, the application of the methodology would result in something significantly positive and maintainable.

First, discounting the philanthropy inherent, the American contractor would be compensated at cost and make a marginal profit, thus incentivizing their involvement beyond altruism.

Second, the natives will have learned a trade that they can then capitalize upon, continuing to build in their community. They will also have built something with their own hands as opposed to being given something outright, resulting in a pride of ownership and sense of accomplishment. They will fight all that much harder when warlords, dictators or radical Islam try to take that away from them.

*Give a man a fish and he will eat for a day. Teach a man to fish and he will eat for the rest of his life.*

**– Proverb**

Helping the rest of the world lift their heads from the deplorable reality of the slums and shanti towns, assisting them to get even the basic necessities of water, food, shelter, and an elementary education is the distribution of hope. As the last best hope for humanity, it is America's duty and honor to do this as best we can. We must do it because, first, and foremost, it is the just and moral thing to do, but also because a person with hope, no matter how slight, will not voluntarily strap a bomb to their chest and walk into a crowd of children for the promise of bliss in an afterlife.

Raising the standard of living for everyone across the world will undeniably increase our security and the safety of all, but it is a daunting task. What lies ahead of us, the road we must take is not the easy route. Building something, providing hope in the here and now is difficult work that often transcends our human nature to take the path of least resistance.

Radical Islam on the other hand, is taking the easy road. What have they ever done? What have they created? Nothing! They only destroy and pontificate a hatred to be assimilated into a society devoid of hope. We must remember this at all times and sleep well knowing that we are on the right side of justice.

Stage three to winning the War on Terror is found in the alteration of our military strategy.

As the Unites States has already withdrawn from Iraq and my purpose here is not to delve into the propriety of having invaded

Iraq in the first place, I will herein concentrate on the war in Afghanistan.

The War in Afghanistan began on October 7, 2001, as the United States launched Operation Enduring Freedom along with HM (Her Majesty's) Armed Forces in direct response to 9/11. The first phase of the war was aimed at removing the safe haven to Al-Qaeda and its use of the Afghan territory as a base of operations for anti-US terrorist activities. In that first phase, coalition forces, working with the Afghan opposition forces of the Northern Alliance, quickly ousted the Taliban regime. Since then, the character of the war has shifted to an effort aimed at smothering the Taliban insurgency hostile to the Coalition-backed Hamid Karzai government.

More than a decade later, we are now amidst a guerrilla war that has claimed the lives of nearly 2,200 American soldiers and wounded nearly 50,000. We are no longer fighting a conventional war, rather one in which the Taliban insurgents are blending into the local population. Instead of directly confronting International Security Assistance Force troops, the insurgents mainly employ improvised explosive devices (IEDs) and suicide bombings to inflict their casualties.

The problem with America's war strategy is the fact that, despite all of our technological advantages, it still is centered around boots on the ground. More succinctly, occupying forces. The failure was not in failing to have an exit strategy before invading Afghanistan and Iraq, the failure was in needing an exit strategy to begin with.

America cannot afford to be an occupying force, especially when our intent is not to colonize. By invading and occupying, even if the intent is to remain in the region only temporarily, we put our soldiers in harm's way as sitting ducks in a foreign land.

The war in Vietnam should have been a lesson to this end. We far outmatched the National Liberation Front militarily, technologically, and financially. Yet, our failure and the fall of Saigon after our exit from Vietnam resulted from our over-dependence on our ground force strength. Our mentality then, as it is now in

Afghanistan, was that of shock and awe. We thought we could just go in there, wipe the enemy off the map, and leave.

But, as the years passed, we found ourselves engaged in a guerilla war. The "knowhow" of waging war learned in the trenches of World War I, the invasions of World War II and the Korean War had not prepared us to fight against an insurgent force hiding amongst the population and in the jungles of a foreign terrain. We lost over 58,000 soldiers in the war as they picked us off from the trees.

In Afghanistan, we do not have the luxury of pretending that we are not in this foreign land, that we did not invade, and that we can simply walk away from the consequences. So how do we get out of Afghanistan victorious?

First, we must recognize that our victory is found not in wiping out every last Taliban, but rather in providing for our own national security. Cutting the Taliban off at their knees, rendering them inept is sufficient to this end.

Our current strategy of training the Afghan police force so they are capable of policing themselves is, in my opinion, proper. My hope is that once we leave, the Taliban is not able to infiltrate their ranks to where we will ostensibly have spent billions to train the enemy how to fight; but it is nonetheless imperative that we leave Afghanistan where they are able to defend against the insurgency, lest the vacuum created by our departure be filled by the very radical elements we've fought so hard to oust.

But, the calculation that the military needs to make should not exclusively focus on whether or not the Afghan police force is ready to defend itself moving forward. Another factor should be considered, and it requires the gathering of massive amounts of intelligence—a talent in which the United States is second to none.

We must continue to compile profuse intel as to the exact or best guess as to the locations of Taliban camps, bases of operations, and strongholds. Understanding that they hide among the innocent population as the cunning cowards they are, it would be honorable of us to publish a general warning to the following effect: "If you harbor an insurgent, you are putting yourself in danger. If insurgents currently occupy or are in and around your territory, notify your local authorities so that coalition forces can assist you to bring them to justice. In the alternative, vacate immediately to avoid unwanted collateral damage." Then, unannounced, on our own secret timetable, we must launch one last, massive offensive on all known Taliban strongholds, coordinated on both sides of the Afghan and Pakistan borders. And we must do this in a way to avoid as much collateral loss of innocent life as possible. With this last offensive, we must cripple the enemy, or at least knock them down for a long, hard count, and then we must get the hell out of there.

Moving forward, we must be very careful not to occupy foreign territory, for to do so makes us a sitting target. Instead, we must utilize the full potential of our technology and the tactical advantages they give us to fight this war as "guerillas" ourselves. We must employ our special forces and our drone aircraft to snipe out terrorist camps worldwide. In and out, like ninjas in the wind. Seal Team 6.

First and foremost, by employing this strategy, we put fewer soldiers in harm's way. We can also reduce the size of our standing army and utilize the extra funds to, one, fund veterans' programs, such as job placement and training, two, develop the technologies of tomorrow's military, and three, pay down the national debt. As a result, our military will become more efficient and advanced than ever, vastly improving our national security, while simultaneously investing capital in advanced technologies that can foster societal wealth and civil advancements at home.

Our policy as conveyed to all nations must be clear—if you harbor terrorists, neglect, or otherwise refuse to disarm or arrest them, and we have clear evidence that they pose a substantial risk to our national security, we will remove them even if it means carrying out a military strike within your borders. We must be most clear as to this ultimatum with Pakistan and Iran, for their failure to deal with the radical elements inside their borders is perhaps the greatest danger we face.

Lastly, it is only through a true understanding of what freedom of religion truly means in America that we stand a chance to win the War on Terror, for each of the stages above delineated hinge upon our society being governed by a strong moral fabric tolerant of and embracing of all morally grounded religions equally protected under the law.

Never, in any nation on this planet, has there been such religious diversity as there currently is in the United States. We lead the rest of the world by this example, as a living, breathing testament to the power of ordered liberty. Men, women, and children of all faiths live in the same neighborhoods, attend the same schools, but in America, unlike in all civilizations before us, we do so in relative peace.

A nation able to host all the world's religions, peacefully, where each is free to practice its creed without interference from law or bloodshed because of the founding fathers' historical and cultural acumen—again, my fellow Americans, that is God's Manifest Destiny!

For in America, we understood at the time of our founding, and now must remember in this horrible hour of humanity, that no benevolent God of any creed wants his followers to convert by the sword. God has never wanted bloodshed in his name—rather he commands love and compassion be spread in his name. As Christians, as Jews, Muslims, Hindi—we must all go forth and lead by the example of practicing philanthropy for all around us, whether or not they share in our beliefs. Not only is this the American way, but history also teaches us that the best way to convert a non-believer is through good deeds and leading by the example of compassion rather than cruelty.

Put the Bible and the Qur'an next to each other and in each one, you can find numerous passages to be twisted into a call for religious war. Many more passages calling for compassion and tolerance can also be found in each. Throughout history, and still today, those desirous of finding passages permitting conversion by the sword can do so merely by taking certain passages out of context. The Crusades lasted from 1095 to 1291, and the religious dogma that fueled the Holy Roman Empire's campaigns on the one side and Muslims on the other, provide us two hundred years' worth of examples highlighting this fact.

But, I ask you this: If God wanted us to convert by the sword, why did he not come down from heaven and give us the order more bluntly? Why has he allowed so much doubt—not only as to his existence and which faith is true and correct, but also as to whether or not he wants us to take up the sword to convert in his name? The answer, I believe, is that he hasn't given the order at all- and would not! Instead, he gave us free will, the choice to do the right thing and the wrong, to believe properly or exist without faith, and he commanded of us above all else that we fulfill the law by love. Therefore, it is between each individual and God as to whether or not he or she chooses wisely and how he or she will be punished or rewarded in the afterlife. That decision, here, on this planet, is not for the governments of men to decree.

Christians, Jews, Muslims, all the peaceful, morally grounded religions of this world, learned this truth in the crusades as well as through the bloody history of man over centuries of religious war and persecution. Radical Islam, on the other hand, remains ignorant of this truth, arrogant and hell-bent on the slaughter of all who do not believe as they do. They aim to have no opposition to their tenets—they aim, literally, to return mankind to the Dark Ages.

This is why the fragile reality of peaceful religious co-existence in America must be protected at all costs. Allowing fear to govern us, turning on each other, will only lead to religious persecution and the destruction of equal justice under the law for all Americans, regardless of faith. Radical Islam wants this—they want us to turn the guns on each other out of fear and ignorance.

Post 9/11 it has only become natural for non-Muslims living in the United States to be leery of Islam. I would be lying if I were to say that I don't get a little nervous when I see a Muslim on the plane. It's unfortunate, no doubt, but the reality we live in is one in which radical Islam is erasing people's faith in the moral grounding of all Muslims. Unfortunately, misguided churches all across the United States now hold lectures on why Islam is fundamentally evil. Out of trepidation and lack of knowledge, more and more Americans now fear all Muslims, failing to understand the immense differences between radical and non-radical Islam. Our overall ignorance as to the true underpinnings of Islam exacerbates this unfortunate apprehension as fear lurks best in the unknown.

This is why one of the most important things that must happen for Western Civilization to succeed in the War on Terror is for non-radical Islam, as a whole, to come forward and assertively condemn radical-Islam at every chance. This war, this clash of civilizations, is Islam's war as well, for they are equally under fire. Now, many have stepped forward to date, many have denounced radical-Islam, but their just position is not sounding nearly as loud as it must.

Followers of Islam need to go out of their way to demonstrate to the remainder of the world just how decent, giving, and law abiding they truly are. They must help all non-Muslims to understand their faith, educate us through their benevolent examples, and they must do this with triple the effort. Is it fair that they need to do this? No! But radical-Islam's actions have made it necessary. So too is it unfair and daunting that America, as the world's greatest superpower, must be the greatest purveyor of freedom and bear the pecuniary brunt of the task. But, fate has tasked us so and so we must.

Education, as is always the case, will be key to succeeding in this task. I for one would like to see Mosques all across this nation hold open houses for Christians, Jews, Hindi—anybody who desires, to come in and learn their faith's moral groundings without the purpose of conversion, but rather with the goal of enlightenment. Synagogues and Churches too, should hold meetings, or clerics should go out into the public and conduct free seminars at local libraries, colleges, etc., educating attendees on the differences between radical and non-radical Islam. For, in this land of opportunity, where the right to assembly and free speech are explicitly protected by the First Amendment, Islam has the greatest opportunity to educate the world as to its true honorable creed.

And so, I call on the nations of Islam to join forces with the rest of us to aggressively fight this war on radical-Islam. They must not remain on the sidelines, but rather lead the fight and join us in the trenches. The moral and faithful people of Islam have a unique perspective with which to help us understand and hopefully return the mind of our enemy to sanity, thereby making Muslims perhaps our greatest allies.

For just as our forefathers took up arms to fight for our unalienable rights in the Revolutionary War, and did so again in the Civil War to procure those same God given freedoms so long denied slaves, our generation must now fight to protect those freedoms for ourselves and for the remainder of the world. Understanding through our own history the horrible realities sectarian violence, blind dogma, and religious crusades present civilization, Christians, Jews, Hindi, Muslim—all Americans, whether agnostic, atheist or devoutly religious, bear the responsibility of taking up arms to protect the liberty afforded us in the First Amendment. The irony of our position as tolerant Americans is that we've sworn not to take up the sword to convert, but now must take up the sword to protect ourselves and others from being converted by the sword. And do so we shall!

CHAPTER SEVEN:

# THE ENVIRONMENT

*As for you, my flock…Is it not enough for you to feed on good pasture? Must you also trample the rest of your pasture with your feet? Is it not enough for you to drink clear water? Must you also muddy the rest with your feet?*

**- Ezekiel 34:17–18**

Hello. My name is John Kidwell. I own a hybrid vehicle, I believe in global warming, and I'm a Republican. Sound like an AA meeting? I make this declaration because, as a resolute Republican, I am extremely dismayed at how many in my party, and how many people across America, are either indifferent to the environment as it relates to the economy or outright don't believe in global warming.

"Did you know that Al Gore's mansion uses ten times more electricity than George Bush's," I've heard numerous people equivocate, calling our former vice president a hypocrite as if that has any bearing on the veracity of his groundbreaking documentary, *An Inconvenient Truth.*

Was *An Inconvenient Truth* a bit sensational? Yes. But documentaries are all designed to be shocking for the purpose of conveying the points therein made, even if sometimes overboard. Yet, despite its sensationalism, Al Gore's message, which won him the Nobel Peace Prize, inexorably fell on many a deaf ear.

Now, a part of me doesn't want to make waves, for it seems the environment, particularly global warming, is an unpopular issue among Republican ranks. People have literally told me that if I plan on running for office, I might want to keep my environmental "beliefs" on the down low. Well, as a Christian, and one who believes that humans, including those of us living in the United States, are failing in our responsibility to be good stewards of the earth, it is my duty to try as hard as I can to expound the issue and work to bring about meaningful, intelligent change, no matter how inconvenient the truth may prove.

To that end, and merely for "sensationalism," let me begin with a thought that continually plays in my head when I think about the tragedy that is our environment. Oil: we are addicted to a toxic, black sludge that oozes from the subterranean and when we burn it, it blocks out the Sun and chokes our lungs. Yet greed and sloth provide us the reasons necessary to ignore this slow death as we pay for our consumption by transferring our wealth to an enemy that has vowed to enslave us or slaughter us if we do not declare allegiance to their twisted worldview of hatred and cruelty. I cannot think of a more hellishly "Apocalyptic" scenario—can you?

The principal reason why so many people find it "inconvenient" to come to terms with the fact that global warming exits as a true and unfortunately real phenomenon, is the negative effect they believe dealing with the issue will have on the economy. This belief, however, is entirely erroneous. In fact, dealing with the issue, I believe will prove the resurrection of America's industrial strength and not only revive but also catapult our economy to new heights.

The energy lobby, specifically gas and oil companies, understandably fear the economic impact shutting off the oil tap would have on their bottom line. It is a result of this fear that they have worked tirelessly to replace sound scientific analysis with a political ideology aimed at promoting doubt as to the authenticity of the science surrounding global warming.

The energy establishment made the calculated resolution to promote doubt within the political establishment as well as to persuade politicians and the public to believe a lie: that addressing global warming means destroying our economy. Cleverly, they took aim at the party historically most protective of their business interests, and it pains me to say, that they've so far successfully used Republican's fiscal conservatism, perhaps our greatest strength, against us to that end. We must not allow this to continue!

In 2004, for example, oil and gas companies contributed over $25 million to political campaigns, donating 80% of that money to Republicans. In the 2000 elections, over $34 million, with approximately the same percentage going to Republicans. All toll, individuals and political action committees affiliated with oil and gas companies have donated an estimated $300 million to candidates and their parties since the 1990 election cycle, with over 75% of that going to Republicans.

Despite the mountains of evidence providing clear and convincing evidence to the existence of global warming, when I bring the subject up out of genuine concern I'm constantly met with pre-packaged retorts: "Did you read Michael Crichton's book *State of Fear*? Antarctic temperature readings contradict global warming because Antarctica is actually cooling." Or, "The hockey stick graph showing the correlation between carbon emissions and global temperature changes has been debunked," and, "Earth's temperature has only gone up by a few degrees. What's the big deal?" The truth—these responses originate from exposure to what I call the global warming "Misinformation Machine."

It is important to realize, further, that the misinformation machine has also been aimed at the general public in order to cast doubt in our minds and spark endless debate. In doing so, they have been able to cloud our judgment, casting a shadow over sound science to where we no longer recognize conjecture and junk science from empirical evidence. Through blogs, tweets, sham Internet sites, etc., we are constantly bombarded with skepticism based entirely on, well, nothing. Unfortunately, this unsubstantiated doubt has permeated the media to where just as many articles question or attempt to debunk global warming as those that put forth sound science as to its existence.

The misinformation campaign launched by corporations that stand to lose money should we alter our energy consumption resembles the tobacco industry's propaganda machine with which we are all too familiar. In fact, it is fundamentally linked. The campaign to attack climate change science, believe it or not, actually has roots within the "Astroturfing" campaigns initiated by the tobacco industry in the 1990s. As part of the campaign, the Advancement of Sound Science Coalition (TASSC), a counterfeit and entirely non-scientific assemblage, was established to link concerns about passive smoking with a host of other anxieties, including global warming. In *Requiem for a Species: Why We Resist the Truth about Climate Change,* Clive Hamilton describes the tactic as a public relations strategy to cast doubt on the science by characterizing global warming science as junk science in order to turn public opinion against any calls for government intervention based on the science.

What we are witnessing, my fellow Americans, is a smear campaign analogous to that of the Roman Inquisition of 1632 that denounced Galileo's theory of heliocentricity. The result of that prosecution found Galileo vehemently suspect of heresy and placed him under house arrest for the remainder of his life for putting forth science contrary to Scripture's established law that Earth is, in fact, the center of the universe.

Let us, then, examine the science of global warming.

To start, consider this fact: the existence of global warming and the fact that human activities are adversely affecting the climate have been endorsed by absolutely every single national science academy that has ever issued a statement on climate change, including the science academies of all, yes, *all* major industrialized nations, including the United States.

In 1997, over a decade ago, the "World Scientist's Call for Action" petition was presented by the Union of Concerned Scientists to the world leaders meeting at that time to negotiate the Kyoto Protocol. The petition was signed by thousands of the world's most distinguished scientists, including the majority of

Nobel laureates in science. Why? Because of some conspiracy to, what, destroy the economies of industrialized nations in favor of the third world? No! They signed the petition because the science is convincing and alarming!

To be clear, I think that based upon the terms of the Kyoto Protocol, the US was in many respects correct in declining to ratify. That being said, the fact that we have still done nothing in over a decade is unconscionable.

One of many methods used to detect global warming is through the examination of ice cores extracted from the tops of glaciers worldwide. These bores contain a climate footprint stomping back thousands of years and by examining the air bubbles contained in each layer of the ice core, climatologists are able to extract the atmospheric temperature of any given year by calculating the ratio of oxygen-16 to oxygen-18. The core samples also provide the level of carbon dioxide in the atmosphere for each year going back 650,000 years.

The results clearly illustrate that at no time in the last 650,000 years has there been a carbon dioxide concentration in the earth's atmosphere exceeding 280 parts per million, nor has there been a temperature variant in the Earth's hemisphere ranging beyond a single degree hotter or colder than the median global temperature—that is until the industrial revolution. Carbon dioxide concentrations in the Earth's atmosphere are now nearly 400 parts per million, and concomitantly, the world's global temperature has spiked to the highest level in the last 1,000 years.

The reason for this phenomenon revolves around the effect greenhouse gases have on our planet's ability to shed infrared radiation, with carbon dioxide being the principal culprit. You see, the Sun sends its vast energy across the vastness of space in the form of light waves that can penetrate through our atmosphere, even greenhouse gases such as carbon dioxide. Our planet absorbs this energy and re-radiates it back into the atmosphere in the form of infrared waves. This is actually a good thing, as this infrared radiation is what keeps our planet from being as cold as Mars. However, with the addition of greenhouse gases, our atmosphere is literally thickening and the infrared radiation is being blocked from escaping our atmosphere in balance to the level of light waves continually entering. It works exactly like a greenhouse, hence the name.

Before I delve into the repercussions of this phenomenon, let me first address the major "debunk" theories put forth by those that don't believe in global warming. These retorts, again, have unfortunately been put forth by the misinformation machine and often center around an attack on the so-called "hockey stick" graph.

Global warming critics have launched a scurrilous attack against a study that illustrates the stark correlation between carbon dioxide in the atmosphere and global temperatures revealed in a graph published by renowned climatologist, Michael Mann. The result is what is notoriously called the hockey stick controversy.

To understand the hockey stick controversy, one must first understand what a climate proxy is. Climate proxies are preserved characteristics of the past that enable scientists to reconstruct the climatic conditions that prevailed during much of the Earth's history. As reliable modern records of the climate began only as recently the 1880s, proxies such as ice cores, tree rings, boreholes, coral patterns, and lake or ocean sediments, provide means for scientists to determine climate patterns well beyond that timeframe.

In 1999, Michael Mann, Raymond Bradley and Malcolm Hughes, all distinguished climatologists, produced a quantitative hemispheric-scale reconstruction from an analysis of a variety of proxies, which they summarized in a graph going back to the year 1,000. This graph, which illustrated a sharp increase in recent measured temperatures from that of a relatively flat median average temperature over the last 1,000 years (resembling a hockey stick) was featured prominently in the 2001 United Nations Intergovernmental Panel on Climate Change (IPCC) Third Assessment Report (TAR).

In 2003, however, a paper, *Proxy Climatic and Environmental Changes of the Past 1,000 Years*, written by Willie Soon and Sallie Baliunas of the Harvard-Smithsonian Center for Astrophysics, was published in the magazine *Climate Research*. The article tried to find evidence for temperature anomalies in the last 1,000 years, such as the medieval warm period, concluding, "Across the world, many records reveal that the twentieth century is probably not the warmest or a uniquely extreme climatic period of the last millennium." The paper investigated the correlation between solar variation and temperatures of the Earth's atmosphere, attributing the medieval warm period to an increase in solar output, and asserting that decreases in solar output led to the Little Ice Age, a period of cooling lasting until the mid-nineteenth century.

However, Soon and Baliunus's paper was swiftly and sharply criticized. For instance, their paper failed entirely to address the fact that the medieval warming period was far smaller than the global temperature increases being experienced today. And while their paper argued that the average global temperature in the twentieth century is essentially unremarkable, they failed to realize that it is not the average twentieth century warmth, but the magnitude of warming during the twentieth century, and specifically the level of warmth observed during the past few decades, which appear to be anomalous in a long-term context. In fact, Malcolm Hughes of the University of Arizona, whose work on dendrochronology was discussed in the paper, called their paper "so fundamentally misconceived and contain[ing] so many egregious errors that it would take weeks to list and explain them all."

In July 2003, the journal *Eos* published a paper authored by many of the prominent scientists cited in the Soon and Baliunas's paper. In it, all of the scientists criticized Soon and Baliunas's "findings" for having "conflated precipitation and temperature proxies while simultaneously attributing regional temperature changes to global changes."

Finally, their paper was sharply scrutinized as it was partially funded by the American Petroleum Institute and the fact that Soon and Baliunas were at the time paid consultants of the Marshall Institute, a conservative think tank that has zealously opposed mainstream climate science since the late 1980s.

And then there's this: over a dozen subsequent scientific papers, using various statistical techniques and combinations of proxy records, both inclusive and beyond the scope of Mann, Bradley, and Hughes's paper, produced reconstructions broadly similar to the original hockey stick graph, supporting the IPCC conclusion that the warmest decade in 1,000 years was at the end of the twentieth century.

Amid the storm of controversy caused by the misinformation machine, the United States Congress itself requested a panel of scientists convened by the National Research Council of the United States National Academy of Sciences to consider current scientific data on the temperature record for the past two millennia, identify the main areas of uncertainty, the principal methodologies used, any problems with these approaches, and the authenticity of the findings. In 2006, the panel's report supported the hockey stick graph, pointing out some statistical failings, but noting that they had little effect on the result. The report affirmed that, "It can be said with a high level of confidence that the global mean surface temperature was higher during the last few decades of the twentieth century than during any comparable period during the preceding four centuries. This statement is justified by the consistency of the evidence from a wide variety of geographically diverse proxies."

Yet, certain members in Congress, such as Senator Jim Inhofe of Oklahoma, remain speciously convinced that global warming is a farce, or are being paid to look the other way. In 2003, and again in 2005, Senator Inhofe made a speech on the Senate floor citing Soon and Baliunas's discredited paper to support his belief that "man-made global warming is the greatest hoax ever perpetrated on the American people." Even as recently as July 2010, despite the clear findings of the abovementioned panel of scientists, Senator Inhofe told ABC News and the *Washington Post* in an interview, "I don't think that anyone disagrees with the fact that we actually are in a cold period that started about nine years ago." What?!

But how can members of Congress and the media make such patently erroneous and unsubstantiated claims when according to NASA—yes, NASA—the past 10-year average was the hottest on record, and with The National Oceanic and Atmospheric Administration independently concluding that the first six months of 2010 were the hottest on record globally, only to be broken by 2011 and 2012? As for some of them, it would seem that they are being paid to do so.

Senator Inhofe just so happens to be the ranking member of the Senate Environment and Public Works Committee—who do you think his top five contributors are? Energy companies. Every single one of them. What industry has contributed the largest amount of money to his political career to date? The oil and gas industry, followed closely by the electric utilities lobby.

"Okay, okay," people will argue with me, "but according to Michael Crichton's book, *State of Fear*, Antarctic temperature readings contradict global warming because Antarctica is actually cooling." Again, this is an unfortunate product of the misinformation machine. First, *State of Fear*, just like Crichton's earlier novel *Jurassic Park* (one of my favorites of all time, by the way) is a work of fiction. The science described in *State of Fear* is no more grounded in reality than the splicing of frog DNA to fill the gene sequence gaps necessary to clone a Tyrannosaurus Rex. Second, Peter Doran, PhD, professor of Earth and environmental sciences at the University of Illinois at Chicago, is the lead author of the paper cited by Crichton in the novel, and he has stated that "…our results have been misused as 'evidence' against global warming."

What, then, is the science surrounding this *State of Fear* controversy? It's this: while the Antarctic Peninsula, site of the now-collapsed Larsen-B ice shelf, has warmed substantially, a few stations located in the interior of the massive continent appear to show a slight cooling over the last twenty years. Crichton's characters in his novel used this bit of evidence in argument to contradict the science of "global" warming. But, we must be more discerning before jumping to such a conclusion.

The fiction is this—a rise in the global mean temperature implies universal warming. It does not. In fact, some areas of the world are experiencing colder weather spells as the climate shifts and dynamical effects (changes in the winds and ocean circulation) impact regional temperatures through the jet stream. However, most are inclined to take the experiences they are having in their neck of the woods as empirical evidence as to the existence or contradiction of global warming. This proclivity is understandable, but misleading.

Take Washington, DC, for instance. In December 2009, we experienced our sixth-worst blizzard in history, only to be followed by "Snowmageddon" two back-to-back blizzards in February 2010, which broke all sorts of records. I can't tell you how many people took this as evidence that global warming is a sham.

Yet, the science of global warming and the climatological havoc it is wreaking on our planet clearly evidences the fact that planet-wide precipitation has increased in the last century by almost 20%. Why? As the temperature goes up, so too does evaporation. The entire East Coast of the United States is experiencing this increase in precipitation and as a result nor'easter storms, massive hurricane-like cyclones that pull their moisture from the warming Gulf Stream, are increasing in frequency. It was three nor'easters that brought the blizzards to DC in the dead of winter—not a cooling of the region!

Additionally, the data signifying a slight cooling of Antarctica's interior is extremely sparse and appears to be restricted to the last two decades because, averaged over the last 40 years, the interior has actually warmed, albeit at a slower pace than the exterior. Furthermore, due to ocean uptake in the Southern Ocean, it is expected that the overall rate of warming in the Southern Hemisphere should be less than that of the Northern Hemisphere where we are seeing alarming rates of warming. Lastly, the Southern Annular Mode (a pattern of variability that affects the westerly winds around Antarctica) has been producing stronger winds in recent years. This westerly wind, likely intensifying due to increased convection currents off warmer seawater, acts as a barrier, preventing warmer air from reaching the interior of the continent.

Here is the truth about Antarctica. The East Antarctic ice shelf is the largest ice mass on the planet and 85% of the glaciers thereon are accelerating their flow toward the ocean. In other words, the ice shelf is melting. The West Antarctic ice shelf, equal in size to Greenland, is slipping off the land mass atop which it is moored. The Larsen-B ice shelf, once standing at over 700-feet thick and the size of a state, has already broken apart entirely and as the ice behind it slipped from the Antarctic continent into the ocean, worldwide sea levels rose.

Now, let us turn our attention northward.

The Arctic ice cap is vastly different from the Antarctic in that it is surrounded by land but covers seawater, whereas the Antarctic ice cap covers land and is surrounded by seawater. While the Antarctic ice cap is over ten thousand feet thick, the Arctic averages less than ten feet in thickness. Why is this important? The positive feedback loop!

Ice naturally reflects sunlight. However, when it melts, as it has been doing at an increased rate since the 1970s in the Arctic, it leaves behind only seawater which absorbs the Sun's heat. In turn, the ocean begins to act like a giant radiator, further melting the ice still floating. So, don't let the name fool you because there is absolutely nothing positive about this trend. While the median global temperature has only increased by one degree Fahrenheit, it has skyrocketed by twelve degrees Fahrenheit in the Arctic and as a result, the Arctic ice cap has dwindled by nearly two million square miles since 1970!

Aside from the well-publicized fact that polar bears are dying off as they starve or drown swimming hundreds of miles only to find the ice from which they fish and upon which they rest melted, permafrost is no longer permanent in many arctic regions.

In addition, the cold that used to hold back invasive species has given way to highly destructive swarms, and vectors such as the common mosquito are spreading a widening array of super-viruses. Yet, the largest threat to civilization is perhaps the rise of sea levels worldwide.

Many people think that the rise in seal levels is something that is relegated only to a prediction of the future, but, in fact, it is already happening. As ice melts and slides off land into the ocean, pulling with it millions of tons of sediment, the sea level rises just as the water level in your glass rises when you add a cube.

Future models of global warming predict that Greenland's ice, which is melting at a dangerous pace, might melt completely and slide into the ocean, raising worldwide sea levels by as much as twenty feet. This would be absolutely catastrophic.

As a result of only ten feet of seawater augmentation, hundreds of millions of people would be displaced worldwide as coastal cities, to include New York, San Francisco, Miami and many others in the United States, would be forced to permanently evacuate. Do you think that we are ready for such a mass evacuation and complete displacement of even our own domestic population, not to mention those that would swarm across our borders as their nations are flooded? Did Hurricane Katrina's destruction of New Orleans not show us that we plainly are not capable of dealing with such an event? Superstorm Sandy?!

With such a threat facing us, and with all of this compelling evidence presented, the only way to dissuade the American public from taking action is to convince them that global warming is a lie and do so with colossal undertaking. The misinformation machine is just that immense and we must understand how invasive it really is in order to tear down the walls of deceit presently impeding our ability to see the danger lurking around the corner. We must understand that the machine has done far more than simply convince laymen of the lie, or even convince politicians, rather, it has inserted itself into the body politic.

On March 25, 2009, for example, Representative John Shimkus of Illinois quoted scripture from the Holy Bible as support of his position that global warming is not possible as God said he would never again flood the planet. Specifically, during the United States House Energy Subcommittee on Energy and Environment hearing on adaptation policies for dealing with climate change, he quoted Genesis 8:21–22 which reads as follows:

**And the LORD smelled a sweet savour; and the LORD said in his heart, I will not again curse the ground any more for man's sake; for the imagination of man's heart is evil from his youth; neither will I again smite any more everything living, as I have done. While the earth remaineth, seedtime and harvest, and cold and heat, and summer and winter, and day and night shall not cease.**

He then went on to quote Mathew 24:31:

**And he will send his angels with a loud trumpet call, and they will gather his elect from the four winds, from one end of the heavens to the other.**

Congressman Shimkus's position is that the world will end when God decides it will end, and therefore global warming cannot exist. First off, I am a Christian and I believe in the word of the Lord and that yes, the world will end when God decides it to be so. That being said, Mr. Shimkus's reasoning is based upon false logic.

Global warming does not presage that the world will end. Rather, it threatens to fundamentally change our planet and render it much less inhabitable. A further reading of the Holy Bible, the Book of Revelations in particular, very clearly shows us that man will play a large role in making hell on earth a reality. Is it not then possible that God, blessing us with the gift of free will, as he has, also gave us the power to poison our environment? Pluck an oil-covered pelican from the Gulf of Mexico and tell me that we cannot. Launch our entire nuclear stockpile and tell me that we cannot destroy this world.

To Mr. Shimkus and my fellow Christians, I say that hiding behind contextual distortion is disingenuous and it disgraces the meaning of the sacred text when it is utilized to deny an obvious truth gleaned from the entirety of the Lord's words. It is tantamount to radical Islam's distortion of the Qur'an to condone terrorism.

Here is another appalling example. In 2001, Phillip Cooney, six years the principal lobbyist in charge of the American Petroleum Institute's global warming misinformation campaign, was selected by President Bush to be in charge of his environmental policy. Despite having absolutely no scientific background, Cooney was given carte blanche authority to amend and redact official assessments on global warming conducted by the Environmental Protection Agency. In 2008, a memo with his notes explicitly stating that a report highlighting the dangers of global warming should be amended with a strategy of emphasizing the speculative nature of the findings was leaked to the *New York Times*. As a result of the political fallout he immediately resigned only to begin working for Exxon Mobil the very next day.

So, here's the difficult truth—Washington, as a result of the misinformation machine's permeation, has collectively decided to burry its head in the sand rather than deal with the perils facing our planet. It's no longer that Washington collectively believes global warming to be a farce, although they are seemingly content to allow us to toil in the convenience of our continued denial. Rather, our government, convinced that dealing with the effects of global warming will bankrupt our economy, has decided instead to wait and see what happens and simply adapt on a piecemeal basis.

The White House's 2002 US Climate Action Report to the United Nations, which explicitly detailed specific and far-reaching effects it admitted global warming will inflict on the American environment, for instance, made absolutely no proposals for any major shift in the nation's policy on carbon emissions. Instead, it recommended adapting to inevitable changes rather than making rapid and drastic reductions in greenhouse gases to limit global warming. The White House's emphasis on adaptation over action was not well received however:

> *Despite conceding that our consumption of fossil fuels is causing serious damage and despite implying that current policy is inadequate, the Report fails to take the next step and recommend serious alternatives. Rather, it suggests that we simply need to accommodate to the coming changes. For example, reminiscent of former Interior Secretary Hodel's proposal that the government address the hole in the ozone layer by encouraging Americans to make better use of sunglasses, suntan lotion and broad-brimmed hats, the Report suggests that we can deal with heat-related health impacts by increased use of air-conditioning...Far from proposing solutions to the climate change problem, the Administration has been adopting energy policies that would actually increase greenhouse gas emissions. Notably, even as the Report identifies increased air conditioner use as one of the 'solutions' to climate change impacts, the Department of Energy has decided to roll back energy efficiency standards for air conditioners.*

**– Report from Government Accountability Project citing a letter from 11 state attorneys general to President George W. Bush**

So, what do we do? How can we deal with such a ubiquitous and massive misapplication of scientific reasoning rising from the base constituency all the way up to the highest levels of government? The answer is, and always shall be, found in the truth.

Let me pause, then, to say this. It is imperative that we put the squabbling and party line propaganda to rest, definitively, and demand the truth instead of allowing those we have entrusted to report and act on honest facts to hide behind shades of mendacity. One side of the media tells us that the other is lying only to turn around and perpetrate another half-baked falsehood for sensationalism. We are eating it up and our government is following suit. We must demand the truth! And we must then act on facts that are grounded in the best of our possible knowledge!

If the findings of the panel of scientists convened by the National Research Council of the United States National Academy of Sciences at the behest of the United States Congress is not enough, then so be it. We must then require the convening of another panel, one presumably more "believable," for a quantitative, empirical, and final analysis as to whether this threat is true or real—or at least more probable than not.

I've spent the better part of this chapter defending the fact that global warming is a real threat, but another person equally as convinced as I to the other end will always be ready to argue the opposite position. And while there can never be any certainty in this world, except for the requirement of taxes to be paid and death, we must put aside uncertainty and convince ourselves above and beyond the preponderance of the evidence one way or the other and take action accordingly. Our plan cannot and must not be to bury our head in the sand and hope that the future tides of global competition, consumption, and environmental degradation bear us manageable predicaments. As our founding fathers took a leap of faith based upon their knowledge that man's unalienable rights were being usurped by tyranny, we must also be willing to take a leap of faith, discounting a modicum of uncertainty in the light of overwhelming evidence.

Lastly, I ask of those that try to convince me that global warming is a hoax—are you willing to bet on the lives of your grandchildren? We have one planet, one chance! Why risk it?

Now, let us put the debate surrounding global warming to the side for a moment. Let's even assume that global warming does not exist, that it is a farce invoked by those with nothing better to do than continuously conjure ways to, "down the establishment." While I clearly don't believe this to be the case, let us entertain it for a moment, because my point in all of this is quite simple.

As a Christian, I believe in my heart, and as I've learned in the study of the Holy Bible, that God put all life that we see on this earth and has required of us that we be the shepherds of his flock. Put aside global warming and still we are monumentally failing in our task. As the dominant species on this planet, we understandably take our well-being into consideration above and beyond all other life. This is the human, actually, natural instinct for all life on Earth from dinosaur to ape. But God gave us the faculties to reason beyond our selfish desires and discern means through which we can adequately provide for our own requirements and at the same time protect the needs of those that share our habitat and rely upon our benevolence.

We are failing in our task as stewards of this beautiful planet we have been blessed to call home. As the population has boomed in this last century to levels never before conceivable, we are clashing with the environment in many more ways than the release of carbon to power our industries. Nearly 30% of the carbon dioxide released into our atmosphere, for instance, comes from the burning of forests such as the Amazon rainforest for the simple purpose of subsistence agriculture and wood fires used for cooking. China, for example, has ripped down a vast majority of their forests and has a continued and seemingly insatiable thirst that drives considerable incentives toward the falling of vast swathes within the rainforests of Congo and Brazil.

Domestically, environmental degradation is equally as horrendous, without considering global warming and its "expected" effects. To start in my own backyard: In the 1970s, the Chesapeake Bay was discovered to contain one of the planet's first identified marine dead zones, where hypoxic waters are so depleted of oxygen they are unable to support life. Millions of fish routinely wash ashore in massive kill-offs. Today the bay's dead zones are estimated to kill over eighty thousand tons of bottom-dwelling clams each year and are robbing the blue crab (my favorite delicacy) of a primary food source.

These dead zones arise in part from large algae blooms that explode as a byproduct of the runoff from farms and industrial waste throughout the watershed. In the Chesapeake watershed, the major culprits are agricultural fertilizers and nitrogen rich chicken manure from poultry farms ubiquitous in the region. The algae prevents sunlight from reaching the bottom of the bay while simultaneously expanding and eventually deoxygenating the bay's water when it dies and rots. As a result, beds of eelgrass have shrunk by more than 50% in the Chesapeake since the early 1970s and much of the bay is a muddy wasteland akin to a flooded snapshot of the lunar surface. A bushel of blue crab now costs me an arm and a leg and crabbers are restricted to an annual catch quota—a quota that directly impacts their economic bottom line.

This hypoxic problem, unfortunately, is not quarantined to the Chesapeake Bay. The Gulf of Mexico dead zone is an area swallowing up over 7,000 square miles between the Mississippi River delta and extending westward to the upper Texas coast. This dead zone is caused by nutrient enrichment from the Mississippi River, particularly nitrogen and phosphorous running off from as far north as Montana and Pennsylvania. The majority of the nitrogen run-off spills into the mighty river from major farming states including Minnesota, Iowa, Illinois, Wisconsin, Missouri, Tennessee, Arkansas, Mississippi, and Louisiana. Anthropogenically increased nitrogen and phosphorus input from fertilizers, animal waste, and sewage have overloaded the natural system capable of absorbing and processing a healthy amount of these toxins. We have fundamentally altered the Gulf of Mexico's ecosystem and it is literally being asphyxiated.

Now, add in the BP oil spill, which leaked an estimated 175 million gallons of oil into the Gulf, and we are on the heels of what is highly considered one of the worst environmental disasters in modern America. Billions were lost as fishermen were unable to captain their boats and the tourist industries along the coasts from Texas to Florida were interrupted. Speaking strictly in terms of the economy, though, the economic impact of the BP oil spill will be dwarfed when the Gulf, which accounts for 72% of United States' harvested shrimp, 66% of harvested oysters, and 16% of commercial fish, chokes to death.

While many continue to dither as to the existence of global warming, the reality is this: discounting global warming, we are nevertheless atrocious stewards of our planet as we allow rivers to flow neon green with toxic sludge, cancer towns to spring up across the globe as cell phone batteries and cathode ray tubes are melted for precious metals, and we rip down our forests without regard for surrounding ecosystems. Worldwide, there is no question that we are currently witnessing a mass extinction never before seen on our planet subsequent to the extinction of the dinosaurs as a direct result of deforestation, habitat intrusion, over-fishing, and unregulated chemical runoff. As shepherds of this planet, there is absolutely no question that we are failing.

I digress—we are pretending, for the sake of argument, that global warming is indeed a farce. Why? Because, as I said, the primary reason why most find global warming, climate change, whatever you desire to coin it, to be an "inconvenient" truth, is because we have all been spoon-fed an utter lie. We've been deceived to believe that fixing the environment necessitates dismantling our economy. That it is one or the other. A false choice.

In fact, the real truth is our economic salvation, the resurrection of our economic fortune, is found in tackling the critical issue that is global warming and the degradation of our environment as a whole. Why? Because the future health and stability of our economy and our national security depends on us harnessing the power of American innovation, recapturing the keys to our own destiny, and weaning our nation from the tit of foreign oil upon which we are so obviously addicted.

The adverse economic impact our addiction to fossil fuel has on this great nation of ours is overt. But it also poses a tremendous national security hazard. Both are reasons why it is vital that we break away from the use of these non-renewable energy sources to power our industries and vehicles, never minding global warming.

The United States is currently spending nearly $200 billion a year to import millions upon millions of barrels of oil from foreign nations. This poses an unnecessary risk to our economy and

173

national security as an outsized portion of that money is padding the pockets of the very people who despise our nation and our Western moral compass. According to the Central Intelligence Agency and the United States Department of Energy, over 20% of the oil imported into our nation, that is $40 billion a year, comes from nations such as Saudi Arabia, a country governed by extreme Islam, and Venezuela, a nation, until just recently, governed by a dictatorial president who has repeatedly sided with Iran's president Mahmoud Ahmadinejad in labeling America the "devil."

While we bankrupt ourselves through the continued deportation of our currency, those we export our money to are literally using our money to invest in ways strategically calculated to weaken the dollar and arm themselves to our destruction. Simultaneously, we are paying exorbitant amounts for our oil and as we are eclipsed by other nations with equal or greater thirst, such as China, our influence over its trade is waning. The result—OPEC is increasingly unresponsive to our demand as it relates to supply and a barrel of crude oil continues to rise at a precipitous pace. Yet again the national average for a gallon of regular gasoline is nearing $4 and is expected to reset at an even higher baseline than after the 2008 spike that insured our descent into the great recession. But it doesn't stop there.

As mentioned in the previous chapter, it is America's consumer market that has traditionally driven our economy, and you, me, the American consumer, as a direct result of increased overhead for shipping commodities, are absorbing the inflation of everyday items. While our economy spirals downward we are paying more to heat our homes, absorbing a 37% increase in the price of food, and the escalating cost of material goods. We are struggling, and it is quickly worsening. Our addiction to oil has the potential to send us into a double-dip recession and ultimately spell our demise.

The answer to these woes, a looming recession and the national security risks inherent in purchasing our energy from the very Islamic fundamentalists bent on our destruction, undeniably, is found investing in clean, renewable, <u>American-made energy</u>.

It is America's duty as the greatest nation on the planet to set the bar and lead by example. But more importantly, it is vital to our survival. It is time that we invest in new and clean energies and build an infrastructure to support those technologies, integrating them into our existing lifestyles.

And if we can do it, through investing in our domestic markets and technology industries the billions of dollars we are currently spending to protect and import oil from overseas, we will be rid of our unhealthy dependence on foreign fuel, drastically improve our national security, and hold in our hands the keys to advanced technologies that will enable our economy to become more self-sufficient and sustainable.

By investing in the development, production, commercialization, and infrastructures necessary for the creation and use of alternative energies, the United States will drastically improve its energy security, generate jobs, and stimulate substantial economic growth, as well as protect Americans from oil price spikes and price gouging.

America can once again become the leader in technology. We did it before, and now it is time for us to do it again. We can create millions of highly technical, well-paying jobs that you and I want, jobs that you and I have steadily been losing to foreign markets.

The truth is that America, the land of the free, the land of the brave and pioneering, is the perfect land from which to engineer the future of mankind. Our policies, from local government on up to Congress, must now be geared toward the promotion of technological advancement, and with a particularly penchant for sustainable domestic energy production.

By dint of hard work and the windfalls that were bestowed upon our great nation subsequent to World War II, the United States built the most advanced and far-reaching system of infrastructure in human history. We were the pioneers of this massive undertaking and the first to do it with such breathtaking breadth. However, this means that our infrastructure is aged beyond many across this world, and hence it is in dire need of renovation. In this era of federal and state indigence, our infrastructure, the medium through which we conduct business, is crumbling in a state of disrepair. There is no question that there is a dire need for a reengineering of our nation's infrastructure—what we must resolve to do is engineer it intelligently and with forward thinking.

Now, many people prevaricate that bio fuels are the wrong way to go. Ethanol does more harm than good. Hydrogen-powered cars require electrolysis for the creation of the energy necessary to propel vehicles; wind and solar power lead to blackouts and brownouts as transformers can't yet manage the unpredictable energy inputs; nuclear is dangerous with the potential for radioactive fallout; oil is hazardous and so too is natural gas, blah, blah, blah. The time for equivocation, for hiding behind the veils of obscurity and complexity is over!

America must approach the necessity of building a new energy grid across our land as if it were our next Apollo project! For so many years, we've collectively told ourselves that it is too hard, too much work, too taxing to roll up our sleeves once more and rebuild our nation better, stronger, and smarter. But, just as Japan woke this sleeping giant by bombing Pearl Harbor, our generation must awake from the siren calls of today's realities so that our children may endure into a better life than we inherited. That is the American way! It is the American Dream!

We must remember that in response to the bombing of Pearl Harbor, the United States literally retooled its entire industrial complex toward producing war machines in a matter of three months. Are you telling me that we cannot do this again? I challenge us to do just that, and heck, even allow us three years total. We owe it to the greatest generation to re-tool our industry toward smart domestic production, consumption, and sale of our own energy!

Let's give our great American scientists the funding necessary to improve on the technologies that will carry our nation into another era of profitability and power. Let's perfect the technologies that will enable our country to become the world leader once more and insure our independence from the influence of foreign oil and the negative political implications tethered thereto.

Instead of transferring our wealth to radical Islam and arming them in their insurgency; instead of continually seeking that one last hit from a "drug" dealer that does not care at all for our well-being, we must regain our moral footing, economic grounding, and advance our national security by redeveloping and reengineering our energy independence.

How do we accomplish this task? Capitalism!

First and foremost, we must not punish industry for conducting business as it has long been doing so under our current laws. Just as we do not condemn the specific commercial use of a parcel of real estate deemed to be operating outside the scope of a newly desired use, we must not condemn the industries that employ our workers for operating in a legal framework that they have invested in and in which they have expended immense capital to drive production. We must instead grandfather in these uses for a reasonable period of time and provide industries incentives to move swifter than mandates require if only to avoid bankrupting those industries and shedding more jobs.

To be clear, I absolutely am not for the repeal of regulations properly pointed at the protection of excess at the unnecessary expense of the many, including the environment, as widespread deregulation for the sake of deregulation is tantamount to anarchy. That being said, we must cut the red tape in America that has for far too long impeded our ability to expeditiously forge new paths as we did in the construction of the intercontinental railroad and the Hoover Damn. Where has our true grit gone when we aren't willing to allow those that volunteer to put their lives at risk to build monuments to man's ingenuity? America was built on this resourcefulness and we must regain this drive and utilize it with tremendous tenacity.

As I mentioned earlier, regulation, properly formulated, warns people that the force of the law will be used against them if they do something untoward. Regulation, improperly formulated, forces people to do something. The proposed cap and trade regulation, which is our current "answer" to global warming, falls squarely in this second, necessarily forbidden category. Our answer is not found in penalizing industry for operating within the means of an energy infrastructure already established, but in giving these industries strong incentives to re-engineer how they fuel their production.

Instead of taxing industry for releasing carbon dioxide into the atmosphere, we should reward them for not. Instead of immediately penalizing production at great expense to our economy, we should instead entice industry to produce "greener" products by making them more profitable to the producer and more affordable to the consumer.

Here is an example: When I bought my hybrid vehicle, the IRS gave me a $1,500 tax credit for doing so. For me, this was enough to entice me to make the dive. However, all things being equal to the gas-powered equivalent of my Ford Fusion, the hybrid cost me approximately $5,000 more. For many, especially in this economy, the extra cost makes a hybrid vehicle too costly for consideration. It also cost Ford Motor Company a lot more to build the hybrid, thereby squeezing out any real possibility of making any net profit on the vehicle's sale. So, what is our government's answer? To continuously up the mpg of cars allowed to roll off the assembly line.

Now, raising the mpg requirements of cars over time is fine if and only if industry is put on ample notice and given reasonable time to absorb the necessary costs in altering their product. Also, given that all vehicles will be held to the same standard, one could argue that supply and demand will not be collaterally affected. But what the government should also do is give American automakers an economic incentive to build alternative fuel vehicles ranging from hybrids to electric and hydrogen- or solar-powered automobiles. How? By agreeing to take less—to tax less!

What do you think would happen if the IRS suddenly told GM or Ford that for every alternative fuel vehicle sold the IRS would levy a reduced capital gains rate on that sale? Suddenly, the sale of the car would be more profitable to the industry and they would be more likely to build more of the cars. This, as economic law tells us, would drive the price of the end product down, increasing demand. Now the consumer has a choice between an equally equipped car with gas mileage that will save them thousands at the pump. Supply has been encouraged to meet demand and the consumer has been encouraged to demand the supply—Capitalism 101!

This same concept can be applied to industry. How about for every dollar invested into the research, development, and manufacture of clean, sustainable energy platforms, the investing company receives an attendant reduction in any series of taxes ranging from income tax to the allowance of larger depreciations on those capital investments? Doing this across the board would entice industry to innovate toward green technology instead of penalizing them for continuing to produce in a global economy where China, Brazil, etc. don't care about the unfair advantages inherent in allowing their industries to operate in an environmentally consequent free vacuum.

This method of tax reductions to induce behavior is analogous to the IRS giving a child and education tax credit to promote those certain behaviors. But applying that same tool to instill in industry the incentive to engineer new technologies will have a vast and far-reaching positive impact on the sustainability of America's economic and environmental future.

Now, the lawyer in me pauses in anticipation of the "other" side's argument. The argument will be the same as the Democrats' argument for not extending the Bush-era tax cuts to people that make over $250,000 a year. "We can't afford it," they argued on behalf of the government's need for more revenue, and they got the tax set at those that make $450,000 or more. They will argue the same—that the government can't afford to give industry the tax incentives to invest in new technologies, especially in this era of trillion-dollar budget deficits. This is just another example of why it is so critically important that Washington changes direction and begins to act with fiscal responsibility.

In reality, what our government can't afford is not to give these tax incentives. Allow me to explain:

One of the most fundamental models commonly referred to in the economics of taxation is the illustration of taxable income elasticity represented in the Laffer curve. The Laffer curve is a graphical representation of the relationship between government revenue raised by taxation and all possible rates of taxation. The inspiration for the curve is actually quite elementary—usually the best theories are. It is clear that a 0% tax rate raises no revenue, but the Laffer curve hypothesis is that a 100% tax rate will also generate zero revenue for the government because there is no longer any incentive for a rational taxpayer to earn any income. Thus, the revenue raised will be 100% of nothing.

If both a 0% rate and 100% rate of taxation generate no revenue, it follows that there exists at least one rate between where tax revenue would be a maximum. What is to be learned from this? Increasing tax rates beyond a certain point will become counterproductive for raising further tax revenue because of diminishing returns—that is, taxpayers will no longer have the necessary incentive to work.

In today's context, we already know that America is going bankrupt, that our nation is facing a $16 trillion debt that is increasing by $1 trillion annually, that nearly every state in the Union is facing monumental budget crisis, and that individually, we are making less as we work harder. As discussed in an earlier chapter, one of the ways our government can deal with this is to raise taxes. Which is what we did to avoid the "fiscal cliff" in January 2013. But I warn against this.

Now, I cannot, nor can anybody else, until the numbers start coming in, definitively state that a tax increase on those that make above $450,000 a year will diminish the drive to work for Americans and cost more jobs than it's worth. And so, to an extent, I found myself relieved when finally the fiscal cliff "deal" had been reached at this compromise, thinking, "hell, at least we can move forward and deal with the debt crisis." I even find myself thinking that, hey, if they're making over $450,000 a year, they can afford it. In fact, to be honest, they probably can.

I hope that they can, because the concern is what happens when we reach the level of taxation where they can't. Many are understandably concerned that we very well could already be at the point of over taxation in this time where we work harder for less income and fewer benefits and our corporations are taxed at a rate higher than anywhere else on the planet.

As a matter of principal, the very same that tied so many republicans to Grover Norquist's Taxpayer Protection Pledge, I believe the instinct must be to avoid taxation unless absolutely necessary. The problem with the Americans for Tax Reform's pledge, although well founded on proper fiscal conservatism, was that it became destructive to the Republican's own ends after thirty years of both camps spending way too much in Congress. Given that the debt is so massive and growing so fast, perhaps we do need to raise taxes if not only out of desperation. Perhaps the richer can afford it and in this time of growing wealth disparities, it is right to ask more of the well-to-do and reasonable for us to expect those that live among the top echelon of society to pay a little more for the freedom they have to enjoy the luxuries they do.

Well, it seems for now that has been decided, at least in the short term. The good news being that we've at least moved forward, for better or possibly for worse, history will tell, but forward nonetheless. As the alternative, which has unfortunately become the norm in Congress, is continued political stalemate and none of the problems facing our nation being timely or intelligently addressed. So let us hope that Congress can now get smart about cutting spending, whereby the extra revenue taxed us is spent more wisely. We can at least move forward with the hope that we are not on the wrong side of the Laffer Curve and with the comfort in knowing that in this great republic we always retain the power to amend our course should we be.

Yet, it is not simply the disincentive to work consequence of raising taxes that causes me to warn against it as the tool to shovel the United States out of our fiscal pit. The problem with taxes is what follows once you raise them above certain thresholds. In short, a downward spiral:

First, government will raise taxes on the rich, that is, industry. Done.

Doing so, as history has shown, will work to strap industry of cash necessary to invest in capital, produce for the market, and create jobs. As a result, industrial innovation will decline in this time when modernization for the development of high technologies for export and domestic reengineering are paramount to our economic survival.

The fear is American industry will continue to stagnate and fall behind in the global economy if taxed further. In order to stay bankruptcy, industry will be forced to shed its American workforce, shut down plants, and in the most severe of cases, look to the government for a bailout. Sound familiar?

But, strictly speaking from the standpoint of tax revenue, what happens when more and more people are laid off and unemployment skyrockets? Two things: 1) the government does not generate tax income from the unemployed but instead must extend unemployment benefits to a growing population unable to find work and support the consumer market; and 2) as the cost of its welfare programs increase (government expenditures on unemployment benefits alone have increased by 150% since 2007) the government is forced to tax those that do have jobs at even higher rates. This scenario spells out a recipe for diminishing returns and it is exactly why we must put down our torches and pitch forks in hunt of the rich. In allowing our government to continue with its economic policies that discourage domestic capital investment, we are encouraging a race to the bottom.

Taxing industry, whether it is the oil industry, farming industry, or any industry, for that matter, is not the answer. Well pointed and calculated tax breaks are!

I live and work in Fairfax County, Virginia. Fairfax County is one of the fastest-growing counties in the United States, or at least it was until adjacent Loudoun County surpassed it. As a "suburb" of Washington, DC, Fairfax has become a preferred home for the federal government's vast workforce and as a veritable city in and of its own, it is called home by over one million people.

There is a major problem facing Fairfax County, much the same as is facing many local governments all across the United States. Fairfax County is facing multi-million dollar annual budget deficits. A major reason is the county's source of revenue, namely the fact that 77.5% of all general fund receipts are generated by property taxes. As real estate values have plummeted, county revenue has fallen.

The crux of the dilemma lies in the fact that only 19.7% of real estate taxes collected in Fairfax County are generated from commercial/industrial property, representing a sharp decline from nearly 23% just a few years ago. Commercial industry is fleeing Fairfax County at a time when taxes on commercial properties (which tend to generate a more reliable source of tax revenue) are needed all that much more. The predominant land use in Fairfax is residential and a compounding issue arises when commercial businesses abscond, taking jobs with them. As a result, fewer residential units are generating taxable income as the owners face foreclosure and cannot pay their taxes.

If I were on the Fairfax County Board of Supervisors, I would strongly consider temporarily reducing the commercial/industrial tax rate for desired uses in order to entice certain industries to take root in the county. As an example, the board of supervisors could reduce the commercial real estate tax rate from $1.075 per $100 of assessed value to $0.85 per $100 of assessed value on narrowly defined green energy, light industrial uses for five or ten years.

Now, all of a sudden, a high-tech recycling plant or photovoltaic (solar) panel manufacturer decides to take advantage of this phenomenal deal. They establish roots by either buying property or entering into an extended lease agreement and invest capital to improve the property to meet their needs. This, in turn, increases the assessed value of the property. If the property was assessed at $1million before the capital investment, let's assume it is now worth $2 million. Instead of generating $10,750 in real estate tax revenue on that parcel for five years, the county will now receive $17,000 annually. Further, the solar panel producer will likely hire a local workforce, resulting in higher incomes, more spending power for county residents, and yet another windfall to the county's purse through sales taxes and residential real estate taxes as those workers take up residence in the county and purchase commodities from local vendors.

Multiply this modus operandi across the nation, from city to county to state, all the way up to the federal government, and we can provide an opportunity for businesses to invest the capital necessary to develop and produce tomorrow's technologies all across our great land. By adopting a mentality of encouraging mutually beneficial behavior rather than punishing behavior that meets current societal demand in a legal supply chain, we can regain our industrial strength in America. We can return to a healthier balance where the ratio of service-to-industry production is sustainable.

With each infusion of capital, more jobs will be created. Imagine, for instance, the sheer number of jobs that would be created by a project such as erecting a wind farm in the Shenandoah Valley. Some jobs would be temporary, such as the surveyors, construction crews, etc., but a whole host of high-level engineering and maintenance jobs, for instance, would also be created. Now multiply that across the board—millions of jobs, blue and white collar, will be created in America. Those newly employed will no longer be taking money from the system via the collection of welfare but will instead be contributing to the system and closing the budget gap (provided we also force the government to be fiscally conservative on their end).

Now, in the beginning of this chapter, I spoke of the ubiquitous influence the oil and petroleum industry has over our elected officials. And while I do believe their interests, as played, have been squarely at odds with the interests of the American people, and Mother Nature herself, I again caution that the road to our salvation is not found in punishing them.

Instead, what about this rough idea? The federal government can team up with the oil and petroleum industry, among other key energy industries, with the goal of building an entirely new energy grid. In this joint venture, the government can promise to match $1 million for every $50 million (arbitrary numbers) invested into the erection of a natural gas energy plant, wind farm, solar farm, or a hydrogen electrolysis plant, etc. The government would then grant these industries royalties which would earn them a positive return on their initial investment for a defined duration (almost like a patent). Further, the government would not be an owner or stakeholder; instead, contracts would be ratified wherein the government's investment is paid back plus a defined percentage within a reasonable period of time taking the exigencies of the project into consideration.

Instead of casting the oil and petroleum industry as the monster, I propose that we help them to use their vast reserves of capital to invest in America's new energy grid, thereby giving them an ownership stake therein. By doing so, we not only get what we need, a new, more efficient energy grid, but the oil and petroleum industry, as part owners of these new energy sectors, will no longer find technological advancement toward "green energy" as a threat to their bottom line. A win-win!

In keeping with the approach above described, that is not to malign the oil and petroleum industry, we must also understand how essential the industry is to our very way of life in America. Even the most ardent tree hugger must understand that we cannot simply shut off the tap. While the BP oil spill makes it easier to vilify the industry, our economy would collapse without them. Oil and petroleum accounts for 94% of our transportation energy source, 41% of our industrial power, and 17% of residential and commercial power. Our nation is built on and runs on their technology.

It is for this very fact that I support offshore drilling and increased domestic production of oil, natural gas, and coal as a stopgap until the use of cleaner renewable energy sources become more ubiquitous and economically viable. The six-month moratorium on offshore drilling after the BP oil spill, for instance, resulted in an economic loss of $2.7 billion in the United States alone.

Yet, while everyone else is drilling around the world (and off our shores), America is being forced to import petroleum to meet our energy demands as a consequence of government policies hindering domestic production. The result: increased trade deficits, commodity inflation, and, as we are all noticing each time we go to the pump, gas prices are skyrocketing. This is what I like to call shooting ourselves in our own feet and cutting off our nose to spite our face—if we are going to use petroleum at all, why would we use foreign sources over domestic? Doing so, as we currently do, is obtuse.

It is also important to consider that fact that our domestic regulations are far more protective of the surrounding environment than are the restrictions imposed by the governments of the regions from which we import our petroleum. Therefore, even from a strictly environmental perspective, it is better for us to produce domestically rather than import.

However, while the United States consumes over 30% of the world's petroleum, we possess less than 4% of the world's known and proven reserves. This fact alone necessitates that we invest heavily in alternative fuel sources and do so expeditiously. Coal, for instance, is one of the most abundant fuel sources in the United States as we hold approximately 60% of the world's reservoirs at over 275 billion tons of recoverable coal. Strong investment in clean coal technology to mitigate against the fact that coal power plants generate 93% of US sulfur dioxide and 80% of our nitrogen oxide emissions will empower us to be free from reliance on foreign energy while simultaneously addressing the impact on our environment. We perfect that technology and then sell it to China, not just for the altruistic outcome of reduced carbon emissions from China's ever-expanding coal plants, but also for profit.

Then there's natural gas. Natural gas already accounts for 76% of household energy production, but less than 40% of industrial. We are extremely lucky in America to have vast natural gas reserves. In fact, a natural gas reservoir double the size of Saudi Arabia's oil reservoir was recently found in the continental United States. As such, I believe natural gas has the greatest potential to jump-start America's energy independence in the immediate future.

What about nuclear power? Believe it or not, The US is the world's largest producer of nuclear power, accounting for more than 30% of worldwide nuclear generation of electricity through 104 nuclear reactors spread across 30 states. Yet, there was a near halt in reactor construction for thirty years in the US subsequent to the Three Mile Island scare, and only four reactors are currently expected to come online between now and 2020. The disaster in Japan highlights the fact that nuclear power has its dangers and extreme caution must be employed, but we must also take into consideration the toll of fossil fuel consumption and mitigate against that threat as well. The latter, I would argue, has to date proven far worse.

The convenient truth is that America already possesses the fundamental scientific, technical, and industrial knowledge necessary to solve our energy crisis and curtail global warming. With nuclear power, natural gas, wind, solar, and clean coal technology, we must take immediate steps to reduce our need for foreign fuel to power our industries.

We must get past the unfounded fears of a nuclear meltdown that have paralyzed us since the Chernobyl disaster, understanding that current technologies mitigate against the possibility of such an event to a far better extent, and build nuclear power plants considerably faster than at a rate of four per decade.

In the windier regions of the state's wind farms should be erected with electrifying speed. Where wind is unpredictable, solar, natural gas and clean coal power plants must be erected. All of the tools at our disposal must be utilized with all expediency to create jobs in America and at the same time release us from the clutches of foreign energy dependence. We must work harder than we have ever worked in order to perfect solar, hydrogen and biofuel technologies with a sense of urgency surpassing our race to put a man on the Moon.

With each technology, though, we are met with the naysayers eager to convince us as to the futility of investing. With natural gas, for example, there are the arguments that fracking, the process of fracturing shale to extract natural gas, poisons the water table, despite the fact that fracking occurs two miles beneath the surface and water tables average nowhere near that depth. With hydrogen-powered vehicles, the argument is that in order to convert hydrogen into an energy source, electrolysis is necessary and that electricity comes from the burning of fossil fuels. But what about using hydroelectric power or wind power to generate the electricity necessary to convert the hydrogen through electrolysis?

It is easy to stand aside and criticize, but America was built by entrepreneurs seeking answers, forging ahead and breaking through the barriers of skepticism. All of these technologies require improvement, yes, but the greatest risk of all would be in not taking the risks necessary to perfect and implement them.

We must set free American ingenuity to perfect these technologies and once again become the masters of our own destinies. In doing so, we will revive our economy, substantially improve our national security, curtail global warming, and hold in our hands the keys necessary to drive all of humanity forward. We will once again lead by example!

CHAPTER EIGHT:

# IMMIGRATION

*Remember, remember always, that all of us, and you and I especially, are descended from immigrations and revolutionists.*

**- Franklin D. Roosevelt**

My mother emigrated from Norway in 1966. As the son of an immigrant, I am keenly aware of the unparalleled opportunities immigration provides for the immigrant as well as the benefits conferred upon the nation by immigrants working for a better life.

We must never forget that the first wave of immigrants to America established our thirteen colonies to escape, among other things, religious persecution, and that our Constitution is largely influenced by the emigration of Western Judeo-Christian Culture to our land. In one form or another, we are all descendants of immigrants, and we must remember that in our diversity, our nation's unique strength is found.

Yet, there is a very real and serious difference between legal and illegal immigration. The latter is placing a huge burden on the United States by draining public funds, creating unfair competition for jobs, and by consigning superfluous strains on services designed to provide assistance to honest, tax-paying American citizens. Worse yet, the illegal immigrant crisis is creating a rift of needless and disconcerting racism between our people.

The melting pot, a widely used metaphor to describe our heterogeneous society becoming more homogeneous with the different immigrant cultures "melting together" into a harmonious whole with a common culture, was commonly used to describe the assimilation of immigrants into the "American Dream." Yet, boiled down to its roots, the problem with America's immigration policy is the proximate result that in reality, immigrants are not assimilating. This, unfortunately, comes as a result of immigration policy as a whole, not simply the lack of policing illegal immigration.

Subsequent to the enactment of the Immigration and Nationality Act of 1965, the number of immigrants flooding into the United States multiplied exponentially. Immigration into the United States doubled between 1965 and 1970, and doubled again by 1990. The most dramatic effect has been the shift from European emigration to Asian and South American, resulting in a massive demographic alteration of American society and an infusion of diverse cultures.

Almost overnight the traditional melting pot model was under attack and multiculturalism, a belief that cultural differences within a society are valuable and must remain distinct, was born. I for one believe in the value of multiculturalism, wanting never to forget the traditions of my Norwegian ancestors. However, assimilation of all peoples living within the United States into a common, moral, democratic culture that holds ordered liberty and justice above all else is absolutely critical to the future prosperity of our great nation. Yet, assimilation has seemingly been cast aside as the evil stepsister of multiculturalism, instead of its protective brother, as was our founding fathers' sage design.

Immigrants should not abandon their culture and traditions, but in order for us all to live together, whether as first, second, third or fourth generation immigrants, we must all consider ourselves a citizen of this nation first and place our loyalties to our "native" land and cultures second. We must resign ourselves to the truth that our heritage, here and now, is this land, this country, under the American flag.

Unfortunately, federal, state, and local policies, as they pertain to immigration, both legal and especially illegal, form a powerful and unconscionable barrier to this fundamental necessity of assimilation in our society.

To begin, the United States must restructure immigration policy to stress the importance of assimilation—that is adopting policies to encourage our increasingly heterogeneous population to become a more homogeneous, harmonious society with a common, patriotic culture. How?

I believe that the principal hindrance to assimilation of immigrants, regardless of legal status, is our reluctance to officially and legally declare English as our national language. The United States of America, contrary to 92% of all other nations on this planet, does not have an official language at the federal level. English, therefore, is our official language only in a de facto sense, not de jure.

Why is this important? First, declaring English as the national language would enable our government to provide information and services in English only, and remove any right of non-English speakers to receive government information and services in another language. This alone would reduce the federal budget by hundreds of millions. For instance, the US Office of Management reports that it costs the government over $1.86 million annually to prepare written translations for food stamp recipients alone.

Money, however, is but a side note to the bigger problem caused by the lack of an official language declaration at the federal level. An enormous strain on public education results from the failure to declare English as our national language and it results in a stark decline in the level of education provided to our students. Here is an unfortunately personal example:

My niece used to attend McNair Elementary in Herndon, Virginia. At the time of her enrollment, Caucasians comprised the minority at only 23% of the student population, with Hispanics and Asians in the majority. A swathe of students in each elementary class either spoke English as their second language, did not

191

speak English at home, or were below proficient in English. A phenomenon emerged that was undeniably exacerbated by the school's desire to obtain funding through satisfying the requirements of the No Child Left Behind Act of 2001.

In each class, the teachers began to teach the same material over and over again until each child in the class understood the subject material. With a majority of children in my niece's class barely able to speak English, she quickly found herself unchallenged and outright board having grasped the material while the remainder of the non-English speaking students struggled to understand the subject matter.

Instead of requiring the non-English speaking students to participate in specialized education classes designed to address their language deficiencies, all of the students, English-speaking included, were drilled the same material over and over for purposes of rote memorization. The result: while no child was "left behind," many children, including my niece, were held back from progressing.

What are the options for dealing with this particular dilemma? This is a rhetorical question because there are two obvious answers, one of which would run contrary to public policy. The first option would be to segregate non-English speaking children from English speaking. However, this would be tantamount to the institutionalized apartheid that was banned in *Brown v. Board of Education*, especially considering the fact that it would logically follow that the English speaking students and the non-English speaking students would necessarily have to be held to different standards of achievement within the No Child Left Behind matrix.

The other obvious option is to establish English as the national language, hold all children, at all levels, to the same high standards of proficiency and hold those that refuse to speak or fail to learn English back while allowing those that attain proficiency to progress.

Admittedly, it would be unjust to levy this rule without an adjustment period whereby non-English speaking students were ostensibly cast aside like lepers. Such a ruling would necessarily be accompanied by sort of a grandfather clause: a well-designed system of special education/tutoring programs to assist the non-English from being immediately "left behind" by a system that has changed its perspective overnight. Such a system, whether spanning three, five, or ten years, would necessarily cost the government hundreds of millions of dollars.

Hence, my argument for making English the national language is not founded merely upon economics, but rather upon unity. Together, speaking the same language and thereby assisted in our collective ability to communicate the free ideas fostered by our constitutionally protected multiculturalism, we can harness the true power of the United States of America!

Now, many will argue that establishing English as the national language will actually harm non-English speaking citizens. Will it make it tougher for them initially? Yes. Hence, the need for a comprehensive system geared toward teaching English as a second language to fill the gap. Community college programs, church programs, and classes held at public libraries, for instance, should be encouraged and subsidized.

That being said, failing to establish English as the national language actually hinders the non-English speaker the most, making the reform all that much more necessary. For instance, the National Adult Literacy Survey found that immigrants with a low English proficiency earn on average 50% less than those with a medium degree of proficiency and 33% less than immigrants with high levels of English proficiency. The US Department of Education's 2001 English Literacy and Language Minorities in the United States Report found that those with limited English proficiency are less likely to be employed, less likely to be employed for a continuous period, tend to work in the least desirable sectors, and earn less than those that speak English.

Finally, and perhaps of utmost importance, it is vital that we declare English as the national language in order to foster assimilation of immigrants around a common language so as to tear down the divide between English- and non-English-speaking residents. The United States is the single most diverse population in the world, home to countless cultures, creeds, and languages, and while it is that diversity that forms one of our greatest strengths, it also tends to segregate our populations from each other. A common language, on the other hand, and a concomitant understanding of the ideals that shape our Republic, can form the universal bond between us all, thereby exponentially strengthening our diversity.

When people can no longer communicate with each other, they have no way of conveying their common moralities, sharing their ideas, and spreading what good their culture has to offer. One need only read the biblical story of the Tower of Babel to understand this truth.

According to the biblical account, a united humanity of the generations following the Great Flood, speaking a single language, resolved to build a city with a tower to the heavens. The Lord came down to see what they were doing and said:

> *Behold, the people is one, and they have all one language; and this they begin to do: and now nothing will be restrained from them, which they have imagined to do. Go to, let us go down, and there confound their language, that they may not understand one another's speech. So the LORD scattered them abroad from thence upon the face of all the earth: and they left off to build the city.*

> **– Genesis 11:6–8**

Making English the national language would enable all of our diversity to have a nexus, a common thread through which to move forward with a collective, patriotic purpose understood by all. This is of extreme importance in an era where our nation is under attack from beyond our borders and from within, for our ability to move forward as a nation hinges upon our ability to do so cooperatively without the unnecessary divisiveness caused by the simple breakdown of communication between our people and our institutions.

At the very least, should we fail to officially make English the national language, we must require all legal immigrants to have a certain defined proficiency in English before earning the privilege of citizenship.

The second most critical step toward promoting assimilation is addressing illegal immigration.

Currently there are approximately fifteen million illegal aliens residing in the United States. According to the Census Bureau, there were an estimated 8.7 million illegal aliens living in the United States in 2000 but their numbers are growing at an alarming rate. It is important to note that the population of "illegal" aliens would statistically be higher than the numbers above, but in 1986 amnesty was granted to nearly three million illegal aliens, allowing them to become legal.

Now, let me be clear. Many will argue that those opposed to illegal immigration are simply being protectionist or even go so far as to argue that we are flat out racist. Anticipating this rudimentary attack, I say the following: I do not blame illegal aliens for jumping the fence. To usurp an old adage, the grass is in fact greener on our side of the border. In fact, it is many of our own policies, which are driven by our shortsighted economic desires that entice them to sneak onto our land. Simply put, from agriculture to construction, Latin America has become the new source of America's slave labor. Arguing otherwise is not only disingenuous, but also flat out naive. I wish this were not the case.

Yet, the fact remains that the first act of any illegal immigrant's trespass onto our land is just that, an illegal act! While the grass is currently greener on our side of the fence, this truth results from the fact that our side of the fence has a longstanding tradition of adherence to ordered liberty, that is, the rule of law, and with each illegal border crossing that is allowed to go unprosecuted, our grass withers and browns. This truth is playing out right in front of our eyes.

I will begin in an unlikely place. Many politicians have avoided the issue of illegal immigration out of a fear that cracking down on it would mean a loss of the Hispanic vote. This, however, is a fundamentally flawed belief.

One of my best friends, Edgar Santiago, was born in Puerto Rico. Technically, then, he is considered to be Hispanic American. When I was born, his family lived two doors down from mine and he was a little over three years old. One day, his mother called mine, wondering if she'd seen Edgar. He was there one second, she said, and the next, he was gone. Well, as it turned out, he was curled up on our front doorstep sleeping in hopes that when he awoke, his new friend would be able to play. I can plainly say that our friendship is a rare one—he and I have been the best of friends, literally, for my entire life.

Edgar and I usually don't talk politics. Usually, we talk sports, in that he played semi-professional football and I played college basketball. But, every once in a while, we talk politics and on one of those occasions, I asked him what he thought about illegal immigration. What he told me, honestly, was eye opening.

He told me that he couldn't stand illegal immigration, especially those from Mexico. It wasn't a matter of racism, or any ire toward Mexican culture as compared to Puerto Rican, rather, he articulated plainly that they were making him, as a tax-paying Hispanic American, look bad. Their breach of the law, never minding their reasons, is proximately impugning his integrity and making it harder for him to get a job. "John," he said, "if someone were to institute real immigration reform, they wouldn't lose my vote, they'd gain it!" I could not have said it better myself.

We must understand that fundamental immigration reform is not about race, it is about justice under the law and the ability to provide for that equally among our citizens, regardless of where they come from. My bleeding heart, the righteousness in all of us, would love to embrace all the huddled masses of the world suffering from tyranny, poverty, etc., but in doing so, we are stripping away our ability to provide tenable shelter for them and for ourselves. We are doing ourselves and them a disservice by allowing our ideals and our laws to be eroded by waves and waves of immigrants not invested in our language, our culture, our set of values, and most importantly, in our system of law and justice.

For instance, illegal immigration undermines legal immigration, depriving the United States of constituents able to contribute to our society on multiple levels. Currently, there are millions of eligible people waiting on an endless list to be legally admitted as immigrants to our country, some of which have been on that list for many years. Yet, while these law-abiding individuals wait for one of their numerically limited visas to become available, illegal immigration makes a mockery of those people's adherence to the rules.

The inflow of illegal immigrants into the United States makes a mockery of those adhering to the "rules" for two reasons: (1) the first signal it sends to immigrants coming into our nation legally is that America does not enforce its laws; and (2) because of the staggering amount of illegals allowed into our nation, it is now necessary to cut down on the amount of legal immigrants granted access per year.

Strictly speaking, the current admission of approximately one million legal immigrants each year into the United States is not necessarily by itself too high, but it is when considered in conjunction with the confounding swarm of approximately 700,000 illegal immigrants annually. We cannot assimilate this many people fast enough and as a result, we are losing what it means to be American.

Immigration, we must remember, is a discretionary public policy, not a national mandate. The primary purpose of immigration since our founding has always been to advance the interests and security of our nation. Unfortunately, the influx of countless cultures, both legally, and especially illegally, and at such overwhelming rates, has impeded our ability as a nation to assimilate under the flag to a common, patriotic purpose, and the results are devastating.

Instead of working together, more often than not, we utilize the freedoms afforded us in the Constitution to voluntarily segregate ourselves. Overwhelmed with change in every direction, America is losing any sense of what she once was, and in radical attempts to hold on to our own culture, we close ourselves off to our neighbors and denounce or outright fear their traditions. This reproving spans not only the demographics of religion but nationality, and the primary reason is because so many of us think of ourselves as African American, Asian American, Hispanic American, or Norwegian American before we think of ourselves as just plain old American!

Christians fear the cultural complexities of Muslims and vice versa, just as blacks and whites, Asians and Hispanics tend to close themselves off to the other's cultural divergences. To censure that which is different is human nature, and it is only with time, education, and understanding that the barriers of ignorance and the fear and chaos that stem from that lack of knowledge can be broken down. As such, the second prong to tackling the problem of immigration in the United States must be to cut down on the number of immigrants, both legally, and especially illegally, if only to grant us the time necessary to understand and embrace our diversity.

Note that I am not espousing the need for an outright hiatus on legal immigration. Instead, a temporary cut in the number of legal immigrants from one million annually to five hundred thousand, for example, would afford us the opportunity to pick the very best immigrants that fit the needs of our nation and, more importantly, allow us the sorely needed time to effectively curb illegal immigration, reform our immigration policies, and deal with the question of amnesty. This breathing room is necessary to further formulate how we, as a nation of such wonderful diversity, can move forward collectively and assimilate around one national, patriotic cause.

But how do we stop the migration of illegal immigrants across our borders? The first, and most critical component, is found in securing the border between the United States and Mexico. How?

First, it is critically important that we understand the US-Mexico border and the challenges to security it poses. Understandably, many will argue simply that the answer is found in erecting a wall from the Pacific Ocean to the Gulf of Mexico. In fact, polls indicate that nearly 70% of Americans favor such construction. A part of me, despite my better judgment, agrees. Yet, the fact remains that the answer to the US-Mexico border problem is not found only in the erection of a twenty-one foot tall fence grounded in three feet of re-enforced cement.

On October 26, 2006, President George W. Bush signed H.R. 606—the Secure the Fence Act—authorizing, and partially funding the "possible" construction of 700 miles of physical fence/barriers along the 2,000 mile border. Of particular import, the bill called for a down payment of $1.2 billion to the Department of Homeland Security marked for border security in lieu of construction of a fence, calling the combination of actual fence and integrated technology with an increased border patrol presence, the "virtual fence."

The virtual fence, though, has turned into a multibillion-dollar mess falling well short of its promise of delivering a sophisticated system of cameras, sensors, and radar that can zero in on people crossing.

According to the original timeline, the system was already supposed to be working but with over $1.1 billion spent, there is almost nothing to show beyond two Boeing testing sites in the Arizona desert and radar that does not function properly in the rain.

Yet, while the government states that it is revamping the system to address the successive problems, the Obama administration has scaled back financing for it to a tune of nearly 40%. The reality in Washington is that our leaders are not dealing with the illegal immigration problem with any sense of urgency and committee chairs continue to hold up funding for the Secure the Fence Act until a comprehensive border security plan that never seems to materialize is presented by the United States Department of Homeland Security.

A fence spanning the entirety of the 2,000-mile border between the US and Mexico is admittedly, in many respects, ill advised. There are myriad environmental concerns as well as regional economic impacts to start, but whether the comprehensive plan consists of one long fence with land mines plastered around it like a militarized zone between the Mexican drug cartels on one side and gun-toting Americans on the other at one extreme, or a fully automated virtual fence monitored by satellites and drone aircraft on the other end of the spectrum, we simply cannot afford to allow the border to remain as porous as it is.

Yet again, this is an example of why it is so fundamentally important that we draw back government spending in the United States. Here, ironically, the problem is that additional funds are requisite to address the border problem, both insofar as erecting fence where appropriate, but also in employing qualified patrols and equipping them with functional tools that enable them to perform their duties. Yet, these funds cannot be forthcoming when our government is spending hundreds of billions more than it should on entitlement programs, thereby hampering its own ability to perform its proper duties—that is to establish justice, insure domestic tranquility, provide for the common defense, promote the general welfare, and secure the blessings of liberty to ourselves and our posterity.

Once the border is secured, though, the question that presents itself is what to do with the fifteen or so million illegal immigrants already here. Amnesty?

In 1986, Congress passed the Immigration Reform and Control Act (IRCA) giving amnesty—legal forgiveness—to all illegal aliens who had successfully evaded justice for four years or more or were illegally working in agriculture. As a result, 2.7 million illegal aliens were admitted as legal immigrants to the United States.

Now, many will argue that the granting of amnesty in 1986 was an economic letdown. According to a study by the Center for Immigration Studies, for instance, the total net cost of the amnesty (the direct and indirect costs of services and benefits to the ex-illegal aliens, minus their tax contributions) after ten years came to over $78 billion. However, this study did not take into consideration the thousands of jobs those legalized aliens created for others, and how much revenue that brought into the system, or reductions of illegal alien borne crime which resulted in decreases to the necessary cost of law enforcement, to include prison management, for instance. The economic argument, for me, then, is a non-starter and unconvincing as a reason not to grant amnesty. It is simply too tenuous and speculative to quantify.

Most people resort next to what I believe is a logical fallacy to argue against amnesty. They will argue that rather than reducing illegal immigration, the 1986 amnesty led to an increase. Any new amnesty measure will further weaken respect for our immigration law and therefore, all amnesty measures must be defeated. This is not necessarily true.

To start, the lack of respect for our immigration policy results not from whether or not we grant amnesty, but our failure to police our borders and enforce our laws in the first place. Further, people do not sneak across the border because they have a lack of respect for our immigration policies; they do so because they are in search of a better life.

Laws against illegal immigration must be enforced, but the enforcement thereof, we must understand, is not so much a deterrent, but a necessity to ensuring that our domestic tranquility remains possible for all of us moving forward.

The simple fact remains that it is entirely cost-ineffective for us to evict fifteen million individuals who have, for various reasons, established residency and roots in the United States. Does it leave a bad taste in my mouth to allow illegal immigrants to get on a road to citizenship? Yes, absolutely. That being said, it is a failure to enforce our existing laws, our aversion to reform, and our conscious decision not to police our borders that have put us in the position of making this choice between the lesser of two evils. We can no longer afford to deny the fact that our years of deliberate blindness to this inconvenient truth requires decisiveness now.

So, let me be clear. Any decision to grant amnesty, or not, must be secondary to securing the border and fundamentally reforming our domestic enforcement. We must not do what we did in 1986; that is, grant amnesty and fail to reform our policies. If we repeat this mistake of recent history, we will be in the same boat ten years from now.

We must secure the border to insure that the population of illegal aliens does not continue to balloon, understanding the adverse impacts having an enormous population living outside the law has on the system.

Immigration reform is critical regardless of whether or not amnesty is granted. Any road to citizenship for an illegal immigrant will necessarily be difficult, and as such, many will wish to instead skirt the system and remain in the shadows. Therefore, comprehensive reform as to how we deal with illegal immigrants already here, and those that come in the future, is absolutely necessary.

Therefore, in addition to border security, we must also invest in a major upgrade in interior enforcement. Our deportation policy is a good place to start. Compared to the size of the illegal alien population, the number of annual deportations is shockingly low at about one in every seven deported annually. Why? The Department of Homeland Security has no plan for identifying and removing the bulk of the illegal alien population. Instead, they rely only upon the ability to identify and deport subsequent to the commission of a crime.

Now, here is where a lot of people get heated. "They are here illegally," people will argue, "so require that they show their papers and if they don't, deport them!" These same people will blow a gasket if you even dream of taking away their right to bear arms or somehow circumscribe their freedoms of religion, speech, or assembly. Yet, what they are advocating is that we circumscribe those same rights for those who wait at a local 7-Eleven for work because they _may_ be illegal immigrants.

Here is an example. I sat down for lunch with Michael Frey, Fairfax County board supervisor for Sully District in Northern Virginia. He had recently been the subject of a lot of criticism for his support of the establishment of a day laborer facility in Centreville, Virginia. "Why are you in support of the day laborer facility," I asked him.

For sake of paper, I will paraphrase by highlighting two key points in his response. 1) A local strip mall owner offered to fund it because the day laborers were scaring away business; and 2) no tax dollars would be spent as that owner was planning to allow them to use a unit he was unable to lease.

I bring this up because in the town hall meeting to discuss the "project," people were less concerned with the pragmatic considerations than they were with demanding that all illegal aliens be deported, period. "Why should we provide any level of comfort for the illegals," people screamed, "just deport them damnit!"

I agree, but as is the case with so many things in America, it just isn't that easy. Hence, the need for comprehensive reform.

You see, in Centreville, the day laborers tend to congregate on the median of Route 29, across from a central strip mall in the town (the one owned by the individual willing to put up the space for free). People don't like this; it makes them uneasy. What they want, what we all want, is for the police to pull up next to them, require they prove their citizenship, and if they fail to do so, throw them in a holding cell for ICE (Immigration and Customs Enforcement) to come and deport them. Here is why it is not that easy.

Put yourself in that crowd of day laborers standing on the median hoping to gain employment. In this economy, in fact, that may not be so hard to imagine. Now an officer comes up to you, demands to see your social security card or your birth certificate and upon your failure to produce valid identification, he detains you for hours or days. You would not be very happy, nor should you be.

Just as a police officer cannot pull you over or raid your house without probable cause to believe you have or are committing a crime, an officer of the law cannot randomly require someone to produce proof of citizenship simply because he or she is Hispanic and therefore *may* be an illegal alien. Ironically, it is our system of justice that protects them. But what is the answer—tear down the protections afforded us in freedom by the prohibition of illegal searches and seizure? No!

The answer is found in preventing further illegal immigration and addressing the removal of the current illegal population by improving the security of personal identification systems and requiring verification of legal work status to filter out those actively breaking the law by working without legal authority to do so.

Most think of illegal aliens as people who snuck across the border illegally. However, over 40% of our illegal population actually entered legally and have stayed illegally past the expiration date of their temporary visa.

Now, once they're in, the problem only snowballs. Theoretically, illegal aliens cannot get jobs or receive welfare in the United States. In reality, they do, because of simple document fraud. Armed with false documents procured for as little as fifty bucks, an illegal alien's eligibility for work or welfare goes unquestioned—providing the employer a veil of plausible deniability to hide behind.

All of this comes at a tremendous cost to honest, tax-paying Americans.

Illegal immigration costs US taxpayers about $113 billion a year, permeating all levels of government. The bulk of the costs, some $84.2 billion, are absorbed by state and local governments with over $50 billion of that price tag resulting in the cost of educating the children of illegal aliens.

A vast majority of this cost can easily be avoided through the establishment of a centralized database for determining who is eligible for work or welfare. Such a system of ID verification is equally as critical as having a currency that is near impossible to counterfeit, yet we have failed to institute such a system.

By linking government databases on births, deaths, and immigration status, and tracking foreigners on temporary visas to assure they leave when required, we won't have to rely on local police to utilize racial profiling in order to manufacture probable cause to arrest those they think might be in the country illegally. Additionally, we must strengthen enforcement capabilities by funding it properly at the federal level rather than mandating enforcement down the chain to states without providing necessary financial assistance.

Like every other critical issue discussed in this thesis, our ability to properly address the problem of immigration in the United States will hinge on our political will uncorrupted by special interests.

Here is an appalling example of just how ridiculous our enforcement of current immigration law is in the United States. Heavily criticized and lobbied by wealthy corporations upset about work-site raids, ICE instituted the "Phoenix Plan." Instead of raiding companies, under this policy they began to inform companies on the basis of a review of employment documents that they appear to have hired illegal alien workers, and then proceeded to give the companies the opportunity to dismiss the workers. What do you think happens when this "warning" is given? The workers simply walk away with their counterfeit documents to seek employment elsewhere and the companies that employed them get away without so much as a fine.

Employers who knowingly employ unauthorized workers function as magnets that attract illegal entry into the United States. We must reform the current system by actually enforcing employer sanctions through fines, jailing for repeat offenders, and loss of corporate charters, but in order to properly hold firms accountable, we must first establish a system of identification that is resistant to counterfeit.

So, I leave you with this. Immigration reform is not about isolationism or racism; rather, it is about doing what is right. It is about reaffirming our most sacred American ideal, that is, the adherence to the rule of law in order promote equality and justice for the citizens of this great nation.

In order for America to maintain the promise of prosperity now and in the future—in order for us to climb from the abyss of this Great Recession and break free once and for all from the counterproductive cycles of boom and bust, both economic and social, we must all work together, collectively, as Americans.

To accomplish this, we need desperately to stop and take a breath, recall the majesty of America's true manifest destiny, and come together with a shared, patriotic purpose centered on an understanding of what it truly means to be free to attain to our fullest potential. We must become a family, embracing our differences with reciprocal understanding and respect for one another, and, as our guiding light, with mutual democratic principles forming the foundation of our united patriotism. In order to take that breath and reaffirm our American ideals, we need time for our massive diversity to assimilate, requiring an immediate and drastic reform to our immigration policies. In doing so, we can reclaim the American Dream and make it better than ever before.

CHAPTER NINE:

# EDUCATION

*Let us think of education as the means of developing our greatest abilities, because in each of us there is a private hope and dream which, fulfilled, can be translated into benefit for everyone and greater strength for our nation.*

**- John F. Kennedy**

All of the reforms I have proposed in previous chapters will prove wholly futile if they fall upon the ears of an uneducated constituency. The War on Terror, our staggering debt, corruption in our body politic, and the energy crisis—none of these critical issues can be addressed by an ignorant population deaf to the elementary connotations surrounding each subject. As such, the greatest obstruction to our nation's future prosperity, undeniably, is our failing educational system. In order for the United States to lead the remainder of the world by technological example, by moral example, with composed and calculated logic, education must be what guides us.

A government for the people, by the people, and of the people, can only operate by a moral people reticent of historical example and wise to future hindrance. An uneducated populace therefore raises an austere impediment to America's future productivity and, unfortunately, that is exactly the reality we are currently facing in the United States.

America's public school system has remained largely unchanged for decades and as a result, we have allowed our students to fall behind rising global standards. Only 68% of our eighth graders can read at grade level and a staggering one-third of our students drop out of high school. In the 1970s, our students were ranked first across the board but as other developed nations have modernized their educational systems, our public schools have languished. Among developed nations, we now rank 24th in math, 17th in science, and 10th in literacy.

Nationwide, one out of three students scored "below basic" on the 2009 National Assessment of Education Progress (NAEP) Reading Test with 67% of all US fourth graders scoring "below proficient," meaning they are not even reading, much less performing at grade level in math and science. Of all eighth and twelfth graders tested, 26% of eighth graders and 27% of twelfth graders scored below the "basic" level, and only 38% of twelfth graders were at or above grade level.

The reality in America is that we are not preparing our children for college and we certainly are not preparing them for the rigors of a competitive, highly technical, global marketplace. This spells catastrophe as our nation's economic success hinges upon the productivity of a highly skilled workforce.

The economic impact of having an uneducated workforce is cumulative. As jobs are being shipped overseas and as we import talent to staff our hospitals and manage our dwindling class of engineers, America's production gap in the global marketplace has led to multi-billion-dollar foreign trading deficits and a dearth in domestic production.

According to a 2007 Organization for Economic Co-Operation and Development report, the United States ranks eighteenth in high school graduation rates and fifteenth in college graduation rates among developed nations. This statistic, corresponding with a 2006 US Bureau of the Census Report that calculated the average income of a high school dropout to be just over $17,000 compared to a college graduate's of over $50,000, paints a very unsettling picture.

To begin, localities benefit greatly from having an educated workforce, deriving higher tax receipts from their increased purchasing power, as well as enjoying the fruits of heightened worker productivity. Research by Cecilia Rouse, professor of economics and public affairs at Princeton University, indicates that each dropout, over his or her lifetime, costs the nation approximately $260,000 through loss of tax income, drain on social programs, etc. At current rates, twelve million students will drop out of America's high schools over the next decade, costing our nation approximately *$3 trillion.*

High school graduates, on the other hand, provide both economic and social benefits to society. In addition to earning higher wages, which results in attendant benefits to local, state, and national economic environments, those with higher education levels live longer, are less likely to be teen parents, and are less likely to commit crimes or rely on public services such as food stamps or housing assistance. Furthermore, the educated tend to engage in civic activity at higher levels, including voting and volunteering in their communities.

The simple fact is that United States must modernize its public school system and empower our children through education to carry forward our time-honored traditions of innovation and pioneering spirit. Doing so will have the attendant benefits of empowering us to employ our creative talents toward tackling the critical issues facing our nation.

The question that presents itself, then, is how do we unleash our creative genius?

First, we must recognize that money is not the only answer, and it ought not to be. While per-pupil funding for public education in the United States has more than doubled over the past forty years, student achievement has declined, especially in math and science. For example, despite having the third highest spending level per student in 2007, only 8% of eighth graders in the District of Columbia were performing at grade level in mathematics.

In today's taxing fiscal reality, states are being forced to face the fact that school districts long accustomed to budget growth must reallocate resources and in some instances operate on reduced funding. This unfortunate reality requires a concentration of efficiency. To this end, one of the major obstacles to reforming our nation's public school system is therefore found in the structure of government itself. Quite literally, public education is often its own worst enemy.

Far too often, local school boards are exploited and held hostage by teachers unions concerned more with the red tape of collective bargaining than the education of our children. As a result, local school boards, tasked with providing for the welfare of our educational systems, are often obstacles to real reform and properly aligned spending priorities.

The battle between local teachers unions and former chancellor of the District of Columbia Public Schools, Michelle Rhee, is perhaps most illustrative of institutional interference with reform. In 2008, Michelle Rhee sought to renegotiate teacher compensation, offering teachers the choice of being paid up to $140,000 based on student achievement criteria and loss of tenure or, retaining tenure with much smaller pay increases. Her move to end teacher tenure and promote merit pay was hotly contested by the teachers unions.

Finally, in 2010, after two years of circular debate and throngs of misinformation, Rhee and the unions agreed on a new contract that offered 20% pay raises and bonuses of $20,000 to $30,000 for "strong student achievement," in exchange for weakened teacher seniority protections and the end of teacher tenure.

Under this new agreement, Rhee fired 241 teachers for ineffectiveness—a move in conjunction with the closing of 21 dilapidated, under-enrolled, and failing schools that seemed to pay dividends. Soon after Rhee's term as chancellor, secondary schools in DC improved their standardized test pass rates by 14% in reading and 17% in math.

To be clear, I am not making the argument that teachers unions are a bad thing, nor that they are inherently iniquitous. Unfortunately, the recent battle in Wisconsin painted the unions, and by association, the teachers, many of them good ones, in a bad and unfair light. In fact, I believe that collective bargaining is in many respects extremely important and can contribute to educational productivity by protecting the interests of the teachers we call upon to perform in the difficult task of leading our children by shining example.

That being said, teachers unions often have the interest of teacher tenure and compensation at heart with too little regard for the education process and the children effected. Unions, just like any faction (with corporate boards on the opposite end of the same self-dealing spectrum), are prone to promote their interests above all else. One of the largest contributing factors to GM's bankruptcy, for instance, was the high healthcare and pension costs negotiated for GM's retirees by the United Automobile Workers without concern for the effect on GM's solvency and ability to compensate its current workforce. Likewise, teachers unions nationwide often advance their interests without proper regard for their localities' duty to provide a quality education for the children living therein.

A fair and healthy balance must always be struck between the interests of the employer and the union, for anything short of this equilibrium results in worker exploitation on one end and a bureaucratic black hole for innovation and productivity on the other. This is true in industry and it is equally true in our public school system. In the case of education, then, the school board, or its equivalent, must be the voice of the children if the teachers unions remain the voice of the teachers. For, in the case of a unionized public workforce, who protects the interests of the people and the students? Unfortunately, it is often the case where school boards are so heavily influenced by teachers unions that they too become the proxy voice of teachers, effectively removing the children's representative voice from the process of education policy.

In order for school boards to intelligently determine what their schools and the students therein require to excel—in order for the body politic to see above and beyond union influence and institutional pressure, there must be a clear understanding within such bodies as to how modernization of education must proceed.

I believe the first priority in modernizing and improving our public school systems, ironically, is something that should be squarely in line with the interests of teachers unions. As such, it is the logical place to begin meaningful reformation. The first thing we must do to improve education in America is to invest strongly in teachers and properly reward the profession with the end goal of promoting effective teaching practices and continued entry into the field.

Success in this arena hinges upon the development of progressive policies and incentives to recruit, train, support, and measure to reward effective teachers and remove the ineffective. Yet, today's policies are mainly failing to encourage high-quality teachers to stay in the classroom and certainly are not geared toward the discovery and development of new and effective teachers.

Many believe that the issue revolves entirely around teacher compensation. This, in fact, is an issue in many regions where teacher compensation is, for lack of a better word, laughable. These individuals are entrusted with the task of educating our children. How can we expect them to embark wisdom when we compensate them at levels that make it nearly impossible for them to even pay off their own college debt? Yet, compensation levels alone do not paint the entire picture, especially when many teachers are paid high wages, receive excellent benefits and pensions, and the average compensation nationwide exceeds $40,000 per year.

Traditional compensation policies are the problem. The issue is that compensation policies, often at the urging of teachers unions, traditionally revolve around salary schedules that only reward longevity and pension policies that penalize mobility. This clearly is not a structure that encourages talented individuals to enter the profession.

Compensation and pension policies that now characterize most state and local teacher pay systems were designed in an era when the labor force included many talented women and minorities with few other professional opportunities. The demographics of the American labor force have changed drastically, however. Workers, especially younger ones, are less interested in staying in one place or in one type of job for their entire career than were the teachers who entered the profession several decades ago. Younger workers do not shy away from jobs where performance is evaluated and rewarded. Consequently, of all college graduates, the nation's elementary and secondary schools annually employ fewer than 10% as teachers. As compensation packages in other professions have become more and more attractive, teacher compensation has become less alluring.

Mountains of research indicates that teacher quality, as measured by student achievement, rises for the first few years of a teacher's career and then largely plateaus. It seems obvious then that compensation policies should reward effective teaching and provide opportunities for good teachers to receive ongoing professional training and promotion while remaining in the classroom, but must also address the need to recruit talented teachers to all subject areas and schools. The first and best way to do this is to offer attractive starting salaries and incremental bonuses or pay increases based upon teacher effectiveness as measured against student achievement, not mere longevity.

Here's an idea that keeps with my reoccurring theme of reducing federal taxes: In order to attract teachers into the profession, what if all college graduates that enter the profession are given an extended, interest free hiatus on the requirement to pay back their student loans and for the first three years of full-time employment by a public school their income tax rate is reduced by 5%? This, in and of itself, would be a powerful incentive to enter into the teaching profession. And for teaching positions in the "forgotten corners" of America, where salaries are understandably and necessarily lower, repayment of student loans can be fixed at a percentage of income.

Next, a premium must be placed on the expansion of teacher training and certification programs in order to break through the plateaus of teacher effectiveness. In this era when high technology goods and innovation will form the backbone of our economic prosperity, it is vitally important that our teachers remain educated. The current wave of technological advancement is but one example. How can we expect our teachers to teach our children if their knowledge is obsolete?

As an attorney licensed to practice law in Virginia, for instance, I am required to take a minimum of twelve hours of continuing legal education per year. A similar requirement must be placed on the teaching profession in such a way that is not so costly to the teachers that it would detract entry into the profession in the first place.

Lastly, the road to effective teaching must be paved through a reward and compensation system based on each teacher's impact on the performance of their students. Unfortunately, existing policies tend to devalue effective teachers by treating all teachers as if they are interchangeable, discounting credentials and expertise in favor of seniority. Students are gravely hindered by this arcane and misguided system as they often are taught by teachers with little practical knowledge of a given topic and literally only a chapter ahead of them in the subject textbook.

Secondarily, the teaching profession itself is hurt by this approach. Because school systems are not basing their staffing decisions on teacher effectiveness they are hiring from less and less qualified sources, increasing pay in rigid lockstep, and imposing seniority as the paramount of teacher qualities. As a result, less tenured teachers, even highly effective ones, are continually bumped from their classrooms in favor of less effective seniors.

Shifting this dynamic of teacher tenure and implementing systems that place an appropriate premium on attracting highly effective teachers, handsomely rewarding them through compensation policies reflective of the value of the teachers' work while requiring continued effectiveness, surrounding them with highly

214

effective colleagues, and requiring ongoing training to empower them to deliver the requisite effectiveness, all will dramatically change the learning environment for students across our great nation.

With an emphasis on subject matter mastery and a requirement that student teachers spend time in classrooms under the supervision of experienced mentors, both senior and freshmen teachers will renew their vigor and be subject to peer review. Yet new teachers are commonly assigned to the most challenging schools with little supervision and support. Frustrated with lack of help, guidance, and support, nearly half of all teachers in America exit the profession within five years. This is precisely why ongoing professional development is critical, because by keeping teachers up-to-date on new research in successful teaching practices, emerging technology tools for the classroom, new curriculum resources, and supporting both freshmen and veteran teachers, the profession will prove less isolating, less daunting, and fewer effective teachers will leave for "greener" pastures.

The second priority in modernizing and improving our public school systems is one that should only seem natural in our democracy; that is, to guarantee freedom of information and choice. Every family should have access to information reflecting public school performance and have the right to choose among quality schools. It is unconscionable that a child's geographical roots necessarily shackles them to the attendance of a poorly performing public school and betroths them to the mercy of ineffective teachers.

A major problem in America's public school system centers on lack of choice. When there is a lack of choice, there is also a concomitant lack of competition. Without competition, industries fail to innovate (Capitalism 101)—the same is true with schools. Therefore, a premium must be placed on giving parents the ability to choose where their children attend school and extend that choice to all parents regardless of economic position.

This is fundamentally important for one simple reason: parents instinctively put the interests of their children above the interests of any one system. Logically, then, the more discretion parents have over where and by whom their children are educated, the more schools, whether public, charter, private, or otherwise, that will rise to supply the demand for high-quality education.

Across America, we must institute policies that provide parents significant access to performance data about schools and their teachers, and foster competition among schools by empowering parents through the choice to avoid failing schools. But how?

First, we must break down the barrier to good education erected by economic condition. Today, wealthier families have greater choice as to where their children attend school by dint of the fact that they can move to neighborhoods with better public schools or send their children to private schools. In contrast, low-income families have limited school options and their children are forced to attend failing public schools. The result is one in which the poor, often minorities such as African Americans and Hispanic Americans, are continually relegated to economic dispossession generation after generation.

Here is the reality: Nearly 90% of public school enrollment in Chicago is black or Hispanic; 95% in Washington, DC; 85% in St. Louis; 95% in Detroit, 90% in Baltimore; and around 80% in Philadelphia, Cleveland, and New York City. At the turn of the century, of over 11,000 elementary and middle school children taught in the New York City public school precinct that covers South Bronx, not even thirty were white.

In many regions, especially inner cities, not even one percentage point marks the difference between the legally enforced apartheid outlawed by *Brown v. Board of Education* and a current reality of socially and economically enforced apartheid. This, I would argue, is the new "racism" in America—that is, a vicious cycle of educational and corresponding economic inequality propagated by an antiquated system. And while I don't believe the inequality

216

to necessarily be deliberate (and therefore not motivated by actual racism), it is nonetheless enforced through institutionalized policies that ignore the effects proximately caused by lack of choice in public education as it relates affluence.

As Victor Hugo wrote, "He who opens a school door, closes a prison." This is true both metaphorically and literally. It is no coincidence that the lack of quality education not only breeds ignorance and jails creativity, but also incarcerates opportunity. Relegated to the alleyways of economic despondence, the uneducated often turn to crime out of desperation. According to the Department of Justice, although African Americans accounted for only 12% of the total US population in 2009, an estimated 38.9% of all prisoners in the United States were black. America is better than this!

Choice is the answer. The following is how to foster choice: (1) Mandate transparency in school and teacher performance by requiring annual reviews. These "report cards" should be open for teachers and all of the public to review prior to the next school year's enrollment. (2) Local school boards should remove the roadblocks to allow an influx of private and charter schools into their regions, thereby inviting competition in the region. If a school's enrollment dwindles or if a school's performance declines, so too should their funding. This will foster innovation, best practices, and effectiveness in local schools. (3) Empower parents to enroll their children in the most effective schools in the region by allowing vouchers to be used for transfers to private schools performing at or above certain levels based upon public school review standards. If the private school is not performing at said level, vouchers cannot be used by a parent for enrollment in that school. This will challenge public schools to perform at high standards in order to retain and recruit students, and it will also ensure that public schools do not shed students despite effectiveness. (Note: this could be a bureaucratic nightmare if implemented carelessly. As such, standards of performance review should be formulated via school boards working in collaborative panel with private school administration to ensure efficiency.) If schools are transparent about school and teacher effectiveness, then they will have more incentives to keep improving constantly, and parents will be able both to demand better for their children and determine which school is best for each child.

The final priority in modernizing and improving our public school systems is centered on the integration of technology into the classroom. While technology is ubiquitous and changing at near light speed, the majority of schools in America fail to utilize technology in order to help students acquire the skills they need to survive in an increasingly complex, highly technological, skill-based economy.

Integrating technology into instruction supports active engagement, participation in groups, accelerated interaction, and connection to real-world experts beyond the confines of a single classroom. Learning while equipped with technology tools challenges students intellectually by expanding their horizons of creativity and accelerating their ability to synthesize information and solve more problems with greater information at their fingertips. It also infuses an innate understanding of the technologies that comprise the modern-day office and will form the foundation of future innovation.

Something as simple as making sure that each classroom is linked to the World Wide Web will "upload" each classroom with more attention-grabbing, diverse, and continuously updated learning materials by connecting students and teachers to experts and creating myriad opportunities for expression through images, sound, and text.

The utilization of technology along with team project-learning approaches, for example, results in students remaining engaged and on task for longer durations. Innovative visualization technologies will empower students to experiment and examine results in graphic ways that aid in understanding and stimulate the imagination.

Improving public schools, however, is only half of the equation when it comes to the challenge of revitalizing education in the United States. The overwhelming majority of jobs that America will need to create in order to drive our economy into a prosperous future will require a workforce with at least a college-level education. Yet, while we used to lead the world in the number of 25- to 35-year-olds with college degrees, we now rank 12th among developed nations.

The crisis deepens with respect to low-income students and minorities: only 30% of African Americans ages 25–35 and less than 20% of Latinos in the same age group have an associate's degree or higher. Meanwhile, students from high-income families are almost eight times more likely as those from lower income families to earn a bachelor's degree by age 24.

The problem, simply put, is the rising cost of college education in America. Between 1982 and 2007, college tuition and fees rose three times as fast as median family income, completely eclipsing the rate of inflation. According to the National Center for Education Statistics, the nominal costs of attending college (tuition, books, room, and board) increased by 67% at public and 56% at private institutions between the 1995 and 2005 academic years alone. As of 2012, the average cost of a four-year college education in the United States has risen above $42,000.

As a result, fewer and fewer students can afford to go to college and the ones that are lucky enough to do so rely on student loans. The debt of the average college graduate for student loans in 2010 was $23,200. This debt burden limits college graduates in their career choices upon commencement—most notably, it renders a profession such as teaching impractical.

The question that presents itself then is this: How do we rein in the escalating costs of higher education? Well, admittedly, the topic is beyond the scope of this thesis, as there is not one single magic bullet that will remedy the runaway costs of college in America. That being said, what follows are a few proposals:

First, it is critical to reform higher education employment policies to reduce cost. More clearly, tenure for professors ought to be drastically reformed and in most cases, ended, as it imposes economic inefficiencies such as misaligned incentives and reduced flexibility.

Several alternative approaches offer more efficiency, including the use of contingent faculty, post-tenure review, renewable long-term contracts, and fringe benefits. The optimal strategy for one institutional type may be very different from what is most effective at another, however. For instance, research-intensive universities might benefit most from a hybrid of renewable, long-term contracts and fringe benefit trade-offs, whereas liberal arts colleges may want to utilize contingent faculty to reduce costs.

Colleges and universities might also try offering three-year diplomas instead of only four or longer. This shortened time to obtain a diploma could be extended to ambitious students willing to go to night school and summer school as well as students who desire the experience of college and a liberal arts education but are not seeking expertise in highly technical fields. The payoffs could be enormous: (1) students would save tens of thousands of dollars on room and board and other attendant matriculation costs; (2) a workforce comprising of employees with three years of college versus none is far better equipped to compete in the global marketplace; and (3) colleges would enjoy a greater use of their facilities year-round, utilizing the full capacity of their facilities to generate tuition income.

The primary mission of a college should be to generate and disseminate knowledge. In reality, however, campuses often rival small cities in size and are necessarily involved in a number of non-education-related services centered on housing, maintenance, food, etc. The corporate world has long utilized vertical contracts to use the cost-effective service of third-party entities that specialize in a needed service outside the corporation's forte. Our colleges and universities, however, have not. Colleges can counteract these trends by outsourcing more services and functions that are beyond the traditional scope of education with a payoff of greater efficiency at lower cost.

The unsustainable increase in tuition is partly attributable to the fact that administrative bureaucracies within higher education have spun out of control. Colleges have consequently lost sight of their true mission which is to provide a quality education at an affordable cost. As such, one of the key ways to reduce the cost of college tuition is to reduce administrative staffs. To do so will require a renewed focus on worker efficiency and a return to a realistic pay structure opposite a current trend where college administrative expenditures have increased over the last twenty years far greater than expenditures on education. Colleges can consolidate comparable departments and positions and implement an incentive-based compensation system in order to achieve this goal.

There are many other ways to reduce the costs of higher education, such as overhauling FAFSA, promoting online academia, and digitizing school libraries and textbooks, but perhaps the biggest impact would lie in a reformation of state subsidies in the funding of colleges and universities.

Every year, colleges and universities receive billions of dollars in state subsidies. In fact, revenues from state appropriations comprise nearly a quarter of their total revenues. The second largest revenue source, tuition and fees, comprise only 17% of total revenues.

The problem is this: direct subsidization of public universities under legislative discretion provides a disincentive to decrease spending and incentivizes increased spending on lobbying and other non-academic pursuits.

Take two identical universities for example. The first school spends with a cavalier attitude, wasting appropriated funds on high-cost activities without regard for student value. The second school behaves prudently by cutting costs, innovating, and keeping expenditures to a minimum, resulting in a surplus. Under the current system, colleges like the first one will successfully petition state legislatures for additional funding, citing their high operating costs, while it will appear that the prudent school has been over-funded and they will likely have their subsidies slashed in the following year.

As a result, wasteful spending is rewarded in the form of higher state appropriations, while efficient educational practices are incidentally punished with a reduction in state appropriations.

The second perverse effect of the current subsidy system is that it forces colleges and universities to spend billions on lobbying efforts and other non-academic pursuits. The reason for this is simple: when most of their money comes directly from the state, it is critical to an institution's bottom line to place a premium on winning over and satisfying legislators by spending time and money on lobbying and public relation efforts.

It is rare that I say this, but in this situation, state governments would do well by following the federal government's example—such as the GI Bill. Shifting toward a system that provides even half of those educational subsidies directly to individual students would mitigate against the rising costs of college education in America by forcing institutions to compete for subsidy revenues. Colleges and universities would consequently need to refocus on satisfying the demands of students rather than expending their full time and attention to currying favor with state legislatures.

It is in these turbulent times that we must remember the sage words of the English philosopher, Herbert Spencer: "Next in importance to freedom and justice is popular education, without which neither freedom nor justice can be permanently maintained."

Our success as a nation hinges entirely on the education of our people. Without it, we cannot understand our history, learn from our mistakes, or address the issues facing our great nation. I firmly believe, however, that there is no greater force on this earth than an educated American because, in the United States, above all other nations on this planet, a learned man or woman is free to attain to the fullest stature of which he or she is innately capable. It is our collective genius and creative spirit that has always formed the backbone of America's innovative might, and it must remain so.

# A CALL TO CONSCIENCE

It is not easy accepting the task of shining as a light in this dark world. The tasks that lay ahead of the United States—their scope and magnitude—are beyond daunting. But we must always remember that the night grows darkest before dawn's light rises to reveal new hope and possibility.

Mankind faced consummate darkness in World War II as the Nazi war machine spread its sadistic malevolence. But just when it seemed all was lost, that America had waited too long to act and Britain was about to fall, we awoke from our slumber to eclipse fascism in freedom's light. And when the greatest generation returned from the horrors of war, America shimmered as a living testament to the power of freedom, the strength of liberty, and as an awe-inspiring illustration of man's benevolent potential.

Faced with the trials and tribulations of today, it is natural for us to feel choked, cornered, and helpless. It's natural for us to feel overwhelmed and want to throw our hands in the air and simply give up. We find ourselves questioning why, for so long, we've touted ourselves as the greatest nation on earth—why were we so, well, arrogant? If we're so great, why can't we seem to solve anything? Why are we locked in an incongruous political stalemate over how to tackle the copious and swelling critical issues facing our generation? A melancholy sweeps in and takes hold, smiting our seemingly misplaced faith.

We must remember that our self-confidence was born out of the accomplishments of our Greatest Generation. Faced with unimaginable horror, we surprised ourselves, and the world, exemplifying the very best in humanity on the world's stage. Holding steadfast to our moral compass and determined not only to protect our own God-given freedom, but also to preserve it for others, we found a way to navigate through the darkness and overcome. All of the world, including us, still looks back on their shining example.

But, understand this—the United States of America was humanity's last best hope then, and today, it remains the same. I know this to be the truth! We are not lazier than our generations before us. We are not less idealistic and, while the times have certainly changed, we are not now less capable of dealing with society's upheavals. The power that afforded us the ability to save the world in 1945 exists today just as it did then. And that power is found in the spirit of the American Dream!

In America, we are freer than any society on this planet and can call from the unparalleled experience of having been so for centuries. Our extraordinary system of ordered liberty has left us free to innovate and over-indulge to a wider spectrum, bringing with it a wisdom unique to our population. It is the unique experiences our people have endured through the Cold War, Vietnam War, through the civil rights movement, all the way through to today's crises, that makes us more understanding of the need and more capable as a society than all others to again pick up liberty's torch and prevail.

In America, because we are free to dream it, and because we are equally free to pursue those dreams, we are capable of doing absolutely anything we put our minds to. This is not me being idealistic, for I am simply recognizing the true power of our Constitution. There is a reason why our nation is the birthplace of more innovation than anywhere else on this planet, why we can put a man on the Moon, and why we have the unmatched capacity to effectively remedy the issues of our time. We can and will overcome because we are free and protected in our freedoms to pursue and perfect.

We put our minds to it, and we won our freedom from tyranny. We drew a line in the sand, preserved the majesty of our union, and ended slavery. We've stood strong against the seditions of communism and fascism. We've met every obstacle with steadfast determination, blasting through history's mountains to forge a brighter destiny for ourselves and our children.

We must not, and I know it in my heart that we absolutely will not, let the dream die here, now, with us. Our children and their children will not endure into a lesser existence because we were too weak to hold true to our American ideals. I will not allow it—and I know that you will not allow it.

So I challenge you. I challenge all Americans. Wake up from your apathy. What our government does and what it leaves undone—it matters! It matters now more so than it has ever mattered.

Our national voter turnout is barely over 50%, a statistic that is equally as disheartening as it is unacceptable. Get up, make your voice heard, and make a difference. Each of us has the power to start doing the right thing. And we must. Because America's ability to pull back from the precipice of collapse starts with you. Not your next-door neighbor, not your county supervisor, and not your senator. You are the answer.

Each of us is free. We are free to overindulge in sedentary lifestyles; free to ignore the problems of today; free to lie, cheat, steal, and shirk our responsibilities. We are also free to do what is right. We are free to face ourselves in the mirror, accept our deficiencies, and strive to better ourselves and all those around us. We are free to lead by example!

Americans don't wait for their government to do for them that which they are free to do for themselves. We are not a nation of people entitled, but rather a nation of pioneers. Remember the sacrifices that our forefathers made, the freedoms for which they fought and secured for us to enjoy. We owe it to them, and more importantly, we owe it to our descendants to return to our revolutionary, pioneering roots. We owe it to ourselves, for I believe that history will show that this generation, called to our duty, responded with a resilience and a passion greater than all generations before. We can become, and must become, the generation that is even greater than the greatest generation!

Galvanized, there is no greater force than the collective, benevolent will of the American people. Therefore, I am confident that nothing can stop us but ourselves. It is okay that we argue along the way. This is human nature; in fact, it is the lifeblood of democracy, for it is through the conduit of deliberation that our greatest ideas are delivered. However, we must put into action our words.

Too long have we languished in the promised land of empty and unfulfilled political sound bites. It is no longer acceptable, for instance, simply to espouse a family-oriented platform. When public policy decisions ostensibly force both parents to work long hours to pay off the debt encouraged by our consumer economy, then forces them to spend hours on end in traffic, how can we say we are encouraging family cohesiveness? We must invest in the expansion of public transportation, ease gridlock, and actually make it feasible for parents to sit with their children around the dinner table, not simply pontificate in a vacuum that family is important.

Recognizing, as we do, the importance of dealing with education, illegal immigration, the environment, etc., we can no longer allow our representatives to promise reform and fail to deliver. We must revolutionize with lightning speed, the likes of which we have not seen since we completely retooled industrialized America in a matter of months to churn out the bullets, planes, and ships necessary to win World War II.

With equal, perhaps greater resolve, we must retool and revitalize our industrial complex to modernize and erect a new, more efficient energy grid. Talking about the potential of solar energy, wind power, and how we theoretically can rid ourselves of dependence on foreign fuel will no longer cut it.

Talk is cheap. We must take immediate action to revamp public education in order to prepare our children properly for the rigors of a global marketplace. We must finally take steps to remove corruption in our government and demand fidelity in our representatives, rather than perpetuate it through our continued indifference to incumbent fraudulence.

But, to do so, we must all come together, united to the singular goal of prevailing as a cohesive, patriotic force. Together, we can accomplish anything, but in a House divided, we will all fail. We must collectively cast aside our egocentric factions as the critical issues into which I've delved are faced by all Americans, regardless of race, creed, or party.

Guided by our shared American ideals, we must shun our growing predisposition to demonize one another, individually and systemically, to the summit of Capitol Hill. We must stand up, all of us, and demand that our elected officials reach across party aisles, not for bi-partisan reform, but for American reform!

Returning to our revolutionary roots, relearning and reaffirming our core principals as a nation—this is how we will win the War on Terror, revitalize our economy, and advance a more perfect union for ourselves and our progeny. In this dark hour, it is our privilege as a free people and our absolute duty as Americans to lead our families, our neighbors, and the remainder of the world, by shining example.

Let us unite under the flag of the United States of America, remembering all it stands for, and knowing all it must continue to represent. Join me in renovating the American Dream! Thank you, and may God continue to bless America!

www.ingramcontent.com/pod-product-compliance
Lightning Source LLC
Chambersburg PA
CBHW030304290526
45785CB00001B/206